Talking Heads

Talking Heads

POLITICAL TALK SHOWS AND THEIR STAR PUNDITS

Alan Hirsch

ST. MARTIN'S PRESS | NEW YORK

To Marjorie

Production Editor: Mark H. Berkowitz

Library of Congress Cataloging-in-Publication Data
Hirsch, Alan.
    Talking heads.
        p. cm.
    "A Thomas Dunne book."
    ISBN 0-312-05521-8
    1. Talk shows—United States.   2. Television and poli-
tics—United States.   I. Title.
    PN1991.8.T35H5   1991   791.45′75′0973—dc20
    90-49233

First Edition: February 1991

10 9 8 7 6 5 4 3 2 1

CONTENTS

INTRODUCTION

Political talk shows are television's version of the newspaper op-ed page. Television didn't always provide such a service. Until the mid-1960s, political programming consisted primarily of newsmaker interview shows like *Face the Nation* or *Meet the Press* and in-depth feature news reports like *David Brinkley's Journal, The Chet Huntley Report,* and Charles Kuralt's *Eyewitness to History.* On these shows, as on the nightly news, journalists kept their opinions to themselves. But eventually there emerged numerous shows in which political commentators—primarily the very people who populate the newspaper op-ed pages—offer opinions and arguments rather than ask questions or report news.

The McLaughlin Group and *Inside Washington* (formerly *Agronsky and Company*) represent this genre in its purest form. These programs involve no politicians, only commentators arguing among themselves. Several other shows approximate the genre. On *Capital Gang,* one political guest joins four commentators, but as another roundtable participant, not an interviewee. *Firing Line* features William F. Buckley, Jr. and a guest engaging in a dialogue rather than an interview, thus offering the opinions of at least one commentator, Buckley, and frequently a second—the guests are more often commentators than politicians. Similarly, *Crossfire* ostensibly maintains an interview format but, as we shall see, actually resembles the roundtables more than the newsmaker interview shows. *This Week with David Brinkley* devotes a segment to a

1

discussion among commentators, and other shows, such as *Nightline,* occasionally have commentators as guests. (*Washington Week in Review* consists of a discussion among journalists, but they offer straight news analysis without explicitly injecting their political views.)

There is a growing sense that television's op-ed page is supplanting the newspaper op-ed page as the primary source of the public's exposure to opinion commentary (just as the television news has supplanted newspapers as the primary source of the citizenry's information). The columnists who double as talk show pundits report that many more people comment about their television appearances than their written work.

As a result, the importance of television's op-ed page is sinking in. Barbara Matusow, contributing editor of the *Washington Journalism Review* and a close follower of political journalism, recently published a list of Washington's major journalists.[1] The list includes numerous talk show regulars—James Kilpatrick, Morton Kondracke, Robert Novak, Jack Germond, George Will, Fred Barnes, Pat Buchanan, Sam Donaldson, Al Hunt, Cokie Roberts, and Strobe Talbott—and excludes some highly regarded columnists who rarely appear on television. Most revealingly, the list omits Jules Witcover and Rowland Evans. Witcover and Jack Germond coauthor most of what they write, just as Evans and Robert Novak collaborate on all of their written work, yet Matusow regards Germond and Novak, but not Witcover and Evans, as especially influential journalists. The reason is that Germond is a regular on *The McLaughlin Group* and Novak, once the star on *The McLaughlin Group,* is now a regular on *Capital Gang* and frequently hosts *Crossfire.* Witcover and Evans receive limited television exposure.

It makes sense that the political talk shows increase journalists' influence, because these shows assist people in sorting out their political views and help establish the conventional wisdom in the nation's capital. Americans stand to benefit from a class that works full time inspiring us, provoking us, clarifying and changing our thoughts about major issues. If television brings us into closer and more frequent contact with this class, it would seem all the better.

While that perspective is sound in theory, in practice some people look askance at television's op-ed page. In his recent book *Harp,* John Gregory Dunne expresses contempt for political talk shows:[2]

> Robert Novak huffed, Patrick Buchanan puffed. Fred Barnes here, Morton Kondracke there, Michael Kinsley holding up the progressive end. . . . I detested those people I was staring at on the tube, the op-ed grandees who moonlight as talking heads. . . . They are plump of body, plump of mind, the cholesterol of smarm and self-importance clogging every mental artery, bloated bladders of hot air farting the most noxious kind of knowingness. . . . They have nothing to tell any of us about the United States of America.

There is some merit in Dunne's diatribe. To be sure, his portrayal of television's prominent commentators is unfair: many of them possess much knowledge and insight about public issues. Unfortunately, television has not given them adequate forums to enhance America's debate.

This book argues that television's op-ed page makes an inadequate contribution to our democracy. First, most of the shows do a mediocre job of promoting a healthy and robust political debate—indeed, in certain respects, they cause harm. With only a few exceptions, they tend to reduce politics to a source of frivolous titillation. Equally important, they present an insufficiently broad spectrum of opinion.

In addition, television has a negative effect on the careers of some of our best columnists. On the surface, it has been a boon for them: whereas columnists once toiled in relative anonymity for low pay, they now combine writing, lecturing, and television appearances into a lucrative and high-profile existence. (The significance of the talk shows is again illustrated by partners Germond and Witcover: because of his television exposure, Germond's lecture requests outnumber Witcover's twenty to one.)[3] But while television's op-ed page has produced wealth and stardom for pundits, the way it has done so and the effects of that stardom are more harmful than helpful to our democracy. In short, television diminishes the contribution of outstanding commentators by tarnishing their work and reputations.

The nature of the talk shows, and most of their failings, is the focus of part I, The Game. Part II, The Players, profiles six prominent television pundits. Chapters on Pat Buchanan and Sam Donaldson build upon part I by exploring the style that makes these two commentators perfect participants for the kind of political talk show that flourishes today. The subsequent profiles of William F. Buckley, Jr., George Will, James Kilpatrick, and Robert Novak illustrate the problems that arise when television converts major commentators into celebrities or caricatures. Part III, Between the Forty Yardlines, dissects a weakness afflicting not only political talk shows but the major media generally: the narrow range of views presented.

The profiles of the six commentators invite a two-part question: Are the most prominent pundits primarily conservatives, and if so, why? The answer is yes, for several reasons. It is, in part, simply a matter of skill and style. The highly theatrical Buckley would have been a television star regardless of his politics. Will and Kilpatrick received their initial television slots because they are highly regarded columnists; once they hit the airwaves, their vivid television personas, not their conservative views, did the rest.

But the fact that conservative pundits are thriving results from more than talent. The journalist-as-celebrity era has coincided with Reaganism, making conservative commentators, perceived as closer to the president himself and to the heartbeat of the capital, in more demand. As liberal commentator Hodding Carter says, "The left is pretty much out of fashion and favor in the same way the right was hard to find on television twenty years ago. Television is notoriously a whore, going where the power is."[4]

Other forces too have inclined pundit superstardom to the right. As noted, celebrity journalism consists of a mutually reinforcing package of wide newspaper syndication, television appearances, and demand on the lecture trail. In part because most newspapers are owned by Republicans, the most widely syndicated political opinion columnists are conservatives—Kilpatrick and Will rank one, two. The highest lecture fees come from business groups, which tend to have conservative political orientations and thus prefer conservative commentators as lecturers.

But while conservatives have had the greater opportunity for fame and fortune, the celebrity bug has bitten liberal commentators as well. They too do as much television as possible and travel the lecture circuit. If Carl Rowan, for example, is less famous than Buckley and Will, and less in demand on television than Novak and Buchanan, it isn't for lack of trying.

Some of the major problems described in the book might seem intractable: television may be thought not conducive to meaningful political discourse and the conversion of journalists into celebrities an inevitable outcome in a celebrity age. In each case, though, there are sufficient counterexamples to make resignation inappropriate. There are good talk shows and there are commentators who avoid the blandishments of celebrity.

Television does have inherent limitations, and the fact that Americans read less and less while they watch more and more is no doubt an unhealthy development for self-government. But television is here to stay, and its influence on democracy, therefore, needs to be improved, not simply lamented.

I

The Game

ONE

Two Traditions and Two Kinds of *Firing Line*

Television shows featuring journalists debating political issues emerged largely in two stages. First, in the late 1960s William F. Buckley's *Firing Line* and Martin Agronsky's *Agronsky and Company* took to the airwaves. The second phase occurred in the early 1980s with the appearance of *The McLaughlin Group, Crossfire,* and *This Week with David Brinkley.* The first stage did have several antecedents. Indeed, political commentary on television has two different ancestral lines: what might be called the "Friendly" and "hostile" traditions.

The Friendly tradition derives from the efforts of former CBS producer Fred Friendly to provide forums for journalists Edward R. Murrow and Walter Lippmann to enlighten the American public about serious issues. Friendly yearned for television to make a significant contribution to the public's understanding of major issues; his vision was realized in 1951 when he brought Murrow's famous radio commentary *Hear It Now* to CBS television as a regular series called *See It Now.*

See It Now, a forerunner of *60 Minutes,* was a weekly half-hour show, generally devoted to a single topic: tobacco and lung cancer, school desegregation, changes in the Middle East and Africa, among others. As with *60 Minutes,* the presentation of facts was often slanted to make a point, but the host generally did not openly advocate a particular position. On a few occasions, however, Murrow explicitly injected his opinion, most famously on March 9, 1954, when he assailed Senator Joseph McCarthy:[1]

9

This is no time for men who oppose Senator McCarthy's meth-
ods to keep silent, or for those who approve. We can deny our
heritage and our history, but we cannot escape responsibility
for the result. As a nation we have come into our full inheri-
tance at a tender age. We proclaim ourselves, as indeed we are,
the defenders of freedom—what's left of it—but we cannot
defend freedom abroad by deserting it at home.

In 1955, *See It Now* lost its prime-time slot to the popular *$64,000
Question* and lost its primary sponsor, Aluminum Company of
America (Alcoa), which was allegedly unhappy about a *See It Now*
report of a major land scandal in Texas, where Alcoa intended to
expand its operations. From 1955 to 1958, *See It Now* was broadcast
periodically as a special (and thus nicknamed "See It Now and
Then") and departed permanently in 1958. It had, however, left its
mark by demonstrating television's capacity to deal with important
issues intelligently and in some depth.

After *See It Now* left the air, Fred Friendly retained an interest
in providing a forum for heavyweight journalists to discuss important issues. The dominant political commentator of the time was
Walter Lippmann, and Friendly angled to bring Lippmann into
people's living rooms. Lippmann distrusted television, believing it
to appeal to emotions at the expense of reason. However, Friendly
eventually convinced Lippmann that the medium would be put to
good use if Lippmann would provide lengthy interviews on public
issues, especially foreign affairs. From 1960 to 1965, CBS televised
seven one-on-one interviews Lippmann gave to Eric Severeid,
Walter Cronkite, Howard K. Smith, Charles Collingwood, and
David Schoenbrun. The one-hour shows earned CBS and Lippmann a Peabody Award for their "contribution to international
understanding," and were published as *Conversations with Walter
Lippmann.*

Aside from Friendly's work with Lippmann and Murrow, the
first several decades of television supplied only a few doses of serious
political commentary, such as *The Drew Pearson Show* and Hardy
Burt's *Answers for Americans* in the 1950s and *Howard K. Smith,*

News and Comment in the early 1960s. None of these programs survived for even two years, illustrating the fragility of Friendly-style political programs.

Friendly himself left CBS bitterly in 1966 when the network ran *I Love Lucy* reruns rather than cover the Senate Foreign Relations Committee's initial hearings on the Vietnam War. His considerable legacy includes having provided relevant antecedents for *Firing Line* and *Agronsky and Company* by showing the potential of serious journalists addressing important issues.

Even as the Friendly tradition was being established, however, a "hostile" tradition of political commentary was also developing. The hostile tradition derives from talk radio. In the post-World War II period, a number of radio talk shows, hosted by such stalwarts as Barry Gray and Mike Wallace, took to the airwaves. These programs featured a mix of live guests and telephone calls from listeners. The 1950s and early 1960s witnessed a proliferation of these shows, which increasingly took on a political bent. They also took on a combative tone. Jerry Williams, Long John Nebel, Bob Grant, Howard Miller, Herb Jepko, and others achieved substantial followings by aggressively confronting or insulting guests and callers.

In 1964, one of the more raucous radio show hosts, Joe Pyne, took his act to television. His parade of controversial guests and weirdos first aired locally on KTTV in Los Angeles. Before long, the bi-weekly *Joseph Pyne Show* was syndicated to over eighty cities nationwide. Pyne's act was not actually the first of its kind. David Susskind's late night show *Open End,* featuring a slew of often eccentric guests who squabbled and interrupted one another repeatedly, had begun in 1958. But Pyne took the concept of aggressive political discussion several steps further, and his wild show attracted much controversy.

In 1966, a similar show hosted by Alan Burke, who also came from talk radio, was aired by a local New York station and syndicated around the country. *Life* magazine characterized the *Burke* and *Pyne* shows as "a new nationwide parlor game that transforms mere blather into television's own Theatre of Cruelty" and described their modus operandi:[2]

> Both shows begin with a beefing session that provides a chance for orators in the audience who can voice their own petty grievances—or can sit tight until they are given a signal to line up and nip at carcasses of the guests. Should the guest confess authorship of a controversial book or espouse an unpopular cause, Pyne and Burke will immediately organize a posse of open mouths to prove that the masochist-of-honor is either money-hungry, idiotic, homosexual or un-American.

Pyne, an ex-marine, chain-smoked on the air and vented a populist fury through silly insults. He enjoyed telling guests to "gargle with razor blades." On a show during civil rights riots in the Los Angeles suburb of Watts, a militant black guest noted that Pyne, living in his safe middleclass neighborhood, didn't have anything to fear. Pyne responded by opening a desk drawer to reveal a gun, remarking, "I have a gun here in case they start coming." The guest drew back his coat to reveal that he too was armed. (A uniformed guard was on hand for some of Pyne's shows.) Another time Pyne's sidekick, a Los Angeles businessman named Ozzie Whiffletree, was punched in the face by a guest whom he had called a liar and coward.

Despite or perhaps because of the craziness, Pyne had no trouble finding guests. A steady stream of racists, communists, Ku Klux Klanners and other extremists were all too happy to be thrown to Pyne and his audience of lions. Lee Harvey Oswald's mother put in an appearance and was driven to tears. Pyne and his producer Robert Hayward were more than pleased with the array of dubious guests. "The subject must be visceral—we want emotion, not mental involvement," Hayward explained.[3]

Alan Burke was an east coast Pyne clone. His show was on New York's WNEW nightly and syndicated to over twenty cities on Saturday nights. The *Burke* show also trotted out freakish guests who were subject to abuse from the host and the audience. Burke had occasional serious shows, including several on New York's proposed new state constitution, but mostly he whipped his audience into a hate frenzy against oddball guests.

Just as *See It Now* departed, and the Lippmann interviews did not become institutionalized, so too the *Burke* and *Pyne* shows faded quickly, lasting only a few seasons. However, a program that was conceived at the same time and in the same climate—the confrontational mood of the 1960s—would display remarkable staying power.

William F. Buckley, Jr.'s *Firing Line,* begun in 1966, is still going strong. Over the years, it has shown elements of both the hostile and Friendly traditions. In its early years, nasty insults and titillation, rather than genuine intellectual exchanges, often prevailed. During most of the 1970s and beyond, however, *Firing Line* consistently offered deeper, more enlightening (yet entertaining) political discourse than television had offered before or has since.

Firing Line commenced in April 1966, sponsored by RKO, which ran television shows on its own stations in four cities and syndicated them to other stations around the country. The program began with a thirteen-week trial period, but more than 1,000 weeks have passed and *Firing Line* is still with us.

In the early years, Buckley enjoyed a reputation as a deadly conservative gunfighter, and highly touted liberal gunsels were brought in to shoot it out with him. On many of the shows, Buckley and his guest were clearly out to draw blood and score debating points, not to probe ideas. The show's producer, Neal Freeman, concedes that he perceived *Firing Line* as an intellectual version of Friday night at the fights. Buckley's biographer, John Judis, describes the early shows:[4]

The debate between Buckley and his guests often became heated and angry, spurred in part by Buckley's *ad hominem* attacks. The ethic of the boxing ring applied. Buckley was perfectly amiable off camera, but on camera he would do everything he could to discredit his opponent.

In his recent book, *On the Firing Line,* a summary of the show's history, Buckley responds somewhat defensively to Judis's suggestion that the show began disreputably.[5] He points out that the 1960s were unusually contentious, and that his discussions never sank to the level of other talk shows of the time. Buckley goes further, suggesting that the tone of *Firing Line,* then as now, derived from the temperament and attitude of the guest. Many of Buckley's early guests were rhetorical flamethrowers, and he simply met fire with fire. Some guests, he observes, were openly siding with Hanoi in the Vietnam War; Buckley's patriotism made it difficult for him to be polite to them.

Each of these points has some validity. Clearly, the early *Firing Line* should not be analyzed in a vacuum, and Buckley is correct that the "political" shows in vogue in 1966 lacked any sense of decorum. *Firing Line* was never as bloodthirsty or ludicrous as the *Pyne* and *Burke* shows. Indeed, some of the early offerings, especially those with conservative guests but also a few with liberals, presented entirely civil exchanges. Buckley is also correct that the savagery of some shows was hardly his doing; a number of the early guests were both politically and stylistically crazed. It was difficult to have fruitful discourse with Black Panther Eldridge Cleaver, who declared that most people who disagreed with his political agenda were "pigs."

However, the selection of guests was itself revealing. There was, for example, an enormous pool of antiwar advocates to pick from, many of whom were restrained, but *Firing Line*'s producers opted for some with whom Buckley could not possibly have a serious exchange. Buckley points out that guests like Cleaver were invited because they had a significant constituency in the 1960s.[6] However, the same is true of Louis Farrakhan and other extremists today, yet *Firing Line* now almost invariably sticks with guests capable of meaningful and civil exchanges with the host. Beyond doubt, in many of the early encounters the point was combat rather than intellectual discussion. Even the shows featuring civil exchanges with liberal guests tended toward intellectual one-upsmanship and witticisms, not mutual exploration. Shana Alexander, writing for *Life* magazine, made no bones about what she and most viewers saw in *Firing Line*. In an article aptly titled "Even Better than Batman," she wrote: "I like Buckley because he not only doesn't play fair, he doesn't even pretend to. Good talk, not universal justice, is what Buckley is after."[7] (A decade later, Alexander and James Kilpatrick would exchange vitriol each week on *60 Minutes'* "Point/Counterpoint" segment.)

To be sure, even at its nastiest *Firing Line* had far more intellectual content than the other political talk shows of the time, as well as several that emerged in the 1980s. Nevertheless, some of the early programs bore a certain resemblance to the deplorable *Joseph Pyne Show* and *Alan Burke Show*. On one *Firing Line* episode, Eldridge Cleaver, asked why Liberians tolerated what he considered American imperialism, actually responded, "For the same reason I'm tolerating this shit now."[8] Such egregious crudity was rare, but insults and unpleasantness were not.

A magazine review of the *Pyne* and *Burke* shows concluded that "the volatile, sometimes even graceful art of insult ought to be entrusted to wits more finely honed than these."[9] And so it was on *Firing Line*. For the first five years, many of the programs featured exchanges of insults as much as ideas.

The original show consisted of Buckley, a single guest, and a moderator, usually Buckley's lawyer C. Dickerman Williams. Dickerman played the role of lenient referee, leaving almost all of the action to Buckley and the guest. On most shows, after roughly forty-five minutes Buckley and his guest would submit to questions from a three-person panel, sometimes associates of Buckley and sometimes members of the studio audience.

The tone of the discussion was established during Buckley's introduction, which was often both contentious and tendentious. He introduced his very first guest, eminent socialist Norman Thomas, as follows:[10]

Mr. Norman Thomas has run six times for President of the
United States, and six times the American people in their infi-
nite wisdom have declined to elect him. . . . If I were asked what
has been his specialty in the course of a long career, I guess I
would say "being wrong."

In John Judis's words, some of the early shows "teetered precipi-
tously on the edge of intellectual violence."[11] Critic John Leonard
described *Firing Line* as "inspir[ing] a lofty sort of voyeurism: the
conservative matador, the liberal bull, and we are all ears."[12]

A show with radical attorney William Kuntsler as the guest
offered Buckley at his nastiest. After eliciting from Kuntsler that he
is law-abiding, Buckley pointed out that Kuntsler had, in a recent
interview, encouraged students to occupy and even burn down college buildings. Confronting Kuntsler with the apparent contradiction, and exploring his real views, was perfectly legitimate. But at
this point Buckley resorted to insults:[13]

WFB: You see, the trouble with you is that you get very resentful
whenever anybody reminds you of what you say. If *I* said what
you say, I'd feel the same way.

KUNTSLER: Well— [laughter]

WFB: In point of fact, you run around with these bravura statements about revolution and then you come [here] and you say,
"I've never urged anybody to burn down a building." What the
hell—why did you say "Yes" when they asked you, "Do you
condone arson?"

KUNTSLER: Under certain circumstances, so do you. Hell, so
do you. Are you against the war in Vietnam? There's arson every
day there. [Applause] *You* condone arson when it fits your purpose.

WFB: You know nothing about the law. You're about to prove it
again.

Many criticisms may fairly be made about Kuntsler, but Buckley,
in his eagerness to insult, made an unfair and mean one. Although

Kuntsler spoke sloppily in characterizing American activity in Vietnam as arson, his success as an attorney suggests that he knows something about law. (And the full transcripts suggest that Kuntsler was *not* resentful when Buckley confronted him with his endorsement of arson; indeed, considering the fact that he was caught in a blatant contradiction, he was uncommonly serene.)

The Kuntsler encounter was a fine Socratic dialogue compared to Buckley's battle with antiwar activist Robert Scheer. For, in fairness to Buckley, he did follow up his insults to Kuntsler by explaining why the "arson" in Vietnam was entirely different from the arson condoned by Kuntsler. His exchange with Scheer lacked such efforts at analysis.

Scheer helped set the tone for the exchange when he gratuitously informed the television audience that Buckley's introduction was read from a teleprompter. Much of the ensuing conversation consisted of Buckley's efforts to diagnose whether Scheer was anti-American. Scheer kept insisting that Buckley define "anti-American" and they went back and forth, getting nowhere, until Buckley resorted to his reliable fallback position: insults.[14]

SCHEER: Unless you're willing to define the term "anti-American," we're going to sit here for an hour piddling around. But if you're not willing to define what you mean by "anti-American"—
WFB: I *am* willing to define it.
SCHEER: I've waited for twenty minutes now for you to define it—
WFB: I'm willing to define it, but meanwhile I'm rather enjoying your embarrassment.
SCHEER: I don't feel in the least bit embarrassed.
WFB: You sound it.
SCHEER: If you want to get into that kind of thing, I don't feel that merely by having a certain grin on your face or look in your eyes is the opposite of being embarrassed.

As Sheer suggested, they spent the hour piddling around. But in a sense they weren't to blame. The raison d'etre of *Firing Line* in those days was just this sort of gunslinging. Whether Buckley had his opponent down (Kuntsler) or couldn't penetrate (Scheer), his tactic was often a verbal kick in the groin. His *Firing Line* opponents were often equally hostile. Buckley was not only a razor sharp polemicist, but also a consummate entertainer. His upper-class accent, wide and winning smile, slouched seating posture, and sonorous voice all suggested an urbanity that was dramatically belied by his verbal assaults. Critic Joseph Epstein compared him to a stock movie character, the "highly cultivated gangster who keeps an art collection, has impeccable taste, remarks on how he 'abhors violence,' but can be ruthless nonetheless."[15] Audiences took to this character and *Firing Line* enjoyed an ever-expanding syndication around the country, eventually reaching over two hundred outlets.

Despite its success, *Firing Line* changed during the 1970s, gradually becoming consistently cordial and intellectual. Buckley attributes the shift to the times, recalling that "the polarization of the sixties had given way in the seventies to edged but exploratory exchanges."[16] There are supplementary explanations as well: *Firing Line*'s move to public television decreased concern about ratings, and Buckley may simply have been mellowing. Whatever the reasons, *Firing Line* eventually reached the point where it bore little resemblance to many of the early shows. Instead of elevated insult contests, *Firing Line* invariably offered serious and important discussions. The format—a full hour devoted to a single subject—enabled it to achieve depth uncommon in television.

Indeed, during the 1970s *Firing Line* was a model of how television can serve democracy. On one typical show, in December 1976, Buckley and Harvard law professor Alan Dershowitz made some important distinctions in a discussion about pornography. The healthy exchange began when Buckley asked whether films were entitled to the same constitutional protections as the press.[17]

DERSHOWITZ: If we simply passed a law saying, "From now on, films are not covered by the First Amendment," that wouldn't convert us into a totalitarian society automatically. But it's a better society which [gives] vigorous support of *any* media, any film, no matter what its content.

WFB: Well, *I* don't think it's necessarily a better society. Surely a society that condones—it having the presumed power not to condone—the reduction of sex to its exclusive biological dimensions is no more commendable than a society that reduces liquor to its pure alcoholic effect?

DERSHOWITZ: See, here's the essential fallacy of your view. Your view suggests that by *allowing* something under the First Amendment, the society condones it. My view is that society does not condone something just because it *permits* it. . . .

WFB: I shouldn't have said "condone." That's a legitimate point. I should have said "licenses," and I think that's an important distinction.

Then Buckley observed that pornography coarsens sensibilities and suggested that a coarsened citizenry may be unable to sustain a democracy. Dershowitz responded:

I don't disagree with you on that. You may be surprised to hear that. I really do believe that words have impact on conduct and that pornography, in fact, may coarsen sensibilities. I think that there are a great many things in our world that coarsen sensibilities, and that I would prefer to do without. On the other hand, the real issue between us is whether it is an appropriate tool of society to ban the kind of speech which may, in fact, coarsen conduct. . . . Because to move toward a regime of censorship on the ground of heightening sensitivities — I think the cost simply isn't worth the very, very problematic benefits that one might expect in return.

The most notable contrast between this exchange and those on many of the earlier *Firing Line* broadcasts is the good will and open-mindedness of the participants. Dershowitz twice made concessions: first, that our republic can survive limits on films, and second, that pornography likely does coarsen sensibilities. For his part, Buckley readily conceded that he misspoke in suggesting that legalized pornography amounts to a societal endorsement, and granted that the distinction between society licensing behavior and endorsing it is important. (Today, Buckley, in calling for the legalization of drugs, emphasizes precisely this distinction.)

Buckley and Dershowitz wrestled with the nuances of the issue and at least got beneath the surface, which is more than usually takes place on television. They did so because they neither interrupted one another nor engaged in one-upsmanship; they seemed genuinely interested in what the other had to say and in getting to the bottom of the issue. As one critic conceded in an unfavorable review of *On the Firing Line,* "When Buckley doesn't feel compelled to score debater's points, he shows a real talent for educating *specific* political differences with figures like [Allard] Lowenstein and Alan Dershowitz."[18]

In the 1970s *Firing Line* also benefited from slight changes in the format. The moderator was dropped and the three-person panel of questioners eventually was replaced by a single "examiner." The examiner, generally an astute liberal (frequently Jeff Greenfield, Mark Green, or Michael Kinsley), was called in for the last quarter-hour to direct sharp questions at both Buckley and guest. Thus, in the course of the hour viewers were treated to a relatively lengthy exploration of the opinions of both Buckley and his guest, then given the benefit of sustained, skeptical questioning and commentary from another source.

To be sure, even in the later years *Firing Line* occasionally regressed, especially during sporadic special debates, usually consisting of Buckley and several partners taking on various opponents. For example, none of the early shows proved any more ludicrous than the following exchange between Buckley and liberal speechwriter Robert Shrum during a 1985 debate on the Strategic Defense Initiative (Star Wars).[19]

WFB: Would you detail an expenditure which you think is preposterous?

SHRUM: I think a perfectly reasonable and sensible—

WFB: No, no, a *preposterous* one.

SHRUM: When you deal—

WFB: In other words, you can't. You can't. [Addressing the moderator] Can you make him, Mr. President?

SHRUM: When you deal with—yes, I can, Mr. Buckley. [To the moderator] Can you make *him* be quiet for a minute and I will *attempt* to answer his question? [Laughter]

WFB: No, you *won't* answer the question.

SHRUM: I *will* attempt to answer your question—

WFB: Oh, I know you *can't,* but—

SHRUM: —if *you* will attempt to be *quiet* for about fifteen seconds. [Laughter]

WFB: Fifteen seconds. Okay.

SHRUM: The same difficulty occurs with domestic spending. You would regard spending one more dime than nothing on most social programs in many cases as preposterous. I'm telling you we shouldn't waste money on Star Wars. I can define a reasonable level of expenditure—

WFB: How?

SHRUM: —and to spend beyond that—

WFB: How? *How?*

SHRUM: Because I think we can reasonably—

WFB: Now, Mr. Shrum. Don't try to fool anybody. You don't know the slightest thing about—

SHRUM: How did you define *your* reasonable level?

WFB: —what expenses are required to research this program. [Pointing to his debate partner, General Daniel Graham] *He* does.

SHRUM: Do *you?* Do *you?*

WFB: No.

SHRUM: I know you don't, but [pointing to his debate partners] they do. [Laughter, applause]

WFB: But—

SHRUM: Which leads Mr. Buckley, to the question, what are you and I doing up here talking about this?

Of course, Shrum knew exactly what he and Buckley were doing up there: engaging in a silly "so's your old man" exchange. But these special debates, where Buckley and guests were intent on outscoring one another—especially in the laugh and insult department—were the exception. By the mid-1970s, there were generally no insults, few interruptions, and a genuine effort to probe the issue under consideration. An additional strength of the show was that, unlike almost all of the political talk shows that followed, *Firing Line* did not revolve around transient crises and current events; it addressed enduring political, cultural, and philosophical questions as well.

In *On the Firing Line,* Buckley describes his idea of a good show:[20]

I am myself most pleased when, after an hour, I have the sense that analytical construction has actually been going on. That, at the end of a quarter-hour, a foundation has been built on which we proceed in the succeeding quarter-hour to build. And when, arriving at the end of the third quarter-hour, it is intuitively acknowledged that the talk goes on with direct reference to argumentation that came before.

On another occasion, Buckley explained his delight when he and the guest "midwived an insight."[21] As we shall see in chapter 2, it is a rare political talk show that displays interest in analytical construction or the midwifery of insights.

Writer Christopher Hitchens points out that there are three conditions necessary for meaningful discourse: sufficient time, interesting people, and the rules of civilized discourse.[22] *Firing Line,* at its best, has all three. Indeed, it always had the first two, and over the years it unofficially adopted the rules of civilized discourse. As *Firing Line* producer Warren Steibel says, "Bill can be very argumentative, and he can cut people down, but I think what emerged was something more."[23]

In his introduction to Buckley's book about *Firing Line,* Alistair Cooke observes that the show's evolution toward seriousness is especially useful because it comes at a time when political discourse on television—such as *The McLaughlin Group, Crossfire, Capital Gang* and, for a limited time, the *The Morton Downey, Jr. Show*—is moving back in the direction of the Joe Pyne/Alan Burke/early-*Firing Line* approach. Cooke concludes that[24]

> In the era of the sound bite and the TV free-for-all . . . we must be all the more grateful for any arena of public discussion that pits the most intelligent and convinced advocates, on different sides of every public issue, and allows them to go on at length, agreeing to disagree short of actual mayhem.

But the "actual mayhem" shows have taken their toll on *Firing Line.* In July 1988, the program was reduced to thirty minutes. Buckley explained in *National Review* that program managers, "obeying national habits, frown on one-hour talk shows."[25] In his book about *Firing Line* he writes that this was "an acknowledgment of the hectic metabolic schedule of almost all television geared to public policy."[26] Partly because of shows like *The McLaughlin Group,* Americans have become conditioned to expect political discourse in aggressive, bite-size chunks. Even the consummate entertainer William F. Buckley, Jr. cannot keep an audience for an hour of civilized, meaningful discussion of public issues.

To be sure, there may be another partial explanation for the reduction of *Firing Line* to thirty minutes. Buckley is not impervious to age. In the last few years he has lost a little of his edge, and some of the programs have been less than riveting. Nevertheless, *Firing Line* endures, and even at its worst is a cut above most political talk shows. Its shortened format bespeaks a trend in television toward the diminution of serious political discussion but its existence reminds us of a superior, alternative direction.

At the moment, *Firing Line* serves this function almost by itself.

Its exemplary format—lengthy and serious discussions between two people on a single, often enduring subject—never took hold as the model for political commentary on television. The model became, instead, the shorter, faster-paced political roundtable that juggles a handful of current events.

TWO

McLaughlin and Company

Martin Agronsky does not look or sound like a pioneer, but his show *Agronsky and Company* was the first of its kind and ushered in a new genre of political television program. Agronsky was a respected television and radio journalist for several decades before coming up with the concept for which he will be most remembered. Today he says nonchalantly, "I just thought it would be a good idea, that's all. Nothing mysterious about it."[1]

In 1969, *Agronsky and Company* took to the airwaves on a CBS affiliate in Washington, D.C., and was syndicated to a handful of public television stations around the country. Like *Meet the Press, Face the Nation* and *Issues and Answers, Agronsky* featured several distinguished political journalists, but the similarity ended there. On other shows, the journalists' function was to interview newsmakers; on *Agronsky,* the journalists *were* the show. Rather than plumbing politicians for information and ideas, the *Agronsky* participants advanced their own ideas and debated issues with no newsmakers to get in the way.

The weekly half-hour show consisted of a roundtable discussion of current events by four journalists, moderated by Agronsky. Although it spawned a series of political talk shows that tended toward verbal warfare more than relaxed discussion, *Agronsky* itself was relatively sedate and civilized. Indeed, no show moderated by Martin Agronsky could get too out of hand. He seems like everyone's favorite uncle, his gravelly voice and gruff exterior not concealing a warm heart, and his demeanor suggesting a mixture of confusion and amusement. His job was to move the show along and showcase the talent, not to inject his own views too often.

The original participants were Hugh Sidey, who wrote a column on the presidency, first for *Life* and later *Time* magazine; Peter Lisagor, the respected Washington bureau chief for the *Chicago Daily News;* and James Kilpatrick and Carl Rowan, syndicated newspaper columnists.

For the first several years, the centerpiece of the show was the erudite Lisagor, whose sense of humor stood out in the otherwise somber environs. Yet *Agronsky* withstood Lisagor's death in 1976, because he was replaced by another star, George Will, who, beginning in 1974, had sometimes substituted when one of the regulars could not appear. Will, then a columnist for *National Review* and a frequent contributor to the *Washington Post*'s op-ed page, was rapidly becoming the most respected political columnist in the country. He assumed Lisagor's mantle as the show's most erudite and witty participant.

Each show began with Agronsky intoning in deadly earnest the week's major events, then directing the first question at one of the participants. After each person made his initial comment, all of the participants were free to jump in. They occasionally had to work doggedly to maintain the floor, but voices were rarely raised. Every so often, Agronsky stepped in to restore control or to introduce a new subject. And so it went till the end of the half hour when he would cut in to declare, "That's the last word." Some viewers took to wagering over who would get the last word on a given show.

Though at different ends of the political spectrum, James Kilpatrick and Carl Rowan displayed similar demeanors: each seemed to feel strongly about most issues and unhappy that the world did not conform to his vision. They both winced and snarled frequently. Although Kilpatrick writes his widely syndicated column in measured tones, on *Agronsky* his style resembled that of the hockey player who said he took the shortest route to the puck and arrived in ill humor.

Rowan, Ambassador to Finland and Director of the United

States Information Agency in the Lyndon Johnson administration, was the sole liberal among the regulars (not counting Agronsky). He seemed bewildered that his views fell on deaf ears. To seize the floor and straighten out the misguided souls in his midst, he would plead with what seemed like agony and desperation, "Can I get a lick in?" His brows furrowed, he spoke in breathy, heavy tones.

Hugh Sidey shared some similarities with Kilpatrick and Rowan. He too was a Washington insider—few reporters had greater access to presidents Kennedy and Johnson—and seemed in danger of dying from earnestness. However, his outlook and tone were different: objective and unimpassioned. His glowing pieces on Ronald Reagan in *Time* later earned Sidey a reputation as a conservative, but during *Agronsky's* first decade he did not play the role of partisan. He was the master of ambivalence and, as in his writing, devoted to intangibles. His column in *Time* is more likely to dwell on the ambience of the White House Rose Garden than on the federal budget. On *Agronsky* he would recommend that the United States establish a "presence" in some foresaken area of the world, and when pressed as to what specific actions should be taken he would smile as if to say "that's not my department."

George F. Will was often the show's focal point, partly because he seemed out of place in the *Agronsky* setting. He had a different speaking style from the others. While Kilpatrick often interjected angry one-sentence remarks, and Rowan tended to wander, Will spoke tersely and eloquently, in bursts of roughly twenty seconds, scarcely ever emitting an "uh" or "y'know." His sentences not only parsed, but joined to form pretty paragraphs. His vocabulary was refined, and he sometimes spiced his remarks with a brief anecdote or appropriate quotation.

Whereas Kilpatrick, Rowan, and Sidey are political junkies and journalists by training, Will earned a PhD in political theory at Princeton. Unlike Kilpatrick and Rowan, his every utterance was not aimed at establishing a specific point on a particular issue: he often chose instead to clarify different positions, or place an argument in a more comprehensive context. And unlike the others (but like his predecessor Lisagor), Will consistently displayed a sense of

humor and a sharp needle. While coming across as the most reasonable, civilized, self-possessed member of the crew, he managed to get
the others' goat. Fellow conservative Kilpatrick was a frequent
target of his usually indirect digs: "Unlike Jack, I do not think the
First Amendment protects nude dancing," or, "Jack, I thought
conservatives cared about a balanced budget."

It was rare that anyone laid a glove on Will. When someone
mischaracterized his position, Will would respond sharply but
cooly, "As the world's foremost authority on what George Will
believes. . . ." Will's demeanor also set him apart. Whereas Kilpatrick seemed prepared to take an argument outside, Will, looking
prim and scholarly with bowtie and glasses, appeared concerned
that two people talking at once might be too undignified. One critic
contrasted his professorial charm with Kilpatrick's "fuming bad
temper."[2]

But this perspective was far from universal. Despite or perhaps
because of his dignity, intelligence, and articulateness, for some
viewers Will was the villain. He came across as prissy, condescending, and too sure of himself. Many critics remarking about Will's
television persona share this perception.[3]

LARRY L. KING: Will issues pronouncements and edicts with all the
    certainty of the Pope. . . . Will could read from the Pittsburgh
    phone book and make it sound as if he were declaring policies
    vital to the preservation of Western Civilization.

JAMES FALLOWS: [Will] won a huge following on *Agronsky* with an
    Oxford Debating Union demeanor, harrumphingly dismissing
    those who disagreed with him while giving every indication that
    he had been reluctantly pried away from his books.

LOUDON WAINWRIGHT: George Will, of course, is there with his
    teacher's pet mien of barely concealed disdain for all other forms
    of life.

Love him or hate him, viewers wanted to see Will's face on the
screen and hear his professorial bursts. King observes that "even
should you not agree with him . . . his manner has a way of compel-

ling attention.["4] Roone Arledge, who eventually hired Will to work for ABC, refers to his "reverse charisma.["5]

On occasion, Will's failure to conceal his condescension annoyed other participants, a dynamic vividly captured by one vignette. In a discussion about what the United States could do about Libya's Mohammar Gaddafi, Kilpatrick muttered that we should sprinkle thalium salt to thin out his beard—a reference to actual CIA attempts against Castro. Shortly thereafter Agronsky declared that they would go for a commercial break, but the station's execution was slow and the cast unknowingly remained on the air. There was some talk that was difficult to make out, followed by Kilpatrick audibly snapping with disgust, "I know Gaddafi doesn't have a beard, George!"

If the Agronsky program sometimes seemed a parody of itself, it also brought out the parodist in others. In *The New Republic,* Michael Kinsley produced a stinging parody transcript of *"Jerkofsky and Company"*:[6]

MARVIN JERKOFSKY: Concern mounts in Washington about any number of things. Life on earth continues, but doubts arise as to its purpose or justification. Hugh, how do you like my new tie?

HUGH SIDEWALL: As for all the issues you raise, they're important issues, and they'll all have to be studied with care, with very great care indeed, and in fact, if anything is clear at all—which I doubt—it is that these very troubling questions are being deeply considered by some of the finest minds in town, who agree—to a man, I might say, or a woman, Elizabeth—that these are all very, very difficult challenges for the nation. But as for what comes next, we just can't say, Marvin. It's too early to tell.

GEORGE III: On the subject of Hugh's brain, Marvin, I'm reminded of Samuel Johnson's remark that the prospect of a hanging concentrates the mind wonderfully. Foolish consistency, Marvin, is the hobgoblin of small minds, as Emerson so aptly put it. And I believe it was Pope who said, "Tis education forms the mind: just as a twig is bent, the tree's inclined." But the Bible says, A fool uttereth all his mind. And what fools these mortals be, as Shake-speare so wisely observed.

CARL ROLYPOLLY: Myyy quessssschunnnnnnn issssss thissssssss. Hhhhhhhwat abouuuuuuut blaaaaaaack peeeeeeeee-pulllllll?

JACK CURMUDGEON: Harrumph. Balderdash. Poppycock. Horsefeathers. Et cetera.
JERKOFSKY: That's the last word, Jack.

Kinsley used poetic license in having George III (Will) quote promiscuously. While Will has been known in his writing to use three quotations in a sentence, or five or six in a paragraph, on television he was always more restrained. But Kinsley's spoof successfully captured Agronsky's solemnity, Will's erudition, Kilpatrick's gruffness, Sidey's indecisiveness, and Rowan's loneliness. It generated a number of favorable letters to *The New Republic*, as well as one from Agronsky's son protesting the takeoff on his father's name.

George Will left for ABC's greener pastures in 1984 and was replaced by Elizabeth Drew, a reporter for the *New Yorker* who was a frequent substitute over the years. At the end of 1987, Martin Agronsky retired. Yet the show goes on, under the name *Inside Washington.* The new host is Washington broadcaster Gordon Peterson, whose style is similar to Agronsky's—affable, courtly, serious, almost innocent. The show has also added as semiregulars Strobe Talbott, a dignified and thoughtful *Time* reporter, and Charles Krauthammer, a highly regarded syndicated columnist.

Although Will and Agronsky are missed, the program is not terribly different from what it was twenty years ago. Then, as now, it was doomed by its format to provide more entertainment than illumination. There are thirty minutes in which four participants chop up four or five subjects, and all of the participants are heard from on virtually every subject. Under these circumstances, few discussions of real depth occur. But it is good television, and is carried by CBS affiliates in Detroit, Miami, Hartford, and Jacksonville, as well as PBS or independent commercial stations in over fifty cities, including New York, Los Angeles, San Francisco, Boston, Houston, Denver, and Atlanta.

Many viewers watch as much for an amusing interaction among personas—especially Kilpatrick and Rowan—as for a serious dialogue about issues. But at least a serious dialogue is the goal, and *Inside Washington* is a model of respectability compared to some other political shows. "I'm not looking for shouting or conflict for the sake of it," Martin Agronsky once said.[7] That attitude distinguished *Agronsky and Company/Inside Washington* from the program that became its biggest competitor.

During the 1970s, *Agronsky and Company* had the political roundtable market to itself, but in 1982 *The McLaughlin Group* crashed that market with a vengeance. *The McLaughlin Group* began on a local commercial station in Washington but before long was carried by NBC affiliates in four major cities and over two hundred seventy-five public television stations around the country. Significantly, General Electric's sponsorship made it available to public television stations gratis.

In format *The McLaughlin Group* is similar to *Agronsky*: one moderator and four respected Washington commentators have thirty minutes to bounce around a handful of current issues. But *McLaughlin* added new elements: shouting, insults, constant interruptions, nastiness, and general chaos. Upon Martin Agronsky's retirement, James Kilpatrick composed a little poem comparing *Agronsky and Company* to its competitor:[8]

> For 18 years the show drew fans.
> Why was it widely prized?
> Wiser than *McLaughlin,*
> and so much more civilized.

McLaughlin's biggest fans would not dispute the last line. Nor would the host, who intentionally crafted a show in which civility has no place. John McLaughlin brilliantly recognized that there was a market for a faster paced, wackier version of *Agronsky*.

While *The McLaughlin Group* has its actual genesis in *Agronsky,* stylistically its forebear was a segment that was part of CBS's *60 Minutes* in the 1970s. Beginning in 1970, *60 Minutes,* which consisted mostly of documentary reports, added a "Point/Counterpoint" segment: vicious minidebates between conservative James Kilpatrick and liberal Nicholas Von Hoffman. The segment evoked images of two hungry rats in a cell being tossed a small piece of cheese. Kilpatrick and Von Hoffman were tossed a topic instead, and given ninety seconds each to chew it up. They managed to compress their views on controversial issues into the short time span by speaking in vehement bursts that left no room for qualifications, balance, or subtlety.

In his book *60 Minutes,* Axel Madsen states that Kilpatrick and Von Hoffman "found each other hopelessly muddleheaded,"[9] and so it appeared to viewers. Kilpatrick acknowledges that, in real life, he and Von Hoffman actually agree on a surprising number of issues.[10] However, viewers of "Point/Counterpoint" were never treated to agreement. Nor, for that matter, were they treated to an exchange of opinion. There wasn't enough time even to scrape the surface of the issue, only to bellow belligerently.

The segment was popular, and became even more so in 1974 when Von Hoffman was replaced by Shana Alexander as the liberal flamethrower. Alexander's presence added an undercurrent of gender hostility, and the segment achieved notoriety when it was parodied on *Saturday Night Live* ("Jane, you ignorant slut"). Indeed, when Alexander left the show over a salary dispute in 1979, *60 Minutes* made a point of seeking a female replacement. They couldn't find a suitable one, and elected to discontinue the segment. But "Point/Counterpoint" had already made its mark on television by demonstrating that viewers enjoy aggression masquerading as political commentary.

Although the format of *The McLaughlin Group* resembles *Agronsky,* in tone and mood *The McLaughlin Group* is really "Point/Counterpoint" writ large. The moderator sees to it that discussions are nasty, brutish, and short.

*   *   *

People who know John McLaughlin only from his raucous television show will find his background astonishing. He received two
masters degrees from Boston College and a PhD from Columbia.
Even more surprising, he was a Jesuit priest for two decades until
he opted for matrimony. (His wife, the former Anne Dore, later
became Secretary of Labor in the Reagan administration.) His stints
as a radio talk show host and a troubleshooter in the Nixon administration, however, did more than his educational and religious background to prepare him for *The McLaughlin Group.*

On his show, McLaughlin does not play the part of scholar or
cleric. Rather, he is a master showman and provocateur, insulting
his guests and moving the discussion along at a breathtaking rate.
Because many commentators couldn't possibly keep pace,
McLaughlin's approach places a premium on the right cast of participants. For the pilot show, he tried journalists Robert Novak,
Jack Germond, Judith Miller, and Chuck Stone. However, the quar-
tet failed to provide sufficient electricity, so McLaughlin immediately brought in Pat Buchanan and Morton Kondracke to replace
Miller and Stone. The new team remained intact until Novak left
in 1988, relinquishing his seat to Fred Barnes.

Patrick J. Buchanan, a right-wing newspaper columnist and former Nixon speechwriter, was a sound choice to inject a spark. An
advocate of confrontational politics, Buchanan is incapable of pulling punches. His tendency to go for the jugular and state his views
in their most uncompromising form makes him right at home on
The McLaughlin Group. However, Buchanan is good-natured and,
compared to his fellow conservative Robert Novak, comes across as
a model of moderation.

Novak's politics, at least as portrayed on the show, were devoid
of nuance. A frigid cold warrior, he found a communist or fellow
traveler under every bed, never recanted his view that Mikhail
Gorbachev was a fraud, and derided Ronald Reagan, George Bush,
and just about everyone else as too soft on communism.

But it wasn't Novak's politics that made him stand out on *The
McLaughlin Group,* since Buchanan is also on the far right. Rather,
Novak's manner accounted for the volumes of hate mail he at-
tracted. Although he coauthors a civil newspaper column with

Rowland Evans and is known among his colleagues as being cordial and urbane, on *The McLaughlin Group* Novak played the villain. *Washington Post* television critic Tom Shales observes that Novak's television persona is "as warm and friendly as a tax collector right out of Dickens."[11] Novak rarely completed a paragraph without making a mean-spirited remark about one of his coparticipants. His comments often began unpleasantly—"People of your ilk, Jack" and "Mort's problem, as always"—and grew nastier. When left-winger Christopher Hitchens was a guest participant, Novak outdid himself. He bellowed that Hitchens hates America and, when the subject of drugs was raised, asserted that they had finally hit on a topic about which Hitchens knew something. Such nastiness was not reserved for Novak's ideological foes. He did not hesitate to tell the conservative McLaughlin that the host had proven even more ignorant than Novak had hitherto suspected.

Morton Kondracke, a mild-mannered reporter for *The New Republic,* usually served as Novak's punching bag. Like his magazine, Kondracke began as a liberal, moved toward the center, and now tilts right of center on foreign policy issues. Unfortunately for Kondracke, middle-of-the-road politics puts one in a vulnerable position on *The McLaughlin Group.* It is easy to provide a quick, punchy assessment of every issue only if you have a tidy ideological perspective on the world. The middle-of-the-road Kondracke lacks a clear, comprehensive ideology, and his attempts to grapple with the nuances of an issue opened him up to Novak's contempt.

When, for example, Kondracke took the position that he favored aid to the Nicaraguan *contras* but opposed efforts to circumvent the law to attain such aid, Novak disgustedly insisted that Kondracke figure out whose side he was on. When Kondracke criticized cuts in federal drug and education programs, Novak went to town: "A lot of people think Mort is not a liberal anymore. But I'll tell you something, he is like a guinea pig. You mention money; we're going to spend money; he just reflexes all over the place. Money, money, money, money."[12] Kondracke sometimes tried to hit back, but he spoke neither loudly nor quickly enough to keep pace with Novak's assaults. Now that his nemesis Novak is gone from the show, Kondracke holds his own (although he still must endure the taunts of McLaughlin, who addresses him, Mor-TON).

Jack Germond, who coauthors a syndicated column with Jules Witcover, is a down-to-earth good old boy who brings the *Daily Racing Form* into the studio and doesn't hide his enthusiasm for a drink: when John Tower pledged to abstain from alcohol if confirmed as Secretary of Defense, Germond quipped on the air that he would much prefer his scotch to that government post. Germond seems wholly at peace with himself, and being attacked never dents his complacency. The complacency, however, does not translate into conservative views; Germond goes in for the oldtime liberal religion, delivered in relaxed, soothing tones. Reclining comfortably and seemingly without a worry in the world, Germond looks as if he may never get up from his chair.

Esquire has written that "while *Agronsky*'s panelists slump in their chairs like bloated dinner guests anesthetized by a bellyful of beef and port, *McLaughlin*'s boys fairly levitate from their seats, waiting to jump off the turnbuckle and bury a blow in the next guy's groin."[13] Actually, Germond combines aspects of the two descriptions. Unlike Novak, he delivers his thrusts dryly and with equanimity, not with venom. Many of Germond's barbs are directed at the manic McLaughlin, whom he sometimes counsels, with cool condescension, to "calm down." On one show he refused to answer a question, explaining that "the question is ridiculous, even by your standards, John." On the same show, asked the appropriate criminal sentence for Oliver North, Germond deadpanned: "One thousand hours alone with John McLaughlin."[14] (McLaughlin receives such jabs with an unfazed smirk.) Another exchange between the two nicely captures both McLaughlin's freneticism and Germond's serenity:[15]

MCLAUGHLIN: Jack, how would you have voted on Rehnquist?
GERMOND: I don't know.
MCLAUGHLIN: Come on, 'fess up, Jack, 'fess up. How would you have voted?
GERMOND: I would have voted against him.

MCLAUGHLIN: You would? Wow! Go ahead, quickly.
GERMOND: I forgot what we were talking about.

Novak's replacement in 1988 was Fred Barnes, a right-of-center reporter for *The New Republic,* who had been a frequent participant during Buchanan's absence from February 1985 to March 1987 (when he served as Director of Communications in the Reagan administration). Although no match for Novak as a villain, Barnes is hardly a slouch in the feistiness department. In one respect, he is a perfect replacement for Novak. His colleagues regard Barnes as an exceptionally nice man, but viewers are instead treated to a cantankerous snarler.

The tone of *The McLaughlin Group* is established by bombastic introductory music accompanied by a brief voice-over introduction. The moderator himself offers no welcome; the instant he appears on camera he bellows "ISSUE ONE!" and they're off.

McLaughlin ushers in each topic with a catchy title (when Geraldine Ferraro was picked as vice presidential nominee, the caption was "It's a Girl"; when the subject was whether the United States should deploy the B-2 bomber, it was "B-2 or not B-2?") and a brief summary. He then directs a clipped question at one of the participants. The designated speaker crams as many words in as few seconds and as domineering a tone as possible, knowing that at any moment he may be interrupted from several directions. The host tries to ensure that each participant gets at least one crack at the issue, after which it's mostly everyone for himself in a verbal free-for-all. Before long, McLaughlin intones his exit question, which generally involves a prediction or assessment ("On a scale of one to ten, how much does the Gorbachev visit help the Bush administration?"). This process is repeated through roughly five issues until the final segment, the participants' predictions of the week. Then McLaughlin, a vaudevillian to the end, exclaims with boyish enthusiasm: "Bye-bye."

The McLaughlin Group is, in critic Tom Shales's words, "hectic, electric, eclectic, and occasionally dyspeptic."[16] A less kind critic writes that by comparison to *The McLaughlin Group,* the other political talk shows "seem as substantive as the deliberations of the U.S. Supreme Court."[17] The level of sophistication, the pace, and the electricity are all evident in the following discussion of the CIA's conduct during the Iran–contra affair and what should be done about it:[18]

NOVAK: I love it when Mort polishes up his liberal credentials, which are in very bad disrepair, by trashing the CIA. You ought to thank God for the CIA.

KONDRACKE: Don't pull that stuff! You know, there's a CIA and there's a William Casey, and the fact is that you want pros in there who obey the law, not somebody who's shuffling money around the world like that. You should be ashamed of yourself.

NOVAK: Let me say something about Bill Casey. Bill Casey has done more for this country than you would ever think.

GERMOND: Oh, come on. That's ridiculous!

KONDRACKE: And if he makes mistakes, he deserves to go.

NOVAK: I don't think that this is a CIA operation. And I'll tell you, this group ought to—

GERMOND: Oh boy, naive!

NOVAK: This group operates out of ignorance very often, but they're really ignorant on this one, because the people who are involved are Mr. Khashoggi and all of those pals . . .

KONDRACKE: Do you think that Oliver North by himself made all these connections with all these creepy characters around the world?

NOVAK: I don't know what the answer is, but—

MCLAUGHLIN: Let's get out. Let's have a round robin.

In that exchange, there was at least an issue lurking among the verbal debris. Sometimes *The McLaughlin Group* descends into total nonsense, as when the host asked a peculiar question: whether new Senate Majority Leader Robert Byrd "will prove to be more of a plus or more of a minus than was [Bob] Dole . . . in so far as Ronald Reagan's agenda is concerned":[19]

NOVAK: I don't even understand what that question means.
MCLAUGHLIN: Do you want me to give it to you again? Will it help or hurt Reagan more than Dole helped or hurt Reagan?
NOVAK: Well, that's a silly question.
MCLAUGHLIN: It's not a silly question.
NOVAK: I mean, obviously he is a bigger problem for Reagan than Dole was. Dole was supporting Reagan for the most part.
MCLAUGHLIN: I don't know about that. What do you say?
NOVAK: Oh, come on!
MCLAUGHLIN: What do you say?
GERMOND: I don't know what we're talking about either. That was a crazy question. I agree with Novak.

MCLAUGHLIN: The answer to the question is, all things considered, I think that Byrd will be more of a plus for Ronald Reagan than—
NOVAK: Well, you're really on your game today.

Such malarkey inspires both critics and fans of *The McLaughlin Group* to compete for the best metaphor to describe the show:[20]

JODY POWELL: "An ideological food fight."
MICHAEL KINSLEY: "On the evolutionary scale, *McLaughlin* falls about halfway between *Agronsky* and the primordial ooze."
DAVID GERGEN: "[It's like] the old *Friday Night Fights,* the Gillette *Cavalcade of Sports.*"
TIM RUSSERT (Vice President of NBC News): "The Washington *Gong Show.*"
JOHN WEISMAN (of *TV Guide*): "An opinion-maker's bar brawl. . . . A political *All in the Family.*"
MARTY SCHRAM: "Punch-and-Judy comes to Washington."
FRED BARNES: "A catfight."
RONALD REAGAN: "A political version of *Animal House.* . . . It's nutritional value falls somewhere between potato chips and Twinkies."

The McLaughlin Group has also been compared, more accurately, to professional wrestling, soap operas, and situation comedies. Guillotines and catfights are real; much of *The McLaughlin Group,* as we shall discuss in the next chapter, is put-on.

Like many successful soap operas and sit-coms, *The McLaughlin Group* spawned a spin-off: when Novak left in 1988, after a long feud with McLaughlin, he formed his own political talk show, *Capital Gang,* on the Cable News Network. Meanwhile, *The McLaughlin Group* has survived the loss of its villain. While the show has toned down post-Novak, it remains television's zaniest political talk show.

Although Novak founded and coproduces *Capital Gang,* he made Pat Buchanan (who also remains on *The McLaughlin Group*) the moderator, and himself a regular participant. Actually, Buchanan is a discussion leader more than a moderator; he offers his own opinions almost as much as the other participants. The two conservatives are joined by two liberal journalists: syndicated columnist Mark Shields, and *Wall Street Journal* Washington correspondent Al Hunt. In addition to these four commentators, each week the show features a special guest, usually a member of Congress. The dignitary is treated as a fifth participant in the roundtable, not an interviewee.

The inclusion of the special guest is *Capital Gang*'s one significant departure from the *Inside Washington/McLaughlin Group* format. Some critics of the political roundtable programs lament the idea of journalists throwing their own opinions around, acting like politicians. On *Capital Gang,* the distinction between journalist and politician isn't just blurred but eliminated. The special guest, a politician, and the four regular journalists have identical roles in arguing the issues. However, but not quite right to say that the participants act like politicians; the decorum on *Capital Gang* is less dignified than in the Capitol.

Still, partly because of the presence of the guest dignitary, *Capital Gang* is more decorous than *The McLaughlin Group.* Although the regulars never defer to the special guest, and try to make a point of calling him by his first name rather than title, the guest necessarily has a restraining effect. Even the combative Buchanan could not get himself to call House Speaker Foley "Tom." And it's hard to get down and dirty with someone you keep referring to as "Mr. Speaker." *Capital Gang* displays more civility and fewer interruptions than *The McLaughlin Group.*

Ultimately, however, *Capital Gang* is a chip off the *McLaughlin Group* block, not a real departure from it. (On the evolutionary scale, *Capital Gang* is closer to *The McLaughlin Group* than to *Inside Washington.*) Indeed, the beginning and end of each show make *Capital Gang* readily identifiable as a *McLaughlin Group* offspring. After a voice-over introduces the show, viewers are shown a long shot clip of the four participants in action, exchanging fast and furious crosstalk in which nothing can be understood. The show closes with each participant's "outrage of the week," a twist on *The McLaughlin Group*'s closing predictions.

While Robert Novak is far mellower than he was on *The McLaughlin Group,* his brand of discourse remains less than comely. A high percentage of his remarks begin with an insult of Hunt or Shields, generally approximating the following: "As usual, Shields and Hunt are totally out of touch," or, "I must be losing my mind because I agree with Hunt and Shields."

Hunt more than returns the favor. At least half of his remarks involve a put-down of Novak: sometimes a gratuitous insult, often a charge of hypocrisy. During discussions of a proposed congressional pay raise, which Hunt favored and Novak opposed, Hunt never failed to bring up Novak's personal wealth. Sometimes he even reserves his "outrage of the week" for something Novak has written in a recent column or said on a previous episode of *Capital Gang.*

Shields, an extremely witty man, pokes fun not only at Novak but also at himself and everything that moves. If Novak and Hunt seem more concerned with put-downs than issues, Shields seems most interested in wisecracks of any stripe. A forceful and sincere advocate when he stays serious, Shields very often does not.

Unlike the participants on *The McLaughlin Group* in its Novak days, those on *Capital Gang* clearly like one another. They share the insult-ridden locker room banter of teammates, not rivals. To be sure, the hostility on *The McLaughlin Group* was always largely a sham: the participants are friends off the air. But *Capital Gang* drops even the pretense of hostility. The "gang" are pals engaged in playful joshing and their insults, no matter how heavy-handed, are usually followed by smiles, not snarls.

Indeed, on at least one occasion *Capital Gang* bordered on the sentimental. When the participants were asked for their wishes for 1989, Hunt expressed a desire for the public to see the real Bob Novak—a genuinely warm man with a strong interest in the arts. On *The McLaughlin Group,* Novak would more likely have been depicted as a wife-beater with a strong interest in cockfights and the wish might have been for his house to burn down.

Inside Washington and *The McLaughlin Group* both appear primarily on public television and *Capital Gang* on cable television. But a fast-paced discussion among prominent commentators has also made its way to nationwide network television. ABC's *This Week with David Brinkley* offers political roundtable discourse to a much larger audience.

Brinkley is actually a hybrid between a newsmaker interview and a roundtable discussion. Roughly the first forty minutes of the hour-long program consist of a traditional journalistic inquiry into a single major topic. After a short background report on the day's subject, David Brinkley, Sam Donaldson, and George Will question newsmakers, who more often than not are government officials.

However, *Brinkley* then offers a ten to fifteen minute segment with a format resembling *Inside Washington, The McLaughlin Group,* and *Capital Gang.* The newsmakers having departed, the journalists get down to business: what Brinkley calls the "uninhibited, free-for-all" discussion among himself, Will, Donaldson, and another commentator who joins the group solely to participate in that discussion. The guest participant, often Cokie Roberts or Hodding Carter, is usually a respected Washington journalist. Occasionally, the *Boston Globe*'s Ellen Goodman, the *New York Times*'s Tom Wicker, or the *Oakland Tribune*'s Bob Maynard are brought in and provide a perspective from outside the Washington Beltway.

In both the questioning of guests and the free-for-all discussion, moderator Brinkley cedes center stage to the others. Donaldson and Will have vastly different styles. Donaldson made his reputation as ABC's White House correspondent, where he was an undaunted, hungry hound, ready to shout questions at the president or to discuss the blood in the virus-ridden president's stool. By contrast, it is difficult to imagine the refined Will shouting. He certainly never raises his voice on television, and is probably the journalist least likely to discuss the president's stool.

Will and Donaldson are a formidable interviewing team on *Brinkley*. Donaldson describes the effect: "George Will is the intellect. I am the district attorney. Because of George, no one gets away with delivering a fuzzy argument. Because of me, no one gets a free ride."[21] But while some interviewees have difficulty fending off the one-two of Will's logical dissection and Donaldson's take-no-prisoners inquisition, Will does not always seem to regard himself and Donaldson as a team. When Donaldson's questioning gets impertinent or coarse, it is not uncommon for Will, perhaps unaware that he's on camera, or perhaps very aware, to shake his head disgustedly or to shoot an unhappy glance at Brinkley. Indeed, Donaldson acknowledges that "at first, Brinkley and Will weren't pleased by my participation. . . . They thought I was too pushy and asked questions that were too harsh."[22]

The Will–Donaldson difference carries over to the fifteen-minute roundtable discussion at the end of the show. This segment would seem right up the alley of an opinion journalist like Will; instead of asking questions, he can open up, state his own views, and argue his positions far more than he can on the question end of an interview. However, Will controls the environment on *Brinkley* less successfully than he did on *Agronsky*; he must contend with Donaldson, not always a pleasant task. The fearless Donaldson wades ahead, seemingly eager to engage Will. Here is Donaldson's description of their contrasting debating styles:[23]

Will knits his reasoning together so well that if you accept his initial premise, you can't find a chink in the armor of his logic through which to penetrate. Then, too, Will will hurl two quotations from Locke, one from Gladstone, recite from the *Federalist Papers,* and wrap it all in some folksy saying such as "Nellie kicked the cow." Awesome.

I usually just argue, using basic reasoning, sometimes emotion, and always, I hope, verve.

The format works to Donaldson's advantage. There are usually three issues to be discussed by the three commentators (not counting Brinkley, who apart from an occasional wry remark sticks to moderating), and therefore insufficient time to probe. While he might have trouble matching Will in an orderly and lengthy debate, the feisty Donaldson holds his own in the quick, round-the-table atmosphere of *Brinkley.* There isn't sufficient time to analyze his positions or to unravel his inaccurate descriptions of Will's views. Donaldson frequently mischaracterizes Will's position, then takes dead aim at the straw man of his construction. Will tries to set the record straight but he rarely stops Donaldson in his tracks (notwithstanding better preparation: Donaldson notes with detectable pride that, in the preshow conference, "Will makes notes to himself, mostly phrases he wants to use, I believe. . . . I don't put any of it into words in advance").[24] Donaldson sometimes leaves Will looking like a champion prizefighter struggling with a graceless but spunky sparring partner.

One illustration was a discussion of a remark by Secretary of State George Shultz that America should provide aid to the Nicaraguan contras, lest American troops eventually have to be brought into the battle. Will agreed with Shultz, whereas Donaldson pounced on Shultz's comment as confirming that the administration contemplated sending troops to Nicaragua:[25]

DONALDSON: I want to applaud Shultz for pointing out what has been the administration policy. . . . I am convinced that Ronald Reagan is going to get rid of the Sandinistas if he can by hook or by crook. And if it takes American combat troops in the final analysis, I think he's going to push for it.

WILL: What Shultz was saying was that if the Sandinistas proceed with their well-articulated goal of exporting revolution, of having a revolution without borders, eventually the instability in Mexico, Guatemala, Costa Rica, Honduras, El Salvador will be such that it will be in America's national interest to use its forces—

DONALDSON: By raising the specter of combat troops.

WILL: That's not specter. That's happened before in history. Now, suppose he's right.

DONALDSON: Yes, it was called Vietnam more recently, and we lost 58,000 American boys for nothing.

WILL: Suppose he's right. Now, just consider the fact that he may be right, that the United States cannot live with pandemic instability throughout Central America. Suppose he's right. Is it not better to resist Hitler in the Rhineland, to resist him in Czechoslovakia? Why wait till they're in Brownsville, Texas—

DONALDSON: Suppose he's wrong. Would you consider that?

During one particularly hectic sequence Donaldson joked that "this is not Dr. McLaughlin's *Gong Show.*"[26] Indeed, despite Donaldson's spunk and obstinancy, the *Brinkley* roundtable is tame compared to *The McLaughlin Group* or *Capital Gang,* and its analyses somewhat less superficial. However, the similar format ensures that *Brinkley* shares a major shortcoming of all the roundtable shows: insufficient time to probe important issues.

The Cable News Network (CNN) program *Crossfire* is, on the surface, an interview show of a different type from the roundtables. Like *Nightline* and *MacNeil/Lehrer Newshour,* it is a nightly show that usually focuses on the day's major story and consists of journalists questioning guests: one liberal host and one conservative host grill one or two guests "in the crossfire." But *Crossfire* actually bears more resemblance to *The McLaughlin Group* and *Capital Gang* than to its superficial genre-mates.

First, the actual questioning is invariably tendentious and argumentative. Second, the two hosts sometimes argue with each other rather than with the guests. Indeed, the show occasionally truly resembles a crossfire, with the guests (themselves sometimes commentators rather than politicians or newsmakers) caught in the middle of a fight between the hosts. "The guests are really just there as fodder," says media critic Barbara Matusow.[27] In addition, *Crossfire* operates on the same principles as *The McLaughlin Group*: speed and jousting triumph over substantive discussion. As Tom Shales says, "It's the same genre really. It's how loud you can shout, not how brilliantly you can reason."[28]

Until recently, the regular hosts were liberal Tom Braden and conservative Pat Buchanan. (Robert Novak served during Buchanan's stint in the Reagan White House, and still substitutes frequently.) In August 1989, Braden was dropped from the show and replaced by Michael Kinsley.

Braden, who along with Buchanan was with *Crossfire* from its inception in June 1982, has a colorful resume: former English professor at Dartmouth, newspaper publisher and columnist, assistant director of the CIA, and author of the autobiographical book *Eight Is Enough,* which formed the basis of the television series of that name. Theatrically, Braden made a nice match for Buchanan because he was full of moral outrage, didn't mind raising his raspy voice, and went for the jugular. On one show he called guest Reverend Jerry Falwell a "fraud" and on another branded substitute host John Lofton a "know-nothing."

Buchanan and Braden were longtime professional adversaries; for years they did a radio show together and debated on late night local television's *After Hours.* But these earlier ventures were performed in relative anonymity; *Crossfire* achieved prominence. The show began in an 11 P.M. slot, but eventually Ted Turner moved it to 7:30 P.M. and by 1985 it was one of the top-rated shows in all of cable television.

Crossfire opens with a fiery piece of music that has been likened to background music in a car chase.[29] The music augurs the violence to come. Following a short voice-over introducing the show, either host makes a dramatic opening statement before turning things over to his partner for a loaded question to one of the guests. A typically hostile initial question was framed by Braden to a representative of the National Rifle Association (NRA): "When will the NRA stop murdering children?"[30]

One critic described the initial question as "the dropping of lighted sticks of dynamite into the lap of the unsuspecting guest, an action strictly designed to prompt the sort of equal and opposite reaction that will enliven the program."[31] This description is accurate except for the word "unsuspecting." Most guests on *Crossfire* know what to expect. On one show, Novak finished an opening harangue/question to consumer advocate Ralph Nader by asking, "Aren't you just blowing smoke?" "No," said Nader, who then remained silent awaiting a more meaningful question. But apart from the rare guest like Nader or Congressman Barney Frank (who has taken to lecturing the hosts about the show's excesses), most guests respond in kind to the opening salvo and the show takes off from there.

Crossfire has been convincingly depicted as verbal warfare:[32]

> The format calls for three segments separated by two commercial breaks, but the effect is more like World War I: fifteen minutes of trench-clearing battle, three minutes of regrouping, ten minutes of counterattack, and a final five minutes of sniper fire before falling back to prepare for the next day.

The guests know, or quickly figure out, that unless they shout nonstop they are unlikely to be heard, for the hosts show more interest in asking aggressive questions than in listening to answers. *Crossfire*'s former executive producer Randy Douthit once confessed that "with any interviewer, the golden rule is to be able to listen to your guest, and we break that rule constantly."[33] Before he became a regular on the show, Michael Kinsley described *Crossfire* as "two journalist 'hosts' snarl[ing] and scream[ing] inhospitably at two bewildered 'guests' and each other."[34]

Although Buchanan is well known as an advocate of confrontational politics, Braden actually became embroiled in the most heated exchanges on *Crossfire*; he virtually challenged one guest (a member of the John Birch society) to a fistfight and stormed off the set after conservative columnist Cal Thomas suggested that he is a pornographer. During the next commercial break, Buchanan persuaded Braden to return. The two are friends, but this was a rare occasion where friendship served a civilizing function on *Crossfire*.

In fact, the nastiest part of *Crossfire* is often the last brief segment in which, the guests having departed, the two hosts directly confront one another. This segment, advertised on a graphic as "Braden [now Kinsley] vs. Buchanan," provides the chance for a final salvo. In a show about whether creationism should be taught in the schools, Buchanan quipped, "I don't believe man descended from apes, Tom, but in your case I'll make an exception." Braden responded, "You look more like one every day, Pat." With Robert Novak as a substitute host, the closing exchanges are less pleasant still. Like Buchanan, Novak delivers thunderbolts, but with an icy scowl, not an impish grin.

Like a number of the talk shows, *Crossfire* very often has the issues of the day as subjects but amusement as its raison d'etre. It provides great entertainment and continues to produce excellent ratings for CNN. From time to time, *Crossfire* proves that topflight entertainment and enlightenment are not mutually exclusive, when it achieves the entertainment through a vigorous exchange with a lively and unusual guest rather than through mere raucous hectoring.

One such repeat guest is the "Walkman" (Edward Lawson), a black man who has mounted successful legal challenges against laws permitting policemen to stop and question loiterers. The Walkman, with unkempt shoulder-length hair and untidy dress, looks the part of a homeless hippie. It turns out, however, that he has a mastery of relevant Supreme Court law, a quick mind, and sharp wit. When guest host John Lofton suggested that he shave, bathe, and get a job, the Walkman replied that he would take a step in those directions if the hefty Lofton would lose weight. But rather than leave matters as an exchange of insults, he proceeded to make the libertarian point: his harmless behavior and appearance should not be condemned by people who engage in genuinely destructive conduct.

The Walkman is one *Crossfire* guest who proves that entertainment and informative debate need not be exclusive. The broadcasts he was on provided genuine insight into the loitering statutes, and were certainly never boring. On one such show, after noting that the Walkman had once been in advertising, Buchanan asked if he had any suggestions for *Crossfire.* "You might change the name to *Ambush,"* he teased.

Many *Crossfire* viewers thought that the guests weren't the only ones ambushed, believing that Buchanan generally got the better of Braden. Conservative Lyn Nofziger called Braden "a perfect foil for Pat,"[35] and many liberals agreed that their viewpoint wasn't effectively promoted. If a desire to provide a fairer fight lay behind CNN's decision to replace Braden with Michael Kinsley, the network picked a reasonable replacement. Kinsley, educated at Harvard Law School and Oxford, and the former editor of *The New Republic* and *Harpers,* has a razor sharp mind.

Because his reputation is for keen intelligence and not for belligerence, some people thought Kinsley's hiring would change the tone of the show. However, in this regard *Crossfire* has changed Kinsley more than the other way around. Kinsley basically plays the same *Crossfire* game, interrupting, shouting, hectoring, and indulging in sophistry and ad hominem attacks (albeit usually with a bemused smile). Many liberals are happy that he replaced Braden, but those who hoped the show would significantly increase its ratio of light to heat have been disappointed.

Of course, Kinsley was not hired to change the show's essence, because CNN was not and is not prepared to tinker with a successful approach. In television, imitation is the surest sign of success. Cable station CNBC recently began a new nightly half-hour show, *Showdown,* directly modeled after *Crossfire.* Similarly, the *Agronsky/ McLaughlin Group/Capital Gang/Brinkley* roundtable format has not only attained a foothold on national shows but spawned countless facsimiles that deal with local and state politics on stations all over the country.

The reason, of course, is money. As public affairs programs go, the aggressive roundtables have amassed formidable ratings. Whether they succeed in achieving one of their other putative goals—to enrich the public debate—is a different question to which we now turn our attention more fully.

THREE

Where's the Beef?

Although television producers may think otherwise, doing well is not the same as doing good. While earning reasonably high ratings, the proliferating roundtable political programs make at best a limited contribution to the public debate.

On its face, this type of show seems like a perfect way for television to serve democracy—exposing Americans to top analysts wrestling with major issues. Yet some journalists object to the very concept of political roundtables where commentators toss around their opinions. Tom Brokaw expresses displeasure at the idea of "reporters talking to reporters . . . I always thought we were supposed to be talking to primary sources, not celebrating each other."[1] This sentiment may be expected from a straight news reporter like Brokaw, trained to deliver the news and ask questions of newsmakers, but it is echoed by journalists of various stripes. Both David Broder and James Fallows lament that the political roundtables distract journalists from uncovering, describing, and analyzing events.[2] Instead, they are encouraged to play a role traditionally associated with politicians—tossing around opinions in an effort to broaden or shore up their constituencies. Broder expresses a strong preference for *Washington Week in Review,* where the journalists report what has transpired on their beat while generally keeping their political views to themselves.[3]

However, journalists need not be all fish or fowl. While there is certainly a need for straight news reporting and analysis, there is also great value in opinion commentary. In addition to journalists

who acquire, disseminate, and analyze information, we need commentators who provoke and stimulate us with opinions. There is a
school of thought that people need only information and can make
up their own minds. Fortunately, from the country's early days this
attitude has never taken hold. As the publication of the federalist
and antifederalist essays suggest, it has long been recognized that a
full throttle effort to influence opinion through the dissemination of
ideas is healthy in a democracy. Hodding Carter rightly observes
that giving people information and letting them figure things out for
themselves is only one function of journalism. He notes that "another function of journalism is to provide clear, hard-edged different
versions and visions of reality."[4]

Nor is it wise to consign this process to the political arena, leaving
to politicians the task of providing visions and to journalists the task
of uncovering and reporting these visions. Indeed, it is crucial that
political debate not be left solely to politicians, who cannot be
trusted to provide straight talk uninhibited by concern for election.
Programs like *Meet the Press* usually involve cautious, nimble
politicians determined not to let the questioners induce them to say
anything they haven't already determined to be safe. Opinion commentators need not exercise such caution, and thus are more apt to
contribute to a robust debate.

Opinion commentators are paid to think and argue. The voca-
tions and avocations of most Americans are unrelated to their responsibility to contemplate civic affairs. They stand to benefit from
an exchange of opinions among people who work full time reflecting
upon public issues. As William F. Buckley aptly observes, "Interesting journalists are always . . . worth listening to. They combine the
passions of late-night sessions at college with experience gained as
professional observers of the political scene."[5]

Thus, the infusion of opinion journalism into television was a
commendable development. But somewhere it went wrong. James
Fallows notes that "[in] theory, it is perfectly conceivable that talk
shows could have led to fuller discussions of public issues—as Buckley's *Firing Line* often does."[6] There are a number of reasons why
this hasn't happened.

One major problem, alluded to in the previous chapter, is the format of the political roundtables. Under the best of circumstances, thirty minutes is not much time to explore even a single subject in great depth. Buckley, who has hosted *Firing Line* at both an hour's length and its current half-hour, explains the difference: "What you get in thirty minutes is a quick exposure to what is at the top of your guest's mind. What you don't get is that subterranean layer that sometimes gets fleshed out in a full hour."[7] Similarly, James Kilpatrick says that the *Inside Washington* participants "often have the feeling that if we could just go on for another half-hour maybe we could really get our hands on this topic."[8]

Most of the roundtable shows compound the problem by having several subjects digested—or at least swallowed—in the short time available. The problem is exacerbated by the expectation that all of the commentators be heard from on virtually every issue. *Washington Monthly* editor in chief, Charlie Peters, who has participated on the roundtables, puts his finger on the shortcomings of this approach:[9]

> In the multiplicity of subjects that come up on those shows, there's one or two about which you may really know something and have something to say, on which you should take a lot of time. And the other guys should have similar areas where they really know something. But instead, everyone on every question is asked to speak up. . . . That leads to the most ridiculous results.

On *Inside Washington,* host Gordon Peterson and the other participants show a degree of deference to Strobe Talbott on arms control, since he is a foreign policy specialist who has written several books on the subject. Peterson often mentions Talbott's expertise and directs the first question to him. Nevertheless, Talbott is generally given the same few moments as the other participants to summarize his views on such issues. (And *Inside Washington* is the only opinion roundtable on which any deference is shown to a participant in an area of his expertise.)

Indeed, because of the format, the participants on all of the roundtables rarely speak for longer than thirty seconds at a time. When one participant wishes to rebut another's remarks, he does so in the same thirty seconds or less. They may go back and forth once or twice, but then someone else will jump in and before long it's off to the next subject. In-depth discussions are virtually impossible under such circumstances. As Fallows observes, the lack of sufficient time leads to blustery conclusions with little nuance or follow-through:[10]

> George Will, in the few minutes available to him on air, will always say we need more military spending but will not confuse the issue by pointing out that many weapons systems don't work and are a waste. Anyone who's for aid to the *contras* will not waste time talking about what's wrong with the *contras*.

This phenomenon is most obvious on *The McLaughlin Group,* where the problem of insufficient time is compounded by a self-parodic pace. The exchanges whiz by with such speed that even when a participant manages to offer a genuine insight in his compressed remarks, it is likely to be lost on much of the bedazzled audience. One media critic remarks that *The McLaughlin Group* "leaves the deeper thoughts—the thirty or forty seconds for three or four consecutive sentences—to *Agronsky* [and] *Brinkley.*"[11] However, the difference between fifteen seconds of two sentences and thirty seconds of four sentences is not the difference between deep and shallow discourse. The formats on all of the roundtable shows preclude an in-depth exploration of issues.

On *Brinkley,* George Will and Sam Donaldson sometimes explore an issue of more enduring significance than the events of the day, and push it just far enough to set the stage for a serious, probing dialogue that, alas, doesn't come. One discussion about the legitimacy of a Senate filibuster led to reflections on the relative merits of "pure majoritarianism" versus a republican form of government:[12]

WILL: What the filibuster does, and it's the essential genius of the body . . . is it says the Senate will represent not only numbers— numerical strength—but it will also measure intensity. . . . [You] should not push the country—a big, diverse, regionally, ethni-

cally diverse country—into changes without measuring and allowing for and accommodating deeply felt passions.

DONALDSON: Issues that have been intense in this country—civil
rights, there is no better example—for years and years never got
through the Senate. And people became small children, larger
children, and old men and women without their rights being
protected because there was an intensity factor?

WILL: When a consensus developed in the country for civil rights
legislation—we all agree it took too long—then the law was
passed. Mike Mansfield, one of the wisest of our recent Senators,
said he never knew something the American people really wanted
that they didn't get reasonably expeditiously.

DONALDSON: But not during their time. Not when its time had
come. . . . George, how can you argue for democracy when in fact
you say, "Yes, democracy except for—" and you make four or
five exceptions.

WILL: Let me just end it. If democracy is, by the Donaldson doctrine, simple reflections of sheer numbers, then the Senate has to
be done away with because Wyoming has just as many senators
as California.

The issue was joined, with Will pointing out that the Constitution
has several nondemocratic provisions and explaining the need for
such provisions, and Donaldson emphasizing that deviations from
majority rule have led to gross injustices. But no sooner had the
opposing views collided than the subject was changed and the potential for an enlightening exploration lost.

Even when the subject matter is less intellectual, the head-on
clashes between Will and Donaldson often cry out for elaboration.
When Donaldson argued that terrorism could not be combated
effectively unless America understood the terrorists' grievances, he
and Will were led to a difference not simply on a single issue but
in fundamental perspective:[13]

WILL: The very fact that some people in the Arab world say that
Gaddafi is not a madman is zero evidence for the proposition that
he is not a madman.

DONALDSON: From our perspective, you're right. From their perspective, perhaps no.

WILL: But our perspective, Sam, is correct.

DONALDSON: Oh, well, I'm glad God is on our side, George.

Will obviously regarded Donaldson's perspective as sophomoric relativism, while Donaldson scorned what he saw as Will's dogmatic objectivism. This exchange begged for further analysis, even apart from the foundational issue of objectivism versus relativism. They might have explored the dangers of an ethnocentric foreign policy, with Vietnam as a case study, or the foreign policy paralysis that might result from the relativism implicitly endorsed by Donaldson. But time was not on their side.

Brinkley deserves credit for at least whetting viewers' appetites for serious discussion. Other shows don't leave viewers frustrated by insufficient follow-through because they rarely reach the point where exploration appears imminent. *The McLaughlin Group,* for example, lacks even the pretense of depth. As one critic puts it, McLaughlin's emphasis on ratings and predictions amounts to "a tacit acknowledgment of the program's superficiality."[14]

As noted earlier, meaningful dialogue requires sufficient time, interesting people and the rules of civilized discourse. Measured against these criteria, the roundtable programs do not strike out. All of them have interesting and talented journalists and some of them—*Inside Washington* and *Brinkley*—tend toward civilized and serious discussion. But the number of commentators and subjects, and the limited amount of time, prevent these shows from offering probing discourse.

The lack of time for serious discussion is a contributing factor to a second unfortunate aspect of the political roundtables: their locker room machismo. These shows, unsurprisingly, are dominated by men, even though there is no dearth of women commentators. One needn't be a feminist to agree with political activist Ann Lewis that "when political talk shows, like 1950s sitcoms, depict a world of white male authority figures, they reinforce stereotyped attitudes about whose opinions really count."[15]

The hosts and producers of some of the roundtables would like to include women. However, the macho atmosphere of these shows is generally not conducive to female participation. To make matters worse, women who do participate in aggressive banter risk being stigmatized as "screechy" and "strident." As Cokie Roberts says, "People are not offended by a man jumping in and interrupting another man and making his voice louder and more strident than everybody else's. People are offended at the mere notion of a woman doing that."[16]

It is no coincidence that the more sedate shows like *Inside Washington* and *Brinkley* more regularly accommodate women (though still disproportionately few). Mary McGrory, Eleanor Randolph, and Cokie Roberts have all turned down invitations to appear on *The McLaughlin Group.* [17] Randolph explained to McLaughlin that "I was brought up not to break into people's conversations. I don't have the personality that's necessary for the show."[18]

The three most boisterous programs—*Crossfire, Capital Gang,* and *The McLaughlin Group*—have a total of eleven regulars, all male. *The McLaughlin Group* does bring in Eleanor Clift as a frequent substitute participant. Clift invariably smiles during the raucousness, feeling compelled to assure the audience—especially the female audience—that she knows the journalistic circus is a male joke. "I always have it in mind that I don't want to become one of them," she acknowledges.[19]

Clift avoids being stigmatized as shrill on *The McLaughlin Group* because her winning smile and the twinkle in her eye successfully communicate that she is just playing along. She has little choice. Until more women are included, the few who do participate are unlikely to improve the tone or increase the maturity of the shows. Hodding Carter notes that "women constantly experience the problem that if you're going to play and be successful, you invariably have to play the silly old macho bit."[20]

The one-upsmanship, interruptions, and cocksureness not only discourage female participation (which, in turn, reinforces the machismo), but also present viewers with a misleading and unflattering impression of the media. *The New Republic*'s Jacob Weisberg writes that shows like *The McLaughlin Group* "contribute materially to the trivialization of Washington journalism."[21] Indeed, many journalists complain that the currency is being debased by the rowdier talk shows.

Even the regular participants seem to concede that the new kind of television punditry, at least on *The McLaughlin Group,* brings discredit on the profession. As *Esquire* reports,[22]

> Germond, Novak, Kondracke, Barnes, and the rest all bemoan the fact that when people stop them in airports and restaurants it's not to comment on a column, it's to say, "Hey, bludgeon McLaughlin!" or "You really gave it to the Russkies this time." Television makes public figures out of all of them, and the figures they cut on the air are cartoons. Heckle and Jeckle.

The reputations are undeserved. These men are serious, thoughtful people, and political commentary suffers when the public views them as cartoon figures, persons without gravity.

Of course, the complaint that the format and macho tone of these shows are not conducive to serious discussion presupposes that they aim for serious discussion. As noted, this is not always the case. On some of these shows—again *The McLaughlin Group* is the worst offender, although the other roundtables share the problem in varying degrees—political discourse is so subservient to entertainment that the adjective "fake" may fairly be applied.

The McLaughlin Group is often compared to professional wrestling, which thrives on the same bizarre juxtaposition of violence and buffoonery: blustery denunciations of the enemy and ostensibly vicious combat showcased in absurd theatrical excess. Like professional wrestling, most of the political talk shows involve some degree of rigged aggression. This dynamic traces back to the 1960s when the gracious William F. Buckley, Jr., who enjoys warm friendships with many liberals, came across as a throat-slasher who would run over his grandmother to advance the conservative cause. Similarly, on *60 Minutes* in the 1970s James Kilpatrick and Shana Alexander, who share mutual affection, displayed what seemed like genuine contempt. This tradition of contrived nastiness has been carried on in the 1980s by Robert Novak.

Viewers of *The McLaughlin Group* were led to believe that there was genuine animosity between Novak and both Jack Germond and Morton Kondracke. In fact, Novak is friends with his television adversaries, indeed an old, close friend of Germond's. Viewer of *The McLaughlin Group* and *Crossfire* saw such a mean-spirited and obnoxious Novak that they would never have guessed that he is affable away from the television studio. Novak simply played the role of designated bad guy.

As with the villains on professional wrestling, Novak's punches don't really land. The few exceptions prove the rule. Once on *The McLaughlin Group* he accused Kondracke of putting loyalty to Israel ahead of loyalty to the United States, and Kondracke was genuinely furious. Upon learning Kondracke's reaction after the show, Novak replied: "Mort was really angry? I had no idea." When Kondracke later told Michael Kinsley that he intended to even the score with Novak, Kinsley responded that the script should not be tampered with:[23]

> No! That's not it! It's *I Love Lucy.* People watch the show because every week they see these familiar characters get into funny situations and act out their foibles. The audience doesn't want to see Lucy acting brilliantly all of a sudden. And nobody wants to see Mort beat up Bob.

Actually, Kinsley was only half right: scores of people would love to have seen Kondracke beat up Novak. But Kinsley's essential point is correct: *The McLaughlin Group* is theater and Kondracke, stung by Novak's excess, was taking matters seriously as if the burlesque were real.

Indeed, *The McLaughlin Group* treats the subjects of the day largely as an excuse to set in motion entertaining interaction among the participants. Therefore, it is all the more important for these "actors" to stay in character: their interplay, not the issues, carry the show. For Novak to depart from his role, like Bill Cosby spending a show being serious, jeopardizes the ratings as well as Novak's public "appeal."

The McLaughlin Group is not the only political show with elements of contrivance. On *Crossfire,* the anger expressed by the hosts is not always spontaneous. Before Kinsley became a regular, he told a revealing story about his experience as a substitute host:[24]

> My first show, while I was desperately trying to remember the name of the congressman I was supposed to be harassing, my head suddenly exploded with the voice of the producer, coming through the little thing they put in your ear, shrieking, "Get mad! GET MAD!!"

Although Kinsley is now a regular host on *Crossfire,* the producers still find it necessary to keep his ire up. "They try to goad you like a bull in the bull ring," Kinsley says. "They'll say, 'Are you going to let him get away with that?' "[25]

The aura of contrivance rubs off on guests too. Columnist Richard Cohen, a frequent guest on *Crossfire,* says that some guests take radical positions and after the show confess that they weren't serious.[26] *Crossfire*'s forced theatrics were most evident during a program with a Ku Klux Klan member as a guest. When Tom Braden and Pat Buchanan arrived at the studio, they found the Grand Dragon of the Klan seated, decked out in the full Klan regalia. After Buchanan's introduction, Braden upbraided the guest, angrily asking, "How dare you come in here with that silly costume? Why are you wearing that?" The Klansman replied, "Because your producer told me to wear it."[27]

The regulars on the talk shows don't have to be told that it pays to be on their worst behavior. As media critic Barbara Matusow observes:[28]

> Performers of every description have learned that it pays to mug for the cameras. The same is true for journalists, who used to be taught not to call attention to themselves. These days wit,

looks, and charm are assets for an ambitious reporter, but bizarre and obnoxious personalities create the most interest—think about Morton Downey—which explains why a show like *McLaughlin Group* caught on so fast.

As suggested above, the talk shows' contrivances, as well as their encouragement of unseemly behavior, tend to be in the service of another problematic feature: the reliance on disagreement and confrontation. The "Point/Counterpoint" segments on *60 Minutes* were a case in point. James Kilpatrick and Nicholas Von Hoffman actually agree on many issues, but the producers did not give them just any subject and tell them to chew it over. Rather, they used topics on which the two disagreed. In the rapid-fire exchanges, the subjects got lost anyway; the fight, not the issue, was the point of the segment. *Crossfire* plays a similar game in the closing "Kinsley vs. Buchanan" segment: two intelligent commentators stoop to the level of children trying to get in the last word. On occasion, Kinsley or Buchanan sheepishly confesses agreement with the other's closing remarks. "The producers hate that," Kinsley says.[29]

On *Crossfire,* the lust for combat occasionally becomes so excessive that a guest refuses to play along. Barbara Matusow went on the show expecting a serious discussion of her book *The Evening Stars.* She describes what transpired instead:[30]

> They would ask these two-minute questions, harangue you and you'd say "Well, ah—" and that was it, then the next guy was after you. So finally I said, "Okay, why don't you just sit here and ask the questions and I'll just sit here and listen?"

Richard Cohen has had similar experiences on *Crossfire.* "I've been on with people where during the course of the show I just sort of checked out. I won't even participate because they've gotten so crazy."[31] Cohen cites Congressman Robert Dornan, a frequent guest and occasional host, as a flagrant offender. On one show, Dornan went further than defending the Bush campaign's commercials involving Willie Horton, a black man who committed atrocious crimes while on prison furlough. Dornan shouted that the ads didn't go far enough because they neglected to describe Horton's crimes fully. Not about to show such restraint himself, Dornan bellowed about Horton's use of a machete to sever his victim's genitals, and a good deal more. (Unsurprisingly, Dornan has roots in the hostile tradition of talk radio.)

Crossfire's producers like guests such as Dornan. The kind they don't like is Jack Germond, who refused to help the hosts shape their antagonistic story line. As a *McLaughlin Group* regular Germond knows that certain shows thrive on antagonism, but on *Crossfire* he chose not to exaggerate his views in order to provide drama. He says, "It was very clear that they were trying to get me to trash Dan Quayle and I wasn't going to trash Quayle. Braden started asking me if I thought Quayle wrote his own speeches. That was so unfair."[32]

The emphasis on conflict and combat applies to a number of the political talk shows. On *Capital Gang,* when Novak, Shields, or Hunt find themselves unable to disagree on a particular issue, they usually preface their agreement with an insult: "Amazingly, Hunt is right for once in his life," or "I'm in trouble when I start agreeing with Novak." Any agreement must be subordinated to the larger dramatic scheme.

The *Brinkley* roundtable displays less antagonism than other programs, but sometimes it too reflects a confrontation-makes-the-world-go-round mentality. Perhaps in his determination not to be cowed by George Will's intellect, Sam Donaldson sometimes adopts strange and aggressive tactics. When the subject was unflattering books about the Reagan administration written by ex-White House staffers Larry Speakes and Donald Regan, Donaldson couldn't or wouldn't notice that he and Will were in agreement:[33]

WILL: Well [the books] are also unflattering to the authors and I think that's the key there. It speaks very ill of Ronald Reagan and his attention to what he's doing and his involvement in the process that people like Don Regan can get that close to him, or Larry Speakes, for that matter.

DONALDSON: Well, who hired them?

WILL: That's right, well that's the point.

DONALDSON: I mean, if it's not flattering to the authors, who hired the authors?

A corollary of the talk shows' preference for disagreement is their lack of commitment to the search for truth or edification. Writing in *Life* magazine, Loudon Wainwright was right on point:[34]

> I've always thought the best of journalism involved an open-minded search for information. So many of these talking stars seem already to know exactly what they think about everything. They don't appear the least bit open-minded, and they show contempt for people who aren't sure about things or who disagree with them.

A key word here is "star." The regular participants on these shows do become television stars—recognized in public and highly sought after on the lecture circuit. Their own stardom, coupled with the dynamic of the shows, creates a pressure to "perform." Genuine reflection, uncertainty, and confessions of a change of heart may go over well in a university classroom, but they don't make for exciting television. Sam Donaldson acknowledges, "We're all a little afraid that if we become namby-pamby in our views, people will say 'Why do I want to listen to him'?"[35]

As Wainwright suggests, the discussions never produce changes of heart or even concessions that an opponent's argument might give one pause. The extent of this void becomes apparent if one tries to imagine Donaldson saying, "George has convinced me I was wrong," or Novak saying, "Hunt makes an interesting point. I'll have to think that over."

Not only do the participants rarely give ground, they go to great lengths to avoid doing so. On a *Crossfire* show about whether too much research was being done on AIDS at the expense of cancer and heart research, Braden insisted that the gap was justifiable because AIDS was a communicable disease that all people could catch. Buchanan pointed out that regardless of communicability, people were more likely to develop cancer or suffer heart trouble than contract AIDS. "It's a communicable disease," Braden kept repeating, refusing to admit error. On another *Crossfire* episode, Novak vigorously opposed random spot-checking of cars as a means to combat drunk driving because it would violate the privacy of innocent people. Guest Alan Dershowitz countered that mandatory AIDS testing, which Novak favors, violates the privacy of innocent persons far more. Dershowitz noted that because automobiles pose a grave danger to others, this is an area where civil liberties deserve least protection, yet there Novak adopted a strong civil libertarian position. Novak replied, "You bet." To concede any inconsistency, much less error, would violate the *Crossfire* ethic.

A rare exception is *Firing Line* where, as noted in chapter 1, genuine concessions and progress take place. Asked whether any guests actually changed his thinking about a position, Buckley replied that almost all of his guests at least shade his thinking.[36] The difference, again, is partly format; on *Firing Line* guests can speak long enough to develop their own positions and counter Buckley's. But the difference is also one of expectation. Novak and friends enter the studios of *The McLaughlin Group, Crossfire,* or *Capital Gang* not to learn or explore but to shout, insult, proselytize and, above all, to entertain.

The tendency toward closed-mindedness is reinforced by the fact that the roundtable shows are not spontaneous, although they like to suggest otherwise. The voice-over at the opening of *The McLaughlin Group* announces an "unrehearsed" show, and Brinkley introduces the roundtable as an "uninhibited free-for-all discussion." However, on all of these programs the topics are known in advance. On most of them they are known at least the day before and on *Brinkley* they are reviewed in a conference an hour before the show.[37]

On its face, this preparation might seem harmless or even positive, but in combination with the machine-gun pacing, combative format, and lack of time, it deprives the shows of spontaneity and increases the bullheadedness of the participants. They know exactly what they are going to say and they refuse to be budged off their dime, partly for fear of not recovering. Knowing the topics in advance, the participants are never caught off guard and forced to think out loud. If they were, some flexibility might result. Of course, openmindedness might hurt the dynamic of these shows by vitiating the clashes that are so central to them.

For his book *How to Win Arguments,* William Rusher asked several prominent advocates how debate has been useful to them. The late Michael Harrington offered a surprising and instructive reply: "To the degree that it can promote sophistry, [debating] can corrupt personal life. My ideal is *discussion, exchange, the mutual exploration of truth, not a polite war*" (emphasis added).[38] With the exception of *Firing Line,* today's prominent political talk shows involve virtually no search for truth. *The McLaughlin Group, Crossfire, Brinkley, Inside Washington,* and *Capital Gang* differ only in the extent to which the war is polite.

Most of the participants on the political roundtables, especially *The McLaughlin Group,* have no illusions that their spats contribute significantly to the public debate. Fred Barnes says, "You don't go to *McLaughlin* for the great philosophical insight or a better understanding of political ideology. You go for the catfight."[39] Jack Germond readily concedes that *The McLaughlin Group* does not offer serious, in-depth discussion, and Eleanor Clift has called *McLaughlin* "the Super Bowl of bullshit."[40]

Why do these serious professionals take part in pointless catfights? The basic defense is that it's harmless fun. Germond says, "It's not important. It's just a television show."[41] Kondracke concurs: "It is a successful piece of show business and most of the people who watch it understand it as such."[42]

Caution is in order. First, these shows do not have a typical audience; they are popular among journalists and etched into the itineraries of many people who help run the country. The roundtable participants have received a number of calls—some angry, others supportive—from several presidents, and the *New York Times,* not given to devoting news stories to amusing little television programs, has reported what many in Washington already knew:[43]

They may not reach huge, prime-time audiences, but they reach many of the people who run the country. . . . The Agronsky and McLaughlin programs are both seen in the capital early Saturday evening and are popular with Washington officials and other newsmakers who are known to watch as they dress for a night on the town.

Charlie Peters vehemently disputes the contention that no one takes these programs seriously: "At various times these shows have had an enormous effect. There was a time when *Agronsky and Company* actually determined what would be the consensus [on which issues are important] in the press room the following week."[44] By helping to set the agenda for the media, they help set the agenda for the country's debate.

The influence of these shows transcends their agenda-setting function. Marty Schram, a frequent participant on *Capital Gang,* says, "The talk shows are very influential. . . . The politicians either watch them or have their aides watch them. They want to find out what the public's being told."[45] Schram is not guessing; he, like the other participants, is often approached by politicians and their aides expressing pleasure or displeasure with a discussion they heard on a recent show. Indeed, the White House staff prepares a weekly summary of what transpires on the air; the report includes not only the remarks of influential congressmen on the interview shows, but also summaries of the roundtables, including the one whose importance is denied by its own participants—*The McLaughlin Group.* The Reagan administration regularly fed its loyalists tidbits to use on the shows.

If presidents and congressmen worry about what the participants on the roundtables say, they evidently believe that their constituents around the country take the shows seriously. There is ample evidence that they are correct. The *McLaughlin Group* crew has taken its show on the road, making joint appearances before business groups. Fred Barnes explained that outside of Washington the audiences "look for some real analysis from us but in town the people really know the drill."[46] The fact that people around the country confuse *The McLaughlin Group* with real analysis rebuts the claim that the show is harmless fun and confirms Hodding Carter's suggestion that "serious is in the eye of the beholder, and a lot of people take [*McLaughlin*] seriously."[47] If many people take even *The McLaughlin Group* seriously, undoubtedly greater numbers take seriously the other more subdued programs that share *The McLaughlin Group*'s basic flaws. For a multitude of people around the country, the political roundtables serve as a window into public issues and current events. Americans need a better window.

The greatest harm from these shows is their role in corrupting the way we approach public life. They offer what one commentator calls "the politics of kicks . . . the phenomenon of political discourse drained of content," as substance takes a backseat to style.[48] The politics of kicks can produce concrete damage, which critic Joseph Epstein believes happened in the 1960s:[49]

> Political and intellectual life took on the quality of a boutique, whose main design was the avoidance of boredom. The results were unmistakable: the mainstream of the civil rights movement all but crumbled and the Black Panthers became American martyrs; the redistribution of national income became a less absorbing subject than the effects of marijuana. . . . William F. Buckley, Jr., Abbie Hoffman, and Eldridge Cleaver, all of whom rose to fame during this period, shared one quality: for a time at least, none of them was boring. Somewhere along the line, the American train jumped the main rail, and across its engine was emblazoned the word "STYLE."

Epstein is correct that overemphasis on style and excitement affects the country's substantive priorities, and the talk shows have a palpable negative influence in that regard. The shows love an issue like flag-burning—juicy, partisan, and emotional even if ephemeral and relatively unimportant—and have far less use for an infinitely more important matter such as the problems of the underclass. The latter lends itself less to frivolous and titillating attitudinizing. When hundreds of thousands of Chinese students massed in Beijing's Tiananmen Square, the roundtable programs spent little time discussing the historical and sociological context; instead they dwelled on whether the latest developments helped or hurt George Bush's political standing.

Recently on *Inside Washington,* the subject turned to the furor over material about Martin Luther King, Jr.'s sex life recounted in a new book by King's old friend and ally, Ralph Abernathy. Charles Krauthammer pointed out that these revelations constituted a tiny portion of a book about a majestic man, and the country's focus on them reflected the trivialization of today's political discourse.[50] He was exactly right, but could have added that *Inside Washington* was contributing to the problem by spending time on the transient flap over those few pages.

The show that most subordinates substantive issues to horse race politics is *The McLaughlin Group,* where much of the program is given to predictions and assessments of winners and losers. On a single show, McLaughlin tossed out the following questions:[51]

1. At present, the Iran engine is idling. Question. Will the engine go forward and roll over Reagan and the administration? Or will it go into reverse and roll over the Democrats?

2. [NATO envoy] Mr. Abshire will [now] report directly to the President, not to Donald Regan, Chief of Staff. Is Regan's flag being slowly furled? . . . Is it a plus for Regan?

3. Who will succeed Bill Casey if he is replaced at the CIA?

4. It is strongly bruited about in Washington that Patrick Buchanan will announce his candidacy for president. . . . What does this augur for the future of Republican presidential politics in '88?

5. All right. Will Buchanan run for President of the United States? Yes or no?

By the very nature of the questions (completely apart from the ensuing interruptions and insults), the audience would not learn or be provoked to think about issues.

The horse race obsession on *The McLaughlin Group* often achieves comedic effect:[52]

MCLAUGHLIN: On a scale of zero to ten, zero meaning zero damage, ten meaning Armageddon . . . how badly do you think US–Israeli relations have been damaged by the [Iran-contra] revelations, would you say?

COHEN: Ten is Armaggedon?

MCLAUGHLIN: Yeah. Zero is zero damage.

COHEN: Three.

MCLAUGHLIN: Three? That much? Bob.

NOVAK: Thanks to the political clout of the Israelis, I'd say 0.8.

GERMOND: I like that, yeah.

MCLAUGHLIN: 0.8?

GERMOND: I agree with that.

MCLAUGHLIN: You agree with him a lot lately. . . . What about you [Morton]?

KONDRACKE: Thanks to the realities of the Middle East, 0.7.

MCLAUGHLIN: I'll give it a two.

Later, on the same show, the subject turned to Marlin Fitzwater's becoming Ronald Reagan's new press secretary. McLaughlin actually asked the following question: "In the respect scale of zero to ten, after, say, in December 1988, with zero meaning zero respect, ten meaning veneration paid by a follower to the Dalai Lama, what kind of respect will Fitzwater have?" Novak gave it an 8.4; Germond chimed in, "I'm with Novak again."

The fact that the participants recognize the farce doesn't make it less farcical, or indeed less damaging. Something is wrong when television's limited foray into political commentary is wasted on a ten-point guess/rating scale of how much respect a press secretary will garner. We are, in Neil Postman's apt phrase, "amusing ourselves to death."[53]

* * *

Morton Kondracke concedes that "if I thought America was getting its information exclusively from *The McLaughlin Group* I'd be worried."[54] (To his credit, Kondracke himself hosts a show—*American Interests*—that offers a serious and reasonably in-depth look at foreign policy issues.) We may not have reached such dire straits, but the movement is in that direction. Moreover, the inverse perspective must be considered. If there were several programs like *Firing Line,* especially at its original hour length, *The McLaughlin Group* and its kin would be less of a problem. But *McLaughlin* and company crowd such programs off the air. This is partly because they satisfy the networks' informal quota of public service shows,* and putative public affairs programming that degenerates into pure entertainment takes precious air time away from serious discussion.

Perhaps more importantly, shows like *The McLaughlin Group* make more serious programs less attractive. These shows titillate us and condition us to expect titillation from political discourse. Watching *Crossfire* and *The McLaughlin Group* makes viewers impatient with slower paced, more serious discussions. The reduction of *Firing Line* to thirty minutes reflects this phenomenon.

A cyclical effect is at work here. Television generally has helped make us a less reflective people with shorter attention spans, creating an environment in which *The McLaughlin Group* can flourish and an hour-long *Firing Line* cannot. Shows like *The McLaughlin Group* then serve to reinforce and worsen the condition that originally gave rise to them. Charlie Peters sees our current political talk shows as "adding to and encouraging the cliché-thinking in the country. All of America is beginning to think that way. We're all ready to give that short, pithy answer."[55]

*The Federal Communications Commission has removed formal requirements but all the networks continue to provide some public affairs programming. There are several explanations for their willingness to do so. To some extent they may have internalized the value of providing such a service. Alternatively, they may fear bad public relations if they stop. And a few of the shows provide decent ratings for the Sunday morning period in which they tend to be crammed.

It may not be empty boasting when John McLaughlin predicts that his "spin of the week" approach to political discourse is the wave of the future.[56] But as we have seen, one needn't speculate about the future to recognize *The McLaughlin Group*'s influence. Michael Kinsley maintains that McLaughlin "has had more impact on journalism than all but a very few people."[57] Kinsley points out that the tendency to reduce serious issues to multiple choice games and one-to-ten ratings is "spreading all over the place and sneaking into print."

It is not surprising that *McLaughlin*-style television discourse proliferates while the Friendly tradition of serious in-depth political commentary remains relatively dormant; the medium of television is more conducive to the former than the latter. In his book *Four Arguments for the Elimination of Television,* Jerry Mander lists many biases inherent to television, including:[58]

The personality is easier than the philosophy. The philosophy requires depth, time, development.

Superficiality is easier than depth.

Short subjects with beginnings and ends are simpler to transmit than extended and multifaceted information. The conclusion is simpler than the process.

Feelings of conflict . . . work much better than feelings of agreement and their embodiment in calm and unity. . . . The former is more visible than the latter.

Competition is inherently more televisable than cooperation.

Loud is easier to televise than soft.

These tendencies of television apply directly to the roundtable political programs. First, the shows tend to subordinate ideas and issues to the personalities of the participants. The opening of these shows is revealing: *Capital Gang* prominently displays the names of the four participants; *Inside Washington* displays a montage of its participants; *The McLaughlin Group* shows the participants within the frame of a newspaper front page, suggesting that they themselves are the news. On *Capital Gang* the cult of personality runs especially high. Al Hunt frequently depicts Robert Novak as a silly hypocrite while Novak returns the favor, characterizing Hunt and Mark Shields as fuzzy-headed naifs. The participants, rather than the issues they are discussing, become the central drama.

Moreover, the shows focus on short subjects with clearly marked beginnings and ends, current events that can be tossed around and then left behind with a prediction or assessment of the latest winners and losers. They rarely take on more enduring open-ended questions such as the role of race, religion, or the Constitution in our political processes. As Hodding Carter says, "The talk shows are terrified of discussing anything that is not topical. . . . They are a creature of breaking waves that have nothing to do with anything else."[59] The shows also display several other traits that Jerry Mander deems inherent in television; as we have seen, the discussions tend toward superficiality, conflict and competition, and, in the case of several of them, loudness.

All of these tendencies are subsets of television's seminal principle: don't let the viewer change the channel. In the advertising-driven television business, a single percentage point in ratings can mean a difference of millions of dollars of profit a year. With the advent of remote control devices that make it easy to change channels, and with the increase of choice offered by cable television, producers have redoubled their efforts to keep viewers' attention. After decades of experimentation and study, they figured out what works best: a fiery, sensory blitzkrieg leaving no opportunity for reflection.

This is, of course, especially true of the violence and sex-laden prime-time network dramas, but it also permeates the political shows where, ideally, reflection is precisely what should be encouraged. The hosts of *Crossfire* and *The McLaughlin Group* seem hyperconscious that a dull moment could be fatal. Before going to each commercial, one of *Crossfire*'s hosts promises something dramatic upon the return. If the subject is arms control, he is likely to say, "When we come back we're going to find out if nuclear war is inevitable." Before going to the final commercial, the screen identifies the upcoming segment as "Kinsley vs. Buchanan," a warning to viewers that a change in channel will result in missing the most titillating exchange of the evening.

Sadly, the imperative to freeze the hand that reaches for the switch continues to grow. The Nielsen Watch is introducing a "Passive People Meter" to provide more precise ratings. The device, a machine that will sit atop the televisions in participating households, will take note of when people nod off or leave the room, even when they don't change the channel. John McLaughlin will have to work that much harder not to let Morton Kondracke explore both sides of an issue and producers will be even more resistant to shows like *Firing Line* which give viewers too many opportunities to change the channel or simply avert their eyes.

Assuming for the sake of argument that public affairs programming must be hostage to ratings, we need not concede that we are doomed to unnourishing shows. For however much the political roundtables reflect principles inherent in television, it is demonstrably false that no program can succeed without adopting these principles. There are counterexamples to the boisterous superficiality that dominates political commentary on television today.

Nightline and the *MacNeil/Lehrer Newshour* both demonstrate that the level of political discourse can rise reasonably high and retain a large audience. These programs are closer to news than opinion commentary (actually offering an eclectic combination of newsmaker interview, minidocumentary, and roundtable show) with the hosts offering no opinions of their own and usually interviewing politicians, not commentators. But *Nightline* and *MacNeil/Lehrer* do offer discussions among competing points of view and thus demonstrate how political debate can achieve respectable television ratings without resorting to silliness or one-upsmanship.

Both *Nightline* and *MacNeil/Lehrer* offer considerably more depth than the roundtables. *Nightline* devotes the entire half-hour to a single subject, and host Ted Koppel masterfully discerns and pursues important points. *MacNeil/Lehrer* touches on the major news stories of the day, but it has a full hour, so its feature discussions on a few topics never seem rushed. Mark Shields, a regular participant on both *Capital Gang* and *MacNeil/Lehrer,* explains the difference between them:[60]

> It's all elbows and knees on *Capital Gang.* If you hesitate, you're going to get your neck bitten. What you say has to be compressed, like a tabloid headline. On *MacNeil/Lehrer,* you generally do one subject in an evening and there's a chance to do it in a more reflective way. There is time, a sense of leisure to it. If you don't make the point on this go-round, you're going to have another chance.

Neither *Nightline* nor *MacNeil/Lehrer* descends into silliness, notwithstanding Koppel's good sense of humor and light touch. (Jim Lehrer and Robert MacNeil rarely crack a smile.)

To be sure, these shows are hardly models of political discourse. *Nightline* is simply too short. Between its initial background report and lengthy commercials, there is limited time for Koppel to conduct the interviews. William F. Buckley, Jr. has declined several recent invitations to appear on *Nightline* because "there really isn't much point in staying up until midnight in order to speak for a total of fifty-two seconds."[61]

MacNeil/Lehrer, for its part, risks giving sobriety a bad name; many viewers find the questioners soporific. More importantly, *Nightline* and *MacNeil/Lehrer* both provide an appallingly narrow range of views, a point taken up in detail in part III. But whatever their flaws, both of these offerings prove that respectable ratings and serious, in-depth discourse are not incompatible.

However, the trend is in the wrong direction. As noted in the previous chapter, panel shows modeled after *The McLaughlin Group* keep springing up. More significant than the increase of dross is the diminution of gold. As noted, in 1988 *Firing Line* was reduced to a half-hour, because sixty minutes of serious discussion was considered virtually intolerable.

When *The McLaughlin Group* first appeared in 1982, stations received many calls complaining about these animals who were so rude and kept shouting at each other. At the time, it was a shock to viewers to see people behaving in such a manner on television. Less than a decade later, the shock has long passed. Instead, it is leisurely and serious discussion of a single subject that disconcerts viewers.

The networks, of course, see such shifts in the public's appetite as simple marketing challenges requiring new programming strategies, not as a threat to the public interest. Thus during the 1980s the networks adopted a new approach toward news as well as opinion commentary. Bill Moyers talks from personal experience about what he saw happening at CBS:[62]

> The line between entertainment and news was steadily blurred. Our center of gravity shifted from the standards and practices of the news business to show business. . . . "Entertainment Tonight" was touted as the model—breezy, entertaining, undemanding. . . . Instead of the role of gathering, weighing, sorting, and explaining the flux of events and issues, we began to be influenced by the desire first to please the audience. The object was to "hook" them by pretending this was not news at all.

Moyers, who like Koppel was influenced by the lofty example of Edward R. Murrow, tried desperately to bring serious programming to CBS. He envisioned public affairs programming infiltrating prime time and exposing a mass audience to major political and cultural issues. In 1986, he left CBS because he could not convince the network to go along for the ride. But before leaving, Moyers delivered a parting shot, giving an interview to *Newsweek* in which he criticized CBS and, more importantly, warned that television is headed down a dangerous path. "Once you decide to titillate instead of illuminate, you're on a slippery slope, you create a climate of expectation that requires a higher and higher level of intensity all the time."[63]

One year later, the *Morton Downey, Jr. Show* came along, suggesting that the slope was slippery indeed, and muddy at the bottom. *Downey* represented (one can hope) the culmination of the trend of insult-oriented, fast-paced political discussion. Although critics often grouped *Downey* with the shows of Geraldo Rivera, Oprah Winfrey, Sally Jesse Raphael, and Phil Donahue, it was really closer to the *McLaughlin Group* genre. Unlike the *Winfrey/Donahue/Rivera* shows, *Downey* was not a daytime extravaganza appealing mostly to housewives; more often than not it dealt with political issues rather than the sociosexual material that dominates the daytime tabloid offerings.

Anyone who saw the *Joe Pyne Show* and *Alan Burke Show* in the mid-1960s knows that *Downey* was recycled trash. Both shows drew on the tradition of talk radio, where insults are even more prized and less restrained than on television. *Pyne* and *Burke* were very much products of the 1960s, when confrontation and showmanship were the preferred means of political debate. It is not a coincidence that a cartoon like *Downey* would emerge in the 1980s in an era where shows like *Crossfire* and *The McLaughlin Group* thrive.

Downey personally emerged from talk radio, where he had made big and frequent waves. He was fired from his first radio show in 1983 after he called an abortion rights advocate a "son of a bitch" and decked him with a right hook. He was then fired from twenty stations in the next five years for other failures of self-control. One can see why he was considered suited for television's 1980s-style political "discourse."

The producers who brought us *Downey* first gave thought to hiring G. Gordon Liddy, the Watergate burglar. They were clearly looking for a "character." Although a movie has been made of Liddy's life, Downey's history actually makes Liddy's look bland. In addition to a radio talk show host, Downey has been a radical left-wing activist, right-to-life candidate for president, owner of a basketball team, and singer and songwriter, among other things. In 1987 he entered a new realm, when television producers sensed that the time was right for a return to the *Joe Pyne* formula.

Anyone who has not seen *Downey* is unlikely to accept a description of it as less than gross exaggeration. *Downey* made *The*

McLaughlin Group look scholarly and sedate. It was common for Downey to go nose to nose with his guests in extended shouting matches, and physical violence (usually involving guests, not Downey) actually erupted on the show more than once. Several lawsuits against him emerged.

The show opened to a heavy disco beat accompanied by a collage of numerous images, many violent. A big simulated mouth with enormous teeth (which Downey has) opened, revealing a frenzied studio audience. The host then marched in triumphantly, sometimes surrounded by bodyguards, exchanging high five hand slaps and kisses with members of the first row and greeting some of the guests. He then stared into the camera and gave an introduction that made *Crossfire*'s opening seem marshmallow soft. It usually ended with a shouted command that was some variation of "TONIGHT, WE'RE GONNA KICK ASS!"

The hour-long show had roughly six guests, at various points either seated at "home base" or standing at one or two "loudmouth" lecterns in front of the studio audience. Downey prowled around grilling guests, backed by a raucous audience that roared approval of everything he said and hooted guests who expressed views Downey disliked. After a while, guests would shout at one another—they were instructed before the show to interrupt early and often. Many expletives were deleted, though sometimes they were exchanged so fast and furiously that the censor could not keep up. If *The McLaughlin Group* is a food fight, *Downey* was a brawl at the football team's fraternity house.

Occasionally, Downey outdid himself for boorishness. When, in the midst of a heated exchange, a little spittle emerged from the mouth of a gay rights activist, Downey shouted at him to "keep your bodily fluids to yourself." When the activist said, "Shut up," Downey slapped him in the face, incurring a lawsuit. When the name of the recently deceased mayor of Chicago, Harold Washington, came up, Downey snapped, "Thank God the fat pig is six feet under." Another time he barked, "Shut up, you old hag," at an elderly woman. These remarks are only mildly more offensive than the things he said routinely on the air.

Downey simply extended the core concept of *The McLaughlin Group*—political discourse as locker room banter with an undertone of violence. John McLaughlin recognized that shouts and insults in the guise of political discourse could attract a big audience. The brains behind *Downey* recognized that some swearing and shoving don't hurt either. *The McLaughlin Group* and *Crossfire* tolerate and even encourage obnoxiousness, whereas *Downey* went a step further and glorified it: the rowdy, animalistic crowd cheered Downey wildly not for his wisdom, courage or rectitude but because he was the champion of the boors.

Like Pyne and Burke before him, Morton Downey wore out his welcome quickly, and his show was canceled in the fall of 1989 when too few stations renewed it. *Downey*'s cancellation, however, hardly bespeaks a trend toward superior public affairs programming. *Downey*'s problems stemmed not from its going in the wrong direction but from going ridiculously far; indeed, the fact that it did so well for as long as it did is sadly revealing about political "discourse" in America. Far from being consigned to the ash heap of television history, Downey proved himself a useful commodity.* Cable station CNBC brought him back, first on a show modeled after *Crossfire,* and then on an audience call-in show. The producers are wise enough to avoid the excesses of the original *Downey* show while still trying to appeal to viewers who seek heat, not light.

The demise of the original *Downey* suggests that, at least for the moment, there is a limit to the egregiousness of televised political mayhem. And there are a few other promising developments where television's role in promoting political debate is concerned. C-SPAN provides the valuable service of constant coverage of political events and occasional interviews with commentators, and pub-

---

*Not surprisingly, John McLaughlin has also proven a valuable property. In addition to his roundtable (and his newsmaker interview show, *One on One*), he now hosts a nightly talk show, *McLaughlin,* on cable station CNBC. The new show has a promising format—it devotes a full hour to a single area and has one primary guest—but McLaughlin, as is his wont, usually subordinates substance to schtick.

lic television comes through with an occasional pleasant surprise. Lately Fred Friendly himself has appeared as moderator on a number of lengthy panel discussions of important, enduring subjects.

But, on balance, television is not moving in the right direction. *The McLaughlin Group* and its ilk have carved out an ever-expanding niche, while Americans see less of the enriching political commentary that people like William F. Buckley, Jr. and Bill Moyers try, against the zeitgeist, to bring us.

II

The Players

FOUR

The Perfect Participants

Political talk shows clearly do not bring out the best in all of the participants. They fail, for example, to showcase the talents of Robert Novak and James Kilpatrick. Instead of giving us Novak the able historian and Kilpatrick the craftsman, the political roundtables turn both into cartoon figures.

But that is not to say that all political commentators are out of their element on these shows. The roundtables give at least two commentators, Patrick J. Buchanan and Sam Donaldson, an opportunity to do what they do best. These two would probably not be flattered by the comparison to one another. Donaldson has derided Buchanan as a flame-throwing ideologue, while Buchanan sees Donaldson as embodying the liberal bias of the media. Yet both of these commentators are made to order for today's political roundtables, for reasons that are revealing about the genre.

PAT BUCHANAN

Patrick J. Buchanan is perfectly suited for *The McLaughlin Group* and other shows of the genre. These shows exalt speed. If a participant takes time to collect his thoughts, search for a precise formulation, or give genuine consideration to what someone else has said, he will slow the pace or lose the floor. The people who succeed best can condense their opinions into short bursts. This comes easily for Buchanan, who combines articulateness with a nicely packaged view of the world and thus speaks glibly and quickly on all issues. No producer or moderator must prompt Buchanan to get to the point, and neither other participants nor the audience need clarification as to his meaning.

But there is a more important reason why Buchanan is the perfect participant for these programs. The cardinal rules on the talk shows are to force a fight whenever possible, and never to back down or express a scintilla of doubt. Pat Buchanan lives by these very principles, as eloquently demonstrated by his autobiography, *Right from the Beginning.*

Like all good autobiographies, Buchanan's does much more than recount the events of the author's life; it projects a perspective on those events and an attitude toward life that together paint a vivid self-portrait. *Right from the Beginning* depicts the essence of a man who is made for today's political talk shows.

Reviewing Buchanan's autobiography, Garry Wills observes that "next to Certitude, Buchanan's chief satisfaction seems to have come from fighting, with fists or insults."[1] Indeed, Buchanan's autobiography is, literally from the first to the final sentence, a celebration of confrontation. The very opening sentence of the book is, "Let the Bloodbath Begin!"[2] Several hundred pages later, Buchanan closes with a paean to country, family and faith, "the things worth dying for . . . worth fighting for . . . worth living for." The book that opens with a bloodbath thus closes with a fight to the death. In between are graphic descriptions of children whipped with belts, a bottle smashed over an infant's head, cats savaging dogs, street fights, boxing lessons, hair-pulling nuns, pranks involving butcher knives, war games replete with foxholes and encampments, smashed car windows, football injuries, arrests, political and journalistic brawls, and wars.

The book's opening call for a bloodbath is actually sounded by a Buchanan supporter urging him to run for president in 1988. Buchanan gave strong consideration to such a run before deciding that his candidacy would only damage the best hope of the Right, Jack Kemp. But in light of his agreement with Kemp on virtually every issue, why was Buchanan considering the run in the first place? On this point, as on most others, he is forthright. Kemp, he explains, is not a confrontationalist:[3]

> Jack's rhetoric is sprinkled with phrases like "my distinguished colleague" and "my good friend." . . . To me, the times required that we not only boldly enunciate our agenda for America, but expose and attack, with all the political weapons in our armory, those in Congress driving the United States toward disaster. . . . "Football is not a contact sport," Vince Lombardi is said to have corrected a questioner, "it is a collision sport; dancing is a contact sport." . . . That is how I feel about politics. . . . Among the reasons I wanted to run, then, was not only to make the case *for* us—but *against* them.

Although Buchanan's ideological soulmate, Jack Kemp is not Buchanan's kind of politician because he treats his colleagues politely and would rather advance a program than smash the other side.[4]

In the opening chapter, Buchanan also reflects nostalgically about the 1940s and 1950s, "in many ways a better time."[5] His musings about the specialness of these decades is revealing; it isn't simply that criminal suspects lacked *Miranda* rights and homosexuals remained in the closet, although those things matter a great deal to Buchanan. Rather, the "tone and style" of his childhood were set by the returning World War II veterans who "had crushed the Japanese empire and overturned the Thousand Year Reich; and they gave to American society a toughness and maturity it has long since lost."[6] Significantly, Buchanan revels especially in the martial aspect of America's triumph; we "crushed" the Japanese, which gave us "toughness." To say we "stopped the Japanese and preserved freedom" would ignore the machismo and confrontationalism so central to Buchanan's childhood and to his adult life.

Buchanan's autobiography describes at length his Catholic upbringing and thus introduces the other major theme of the man and his book—certitude:[7]

> Modern theory holds that children should be presented with facts, shown a menu of values and beliefs, and be permitted to

make up their minds, at maturity, as to what is right and wrong, and what they wish to believe. We held to the opposite view. We already had the truth. . . . We began our education with the answers.

Garry Wills notes that devout Catholicism exacts a high price— total submission to the ideas of the Church—but that for Buchanan, "the satisfactions were abundant, especially that of Certitude, to which [he] became addicted."[8]

While Buchanan does not discuss the incongruity of his religious faith and his love of confrontation, he is obviously aware of and not disturbed by it. His choice of the confirmation name Francis instead of Xavier leads to the following digression:[9]

When I got home Pop let me know I had blown it. "Why didn't you take Xavier?" he demanded. Francis could as well mean the pacifist with the pigeons as the great missionary. "Well, don't worry about it," Pop said finally, "Francis is a great name, too." (Later I was relieved to learn the sainted Francis of Assisi had accompanied, and not condemned, the fifth Crusade.)

The twin themes of confrontation and certitude merge when Buchanan reveals that his militant anticommunism derives primarily from his Catholicism:[10]

Either men are, or they are not, children of God, with immortal souls, destined for eternity and possessed of God-given rights no government can take away. If they are, Communism is rooted in a lie; and every regime built upon that lie is inherently illegitimate.

Although Buchanan proclaims the centrality of Catholicism to his political views, he fails to pursue the implications of his vision. Thus he doesn't discuss or even acknowledge that numerous people who do not believe in immortality and God nevertheless recognize the evils of totalitarianism. *Commentary*'s review of his autobiography noted that while many conservatives are atheists and many liberals speak with religious conviction in favor of disarmament and social programs, Buchanan never says "on which side of the 'war' [he] put[s] these two groups of religious and irreligious."[11] By avoiding this question, Buchanan preserves a tidy universe in which "us versus them" and "good versus evil" correspond perfectly to "believer versus nonbeliever" and "conservative versus liberal."

In *Right from the Beginning* the themes of confrontation and certitude also merge during Buchanan's spirited defense of Senator Joseph McCarthy. Actually "defense" is too weak a word; as usual, he takes the offensive, arguing essentially that no tactics in support of anticommunism are too ruthless and that those who disagree fail to appreciate the communist menace. The discussion of McCarthy leads the book squarely into the political arena where, we find, nothing changes. For after lengthy recollections of a fight-filled childhood, Buchanan glides into political discussion with the same instinct for confrontation:[12]

> Just as you cannot explain the virulence of the hatred of Joseph McCarthy by proving he violated Senate traditions or abused Senate witnesses, you cannot explain the hatred of Richard Nixon by proving he authorized Bob Haldeman to tell Pat Gray to impede the Watergate investigation. . . .
>
> No, what was behind both flaming controversies were warring concepts of morality, of legitimacy, of patriotism. Who is the legitimate moral authority in America? Who, by conviction, background, character, and belief, should rightly determine the destiny of the Republic, and which is the illegitimate usurper, incompetent to identify and protect America's true interests from her real enemies? . . . [McCarthy's] lasting contribution was to have ripped the bandages off the underlying wound in America's body politic: them or us.

Buchanan is commendably honest. Not many commentators will defend both Richard Nixon and Joseph McCarthy, much less in the same paragraph. His analysis, however, is disturbingly stark. American politics reflect a good deal of consensus—the Democrats and

Republicans are far closer to one another than left-wing and right-wing parties in most European countries. But Buchanan makes the difference between, say, Hubert Humphrey (who condemned both McCarthyism and Watergate) and Richard Nixon into a manichean struggle between polar forces: one aligned with God, truth, and light, and the other with Satan, falsehood, and darkness.

Buchanan attended Georgetown University, and gave the Catholic school more than it could handle. His college days were replete with violence, and an early taste of Buchanan-style politics. Running for president of a social club, he distributed literature that personally savaged his opponent. The pamphlet went over well, which convinced Buchanan that "in dealing with the smug and the self-righteous, the best defense is not to bother defending anything, just go after them the way Jack Dempsey did, while they are still on their stool taking the applause."[13]

But what's the best defense against smug and self-righteous policemen? Buchanan became involved in a brouhaha that got him suspended from Georgetown for a year. Stopped by two policemen for speeding, he addressed the cops in language that he hadn't learned from the nuns. He concedes that he resisted arrest, which led the police to try to work him over. Buchanan didn't take it lying down, and in the ensuing brawl he gave almost as much as he received.

Brawling with policemen and getting thrown out of school over a traffic violation is an occurrence totally in keeping with the politics of Pat Buchanan, a man who could turn a proposed tax increase into religious and political warfare. But the incident leads to a rare lapse of ideological consistency in Buchanan. He blames the policemen for the brawl, yet if a similar case of police brutality were discussed on *The McLaughlin Group* or *Crossfire* there is little doubt he would side with the cops.

The incident with the police also gave rise to a vignette that beautifully illustrates how Buchanan can hold extreme views and advance them uncompromisingly while remaining likable to many of his ideological foes. A decade after the brawl, when he was writing militant law-and-order speeches for Vice President Spiro Agnew, he received a call from the office of syndicated columnist Jack Anderson asking about the fight with the cops at Georgetown. Buchanan did not share the Nixon administration's instinct for stonewalling. He unhesitatingly told Anderson's assistant, Brit Hume, "I was ahead on points—until they brought out the sticks."[14]

Buchanan claims to have learned from the fight, to have matured and grown more peaceful, but his confrontationalism hardly diminished after college. He took his fists to Columbia Journalism School, and if Georgetown hadn't often seen the likes of Buchanan, neither had the country's most prestigious breeding ground for journalists. When socialist Michael Harrington tried to speak to a small crowd outside of a Columbia library, Buchanan harassed him so impressively that a detective asked him if he would be willing to file reports about campus radicals with the New York City police.

Buchanan declined because he was too busy. Busy fighting, among other things. Buchanan punched and gave a black eye to a classmate who dared to respond to a caustic remark of Buchanan's with a burst of obscenities. Buchanan confesses—actually boasts—that he had it in for the boy because one of Buchanan's friends didn't like him.

A satirical edition of the journalism school's newspaper showed photographs of each student with an identifying word beneath the picture. For Buchanan the word was "Violence!" Noting that his classmates couldn't understand why he punched out the other fellow, Buchanan embarks on one of those reflections that starts with his fistfights and leads, effortlessly, to the crusade against communism:[15]

My brothers and the friends I grew up with would have understood in a second. They would have reacted the same way; a thirty-second fistfight was no big deal. . . . If you took [abusive language] without responding, something was wrong with you, not him. The only reason America sits still for the kind of abuse vomited upon us routinely at the U.N. is because, too often, we have had the wrong kind of Americans sitting there.

The wrong kind of Americans, presumably, do not share Buchanan's affinity for picking fights with people they don't know and don't like.

Buchanan came of age politically during his journalism school days. The conservative movement of the time had, he explains proudly, "a willingness on the part of the faithful to sacrifice, the conviction that the cause was right and just—and must not, *above all,* be compromised" (emphasis added).[16]

After completing an M.S. in Journalism at Columbia in 1962, Buchanan found an effective way to serve the cause, landing an editorial position at the confrontationally conservative *St. Louis Globe Democrat.* (He botched an interview with the *Washington Post* because he was "sidetracked into a foolish argument with the *Post* editor over their biased coverage of everybody from Joe McCarthy to Richard Nixon."[17]) The move from student to professional did not mellow Buchanan. He had barely begun work when he told off the union steward. Before long, he was furious at his boss and itching to punch him out.[18]

Despite or perhaps because of his feistiness, Buchanan moved up in the ranks quickly, impressing his colleagues with his eloquence, intelligence, and diligence. It's easy to see why he loved his job at the St. Louis paper. When a reporter at the rival *Post-Dispatch* "misstepped," Buchanan's boss walked into his office screaming, "Pat, I want you to cut this bastard from rectum to belly button." Buchanan replied, "I'm already working on him, sir."[19]

From the *Democrat,* Buchanan moved to working for Richard Nixon, an undeclared presidential candidate for the 1968 election. He was a Nixon speechwriter and jack-of-all-trades right up until his boss's resignation in August 1974. At that point he became a syndicated newspaper columnist and eventually a television commentator, the positions he has maintained until the present, interrupted only by a two year stint in the Reagan White House.

Buchanan's service in the Nixon and Reagan administrations was true to form: an exaltation of confrontation. Buchanan wrote some of Vice President Spiro Agnew's harshest speeches, savaging the eastern liberal establishment and the media. Both in his speechwriting and his private counsel, John Judis writes, "Buchanan became one of the principal proponents of Nixon's politics of 'us versus them' [and] endowed politics with the imagery of God and devil and the violence of adolescent gang warfare."[20]

In his book *Before the Fall,* William Safire, also a former Nixon speechwriter, explains that when Nixon wished to attack an opponent, he knew he could count on Buchanan to do the deed with relish.[21] Safire also recounts how he and Buchanan were monitoring the first moon landing to prepare the President, when news came in that Senator Edward Kennedy and a passenger had been in an automobile accident. Buchanan casually told one of the news summary aides to keep an eye on the clips to determine whether the passenger was female.[22] This is vintage Buchanan. Neither an imminent monumental event nor a tragedy could move his eye off the ball: the possibility that an enemy might be destroyed. It is no wonder that, completely apart from his impressive speech-writing ability, his boss valued him tremendously.

Shortly after Nixon's reelection in 1972, Buchanan, still working in the White House, wrote a book, *The New Majority,* lauding the accomplishments of the administration and suggesting that the best lay ahead. Even in victory Buchanan could not resist trumpeting the old confrontationalism: "The die was cast. A collision between Congress and the President . . . seems assured."[23] He gleefully predicted that the forthcoming battle with Congress "guarantees that, whatever else occurs, the next four years will find the nation living in what the Chinese characterize as 'interesting times.' "[24]

The Nixon administration would soon face more of a confrontation than even Buchanan wanted: the Watergate scandal that eventually drove Nixon from office. Predictably, Buchanan was a hard-liner in the Watergate matter, counseling destruction of the infamous White House tapes and urging the firing of special prosecutor Archibald Cox. In *The Final Days,* Bob Woodward and Carl Bernstein recount Buchanan's opposition to the suggestion that Nixon concede the House of Representatives and proceed to trial in the Senate:[25]

> If the President had to go down in the House, he should take some Congressmen with him. "We should hold those mothers' feet to the fire" [Buchanan] said. . . ."We've been too nice to those guys, and what has it ever gotten us?"

Buchanan's five hours of abrasive testimony before Sam Ervin's Watergate committee were among Nixon's better moments in the final months. (Buchanan was a rare witness who took the offensive, blaming Nixon's woes on the irresponsible Congress and media.) And Buchanan was one of the closest Nixon aides to escape Watergate with his liberty and reputation—and his fighting style—intact.

That style was much in evidence in Buchanan's next book, *Conservative Votes, Liberal Victories,* written shortly after he left the White House. In the introduction, he predicted that "the comments herein on race and politics will be adjudged among the most mean-spirited of a thoroughly ill-tempered book."[26] Indeed, he charged that the "fabric of American society is being torn apart" by the civil rights movement. A theme of the book was that conservatives need to be more confrontational. Buchanan counseled them to "seek out, not avoid, political conflict with liberals of both parties, on issues, domestic and foreign. We have nothing to lose by confrontation politics."[27] He called for conservatives to consider forming their own political party, a coalition of right-thinking Republicans and George Wallace supporters.

The party never having been formed, Buchanan remained a Republican and returned to the White House in February 1985 as director of communications in the Reagan administration. For the opportunity to serve another Republican president, Buchanan dropped his growing syndicated newspaper column and his positions on television's *Crossfire* and *The McLaughlin Group*. But he didn't drop his sword. Rather, as director of communications he communicated his usual brand of uncompromising confrontational conservatism. Larry Speakes, Reagan's press secretary at the time, believes that[28]

Pat Buchanan caused more trouble in only two years than anyone else who worked closely with Reagan during the first six years. . . . We wasted more time and energy in meetings trying to pacify Buchanan on every conceivable subject than we did making decisions. . . . He was always looking to pick a fight with Congress.

Reagan aide Michael Deaver provides a specific example of Buchanan's approach to governance. When it was revealed that Nazi SS men were buried in the cemetery Reagan intended to visit during a trip to West Germany, many Jewish groups called on the president to cancel the visit. The White House was split between those who wanted the president to cancel and those who wanted him to go ahead as planned (so as not to offend our German allies) but to make other conciliatory gestures toward the Jewish community. Buchanan was a voice of one against *any* conciliation:[29]

Buchanan argued for a harder line, a bigger gesture, a clearer defense of the new Germany and virtually an amnesty for the Third Reich; whatever it took to avoid the appearance that the President was bending under pressure from Jewish or any other groups.

Buchanan's uncompromising approach to policy and politics led many in the administration, as well as the first lady, to want him out. He attracted a great deal of attention during the Iran-contra scandal, hailing Oliver North, assailing Republicans who headed for the "tall grass" rather than backing the president, and blaming the whole affair on a "liberal lynch mob" that sought to do in its second conservative administration in two decades.

Buchanan's final act before returning to private life in 1987 was an open farewell letter to the president published in *Newsweek*, advising Reagan exactly what to do for the duration of his administration. It was vintage Buchanan, attacking the Democratic leadership in Congress, depicting an "us versus them" war in the United States as well as abroad and, above all, warning against compromise:[30]

> If—as you have more than once reminded me—the problem with True Believers is they always want to "go over the cliff with flag flying," the problem with Establishment Republicans is they abhor the unseemliness of a political brawl.

By contrast, Pat Buchanan relishes a good brawl. A year after his complaint to Reagan, he would write ruefully that "the Congressional Republican abhors a political brawl. . . . And, unfortunately, you cannot make an attack dog out of a cocker spaniel."[31]

Back on *Crossfire, The McLaughlin Group*, and eventually also *Capital Gang*, and in his syndicated column, Buchanan resumed his assault on the liberal lynch mobs and sodomites who were almost as much the enemy as the communists. He became homosexuals' public enemy number one for insisting that AIDS was "nature's retribution" for their perversity. He wrote that the Iran-contra affair was an attempted "coup d'etat" by Democrats and "in the aftermath of the failed coup, Ronald Reagan should go on the offensive" because "now is the time to let the jackal pack know what it means to strike a king."[32] McCarthyism is a term that gets tossed around loosely these days, but Buchanan came close to the real thing when he wrote that the vote on aid to the Nicaraguan contras would "reveal whether [the Democratic party] stands with Ronald Reagan and the resistance—or Daniel Ortega and the communists."[33]

This style, indeed Buchanan's upbringing and entire life, prepared him perfectly for *McLaughlin/Crossfire*-type television. When William Rusher solicited tips from skilled debaters for his book *How to Win Arguments*, Buchanan's response was revealing:[34]

The most common error of the amateur is to reveal, by expression, that an antagonist's shaft has struck home—to exhibit that state of agitated confusion known as "fluster." . . . When caught *in flagrante* by an opponent, one should concede nothing—but imitate a motorist flagged down by a foot patrolman for running a stop sign. Look directly ahead and stand up on the accelerator. There is at least the chance you will not have to pay the fine.

Viewers of *Crossfire* and *The McLaughlin Group* will not be surprised by this advice (though, after events at Georgetown it may be presumptuous for Buchanan to offer hints on how to deal with traffic violations). Buchanan never exhibits "fluster" and plows straight ahead when caught "in flagrante." When a *Crossfire* guest wondered why a Buchanan column dwelled on pederasty among homosexuals and failed to mention that it was more common among heterosexuals, Buchanan responded: "I wasn't talking about heterosexuals, I was talking about homosexuals." When another guest recommended economic sanctions against Panama, Buchanan roared, "That's Jimmy Carter all over again." When the guest pointed out that Ronald Reagan, not Carter, imposed such sanctions, Buchanan didn't blink. "It's Carteresque."

In these instances, Buchanan was obviously not searching for truth. Indeed, in his autobiography he comes out against the search for truth:[35]

We were taught that the Church "had" the truth; and that we were there to learn it. Today, one hears the faculty and students at Georgetown are all engaged in a mutual "search" for truth— which suggests they had something in the 1950s they subsequently lost.

Buchanan's television adversaries attest to the fact that he long ago stopped searching for truth. His former *Crossfire* adversary Tom Braden says, "There's no self-doubt in Patrick,"[36] and his current colleague on *The McLaughlin Group* Morton Kondracke says, "I envy him his certitude. If you think you know how the world is put together, you pick up your gun and shoot. You don't agonize over the facts."[37]

Indeed, on his various television shows Buchanan shoots a lot and agonizes rarely—which makes him a perfect participant for *McLaughlin/Crossfire* television. The certitude also produces another tendency common to these shows: it makes Buchanan content with facile, neatly packaged arguments that wouldn't survive scrutiny.

This trait carries over into his writing. In *Right from the Beginning* Buchanan explains that conservatives and liberals "have a different sense of what is truly morally evil. . . . It is not Botha or Marcos or Pinochet; it is the Soviet Union and its genuinely evil ideology."[38] There is a case to be made for America going easy on South Africa, but here Buchanan goes further, suggesting that apartheid is not "truly morally evil" or "genuinely evil." Later in the book he urges that America stop abusing South Africa over the "sin of segregation," implying that apartheid amounts simply to segregation, perhaps even "separate but equal."[39]

If a genuine exchange of ideas can accomplish anything, it should be able to shatter the idea that South Africa's sin is solely segregation and thus ranks relatively low on the scale of evil. Yet on *Crossfire* Buchanan has frequently downplayed the evil of apartheid in the course of urging that America leave South Africa alone. No one has had the time or speed to expose his callow equation of apartheid with segregation before the next commercial or harangue.

Buchanan shows a knack for the glib formulation, as when he says that "the root cause of the rioting of the 1960s was the rioters of the 1960s." But often he uses such witticisms as substitutes for arguments. On the various roundtable shows, he carved out a neat position on the Reagan administration's violations of the Boland amendment forbidding congressional aid to Nicaragua: the letter of the Boland amendment was complied with while the spirit of the amendment—to help the communists—was malevolent. This argument was erroneous. The *effect* of the amendment may have been to assist communism; that was certainly not its spirit. Some congressmen saw support for the contras as a lost cause, while others believed that, even if effective, America had no right to violate Nicaragua's sovereignty. It is inconceivable that more than a few members of Congress voted to cut off aid to the contras in order to assist communism. The idea that the Boland amendment should be circumvented because of its heinous "spirit" is no sounder than a liberal administration confiscating guns because the spirit of permissive gun laws—to kill children—is malevolent.

Similarly, on his various television shows, Buchanan argued that the criminal trial of Oliver North made no sense because North had already come before the American people in testifying before Congress and was acquitted overwhelmingly: polls showed that 60 percent of those questioned supported him. This argument blatantly confuses the court of public opinion and the court of criminal justice (60 percent of the people may have sided with Jack Ruby, too), but Buchanan recited North's massive public acquittal like a mantra. On *Capital Gang* Mark Shields called him on it, saying, "Surely we don't want jurisprudence by Gallup poll." Shields added, "I'm sure you don't want that, Pat"—though if that isn't what Buchanan wanted it's unclear what he did want. On a show like *Firing Line,* he would have had to explain whether he really did want jurisprudence by Gallup poll and, if not, exactly what his point was. In the fast-paced *Capital Gang* roundtable, the point wasn't pursued.

In the final chapters of his autobiography, Buchanan lays down what would have been his presidential platform. It is of a piece with the preceding narrative of his life—the fistfights and chase scenes of the youth give rise to the world view of the adult. Buchanan urges Congress to strip courts of jurisdiction over several issues, relishing the possibility that the Supreme Court would declare such action unconstitutional: "We will have set up an overdue confrontation."[40] He proposes ten constitutional amendments and calls for a constitutional convention not because he believes these amendments will be passed but because it "would reveal which of the two parties is populist, and which elitist, which trusts and which fears the people."[41] Us versus them, black and white.

Buchanan, who must be embarrassed that his two presidents signed arms control agreements with the Soviets, declares that *no* agreement with the Soviet Union will enhance American security. His certitude on this point leads to a rather strong indictment of those who disagree. The idea that arms control agreements can serve the interests of the United States is "contradicted not only by history but by common sense. It is not natural for men to believe nonsense like that."[42]

With no trace of irony, Buchanan laments the savagery of contemporary American politics and the unbridgeable divisions between Americans. He apparently rationalizes his own brand of religious warfare as self-defense. Thus, in his book *Conservative Votes, Liberal Victories,* he declares that "the nation is a divided country; but it was not divided by conservatives."[43] Regardless of who started the battle, Buchanan unleashes poisonous escalation. One reviewer of *Right from the Beginning* went so far as to say that Buchanan "bring[s] to American politics the same tender reasonableness the Ayatollah brought to Iran."[44] That characterization is a bit much but the reviewer is right to point out that "when people disagree with Buchanan in this book, they are 'morally confused' or have a 'mental disorder' or are 'decadent' or 'willfully self-deluding.' "[45]

Liberals are not alone in regretting Buchanan's tone and approach. *Commentary*'s review of *Right from the Beginning* notes that "Buchanan's language of 'religious war,' leaving as it does no room for compromise or diversity," threatens the conservative coalition too.[46] If Buchanan worries that his brand of politics and discourse are divisive, either for his party or country, he hasn't shown it.

Buchanan takes his religious warfare to the airwaves on several different talk shows. He plainly relishes the macho, fast-paced rat-a-tat in vogue today. His notions about desirable television discourse are further revealed when he discusses *Firing Line.* As noted in chapter 1, in the early years *Firing Line* was often a wicked insult contest but eventually evolved into television's most provocative and educational political program, offering civil and intellectual exchanges. Predictably, Buchanan much preferred the early *Firing Line*. Those shows, he recalls nostalgically, were "a masterpiece" because Buckley would "tear [liberals] apart." But now, he says wistfully, it has become "much more academic and intellectual than it is combative. . . . an exploration in issues rather than an engagement."[47]

One would have thought that an exploration of issues would be highly desirable in a democracy, but it isn't the goal of most of today's political programs, which prefer "engagement." Thus, these programs were made to order for Patrick J. Buchanan. Us versus them. Never duck nor rest. Glib and certain. It is no accident that Buchanan is a major player on today's political talk shows.

Sam Donaldson

Few people were more excited than Sam Donaldson about rumors that Pat Buchanan would run for the presidency in 1988. On *This Week with David Brinkley,* Donaldson said that he would take a leave of absence from the White House beat in order to cover the Buchanan campaign.[1] Donaldson may have intuitively recognized that he and Buchanan are soulmates.

They are not ideological soulmates, however. While Buchanan is one of the most ideological members of the media, Donaldson is one of the least. As a White House correspondent he tried to conceal his political views, leading William Rusher to complain that Donaldson "shows signs of believing . . . that his obvious and offensive liberal bias is in fact merely an appearance."[2] Today, Donaldson makes no bones about his liberal leanings. (He wasn't always liberal, having started a Texas chapter of the Young Republicans in 1956 and supported Barry Goldwater in 1964.) He has expressed ardent opposition to the Reagan administration's Central American policies and enthusiastic support for arms control, welfare programs, and the environment. Nevertheless, ideology is not a high priority for Donaldson.

If he were a crusading liberal, it would show in the roundtable discussion on *This Week with David Brinkley,* where he exchanges the cap of objective reporter for that of speak-your-mind pundit. Yet while on *Brinkley* Donaldson's overall views shade left of center, they do not follow a rigid predictable ideological pattern. His tone and style, on the other hand, are quite predictable: he seems certain that the last thought to pop into his head is indubitable, and he enjoys a good tiff. It is these traits—certitude and delight in confrontation—that make him Buchanan's soulmate.

Donaldson's childhood, as recounted in his autobiography, *Hold On, Mr. President!,* evokes Buchanan's early years. He was raised by his mother on a farm in Texas. (His father died before Donaldson was born.) Like Buchanan, he received his share of beatings and grew up tough. At the age of seven, during World War II, Donaldson blew up the family truck thinking it was a German tank. In general, life on the farm was downright Buchananesque:[3]

> One noontime when I was seven, I playfully shot out a front tooth of one of the Mexicano workers with my BB gun. No one was amused. When I was twelve, I got a kick out of letting the horses ride out of their corral so I could chase after them on a farm tractor.

Because of his lack of discipline, Donaldson's mother sent him to the New Mexico Military Institute. The years of hazings, beatings, military discipline, and toting a semiautomatic rifle did nothing to mellow the lad.

Along the way, Sam developed a love of broadcasting. After graduating from Texas Western College (now the University of Texas at El Paso), he did a year of graduate work in telecommunications at the University of Southern California. He then started a magazine called *Television Film,* and although he didn't stay long, the magazine survives to this day under the name *Television International Magazine,* run by his original partner.

In the 1950s Donaldson experienced a tour of active duty in the Army, a brief marriage, and a short stint as an insurance salesman. When he finally made up his mind to pursue a career in broadcasting, he did so with characteristic grit and determination. He pounded the pavement and climbed the ladder, first working in the news department of a CBS affiliate in Dallas, then as a roving reporter for Washington's WTOP. In 1967, having become the station's weekend news anchor, he was hired by ABC.

At ABC, Donaldson covered Congress, the Vietnam War, and Watergate. His big break came in 1976 when he was assigned to cover the dark horse presidential campaign of Jimmy Carter. When Carter was elected, Donaldson was promoted to ABC White House correspondent. It was in that post that he made his mark, paving the way for his participation as pundit on *This Week with David Brinkley.*

True to his nature, Donaldson was not content to be just another White House correspondent. He came to Washington at a time when most reporters were deferential—content to receive press handouts and attend official briefings. Donaldson, however, doesn't know the meaning of deferential. Political comedian Mark Russell jokes that "if you looked up the word 'brash' in the dictionary, you would find only the word and a picture of Sam."[4] With his devilish eyebrows perched atop an otherwise friendly countenance, Donaldson waded in where others feared to tread and helped transform his profession.

Over the years Donaldson questioned Jimmy Carter so aggressively that the departing president semijokingly wished two bad things on his successor: Menachem Begin and Sam Donaldson. Donaldson's reputation as a fearless gadfly grew during Ronald Reagan's presidency. Reagan's aides were not fond of exposing their man to the press; during some of his unavoidable contacts with the media they had the president walk near a noisy helicopter that would drown out questions. Most reporters got the hint, but Donaldson did what came naturally: he screamed questions over the din. On occasion the president, less fearful than his aides, answered.

Donaldson's style caught on and increasingly reporters stopped accepting silences and evasions from politicians. Although Donaldson earned lots of hate mail—informing him that he was an arrogant, obnoxious, boorish, belligerent, grating loudmouth—his example spurred the press to serve its adversarial function noticeably better. Whereas once he stood out as the gauche goon who yelled at the president, today any White House correspondent unwilling to confront the commander in chief abrasively is considered unsuited for the job. Helen Thomas, dean of the White House press corps, says that Donaldson "may be the *enfant terrible,* but it's very effective. It makes them realize we're not all sheep."[5] Three times his colleagues have voted Donaldson the best all-around television news correspondent of the year.

If Donaldson's lack of deference deserves praise, his actual questions often do not. They frequently betray an indifference to gathering information or discovering truth, and a lust for combativeness and entertainment. In his book, Donaldson states that there are no bad questions, only bad answers.[6] He provides ample illustrations of this belief, as when he praises a *Los Angeles Times* reporter for asking President Reagan about the first couple's sex life.[7]

The questions Donaldson seems proudest of having asked are quite revealing. During the Iran-contra affair, he confronted President Reagan as follows: "The polls show that a lot of American people just simply don't believe you; that the one thing you've had going for you more than anything else in your presidency, your credibility, has been severely damaged. Can you repair it and what does it mean for the rest of your presidency?"[8] This "question" contains a few loaded premises. Donaldson confidently asserts that credibility has been Reagan's greatest strength and leaps from the fact that people disbelieved Reagan on the matter of Iran-contra to the conclusion that his credibility has been severely damaged in general. Donaldson didn't invite Reagan to comment on these premises, only to state whether he could repair the stipulated damage. The question was evidently intended to create tension and perhaps get the president's goat, rather than to gain insights. Indeed, Donaldson's follow-up questions at news conferences often ignored the original response, suggesting that answers were not what he was most interested in; confrontation was.

The loaded premise is a major part of Donaldson's arsenal, as when he began a question to Israel's Ariel Sharon by stating, "General, you have a record of insubordination."[9] He is pleased as punch at having once asked Reagan, "Sir, do you think this [an appearance at a wildlife refuge] will limit the damage done by the Burford appointment?" (On that occasion Reagan had the presence of mind to unload the premise, answering that there was no damage to begin with.)

Donaldson loves the "when did you stop beating your wife?" type question. He boasts of asking Caspar Weinberger whether he was antisemitic[10] and of demanding Jimmy Carter to defend himself against charges that "your administration is inept." There was no shortage of good questions to ask Caspar Weinberger about his allegedly anti-Israel positions or Jimmy Carter about his administration's failures. But Donaldson, who justifies his aggressive style by saying that the public deserves answers, framed his questions in a way that couldn't possibly lead to a revealing response; instead, they put someone on the spot and created excitement. Similarly, he was obviously not hoping to elicit information when, on *Brinkley*, he asked two supporters of Israel whether it was the view of the Jewish community "that Israel is always right in these things and . . . the Palestinians are always wrong?"[11]

Another time on *Brinkley*, Washington, D.C., Mayor Marion Barry denied that he uses drugs, prompting Donaldson to respond, "Bill Regardie, a local publisher, says he knows the signs of drug addicts when he sees them because he used to use cocaine. He says you're a drug addict."[12] This, of course, is not a question. And having already categorically (if falsely) denied that he uses drugs, there was nothing left for Barry to say on the subject. Donaldson dropped some dynamite, perhaps in the hope that Barry would pick it up, and certainly with the notion that explosive television is a good thing.

Occasionally, Donaldson will even ask an irrelevant question if it is sufficiently inflammatory. When Bert Lance, a power broker in the Democratic party, was on *Brinkley* to discuss the 1984 presidential election, Donaldson reminded him of his forced resignation from the Carter administration for irregular banking practices and asked, "Do you have any overdrafts today?"[13] Donaldson justifies the question by observing that subsequently Lance was investigated for additional overdrafts, ignoring the fact that this had no relevance to any public issue. Such questions explain why Carter's former press secretary Jody Powell calls Donaldson a "master provocateur."[14]

Sometimes Donaldson goes to ludicrous lengths in his efforts to provoke. When *Brinkley* guest Mario Cuomo opposed the president's proposal to do away with the deductibility of state and local taxes, Donaldson pressed him as to how he would make up the money that would be lost if the proposal were defeated. Cuomo responded that it had taken the president many months to craft a plan and he could not be expected to do so instantly. Donaldson smelled blood:[15]

DONALDSON: Well wait a moment. You're attacking their plan. You're saying that it's not fair. Don't you have an obligation to put forward then how we're going to make up that revenue?

CUOMO: Sure, Sam, you give me six or seven months and 450 pages and I'll write you a better plan. But I'll say this. They figured out where to get the money for oil states. . . . Why can't they figure out the money for us?

DONALDSON: But, governor, under their analysis—since you say you don't have an analysis—

CUOMO: No, I didn't say—no, no, Sam, excuse me. I didn't say I don't have an analysis. I said if you gave me the same time they did I could write you a better plan than theirs.

DONALDSON: If I may, since you can't come up with an alternative and—

CUOMO: I didn't say I can't. I said [if] you give me the time—

DONALDSON: Well, all right, you haven't this morning—

CUOMO: —you gave them. Well, of course not.

DONALDSON: Then why can't we assume that maybe your alternative will be to raise the rates again? Maybe your alternative will hit the middle class again. Maybe they'll have to pay for this one-third who subsidize on state and local taxes.

CUOMO: No, I said the same ingenuity that showed the president how to take care of the oil states, how to take care of capital gains, how to take care of the rich, if you keep using that ingenuity, after a while you can come up with real fairness.

DONALDSON: But you don't have it for us this morning, right?

CUOMO: You give me a little time, Sam—of course not! Do you want a plan written in seven minutes on ABC television when it took them months and months to correct their own? That's ridiculous, but not surprising.

Cuomo was right on both counts.

In fairness to Donaldson, when he opts for reasonable questions he is the best interviewer in the business. His refusal to take "no comment" for an answer and his persistence in pursuing evasive interviewees often yield important results. It was in response to Donaldson's persistent questioning that Ronald Reagan confessed ambivalence about whether Martin Luther King had communist ties and expressed his desire to "remove" the Sandinista government.

Donaldson often comes across as appealing despite his less winning tendencies, largely because of his willingness to play the clown. When Israeli Prime Minister Begin, at an airport departure ceremony following a visit to the United States, declared that he and President Carter had accomplished a lot, Donaldson laughed out loud. United States and Israeli officials looked around in annoyance, Donaldson says, but Jimmy Carter knew exactly where the inappropriate laughter came from. (Donaldson sheepishly admits that, unknown to him, Begin and Carter *had* accomplished a lot—paving the way for the Camp David summit.)[16] On another occasion, as he and the press waited on the White House lawn for Saudia Arabia's Prince Fahd to arrive for a meeting with Carter, Donaldson broke

into a loud rendition of "The Sheik of Araby." Carter emerged and
somberly queried whether Donaldson was having a good time. Donaldson nodded and instructed Carter to "Get the oil!"[17] Garry
Wills's description of Buchanan applies almost as well to Donaldson: "The clown redeems the thug."[18]

An element of goofiness, as well as his confrontational instinct,
carry over to Donaldson's work as an opinion commentator on
Brinkley. Indeed, the lessons he learned as a television correspondent are all on display during the *Brinkley* roundtable. He describes
one important lesson as follows:[19]

> The debate over what's important to tell in a limited time can
> fill hours in the classroom or the seminar hall, but at forty-five
> minutes to deadline, there can be no debate. Deadline television
> reports must be constructed by a dictator who says, "Right or
> wrong, this is the way it will go." If you find it impossible to
> make up your mind about things, for goodness' sake, don't get
> into the daily news business.

Donaldson recounts how when Lyndon Johnson startled the country by announcing that he would not seek reelection, Roger Mudd
told the television audience that he'd like to think about it overnight
before commenting. Donaldson adds that "Mudd, of course, was
kidding. None of us in this business has the luxury of thinking about
it overnight. I often say—only half in jest—that the rule must be to
get the mouth in gear and hope that the mind will follow. If you wait
until your mind produces just the right thought, you'll often sit
mute."[20]

This principle of "talk now, think later," Donaldson's inherent
feistiness and lust for combat, and his cocksureness, are all in evidence during the *Brinkley* roundtable. There, Donaldson resembles
Pat Buchanan. His remarks are glibly packaged, and although some
of them would not withstand scrutiny, he delivers them with total
certainty. And even when shown to be wrongheaded, he never
backtracks.

Donaldson readily acknowledges that the participants on the political talk shows display more intransigence than openmindedness. But asked whether he regards this tendency as unfortunate, he replied, "I don't think so. The viewers have the right to expect that we have something to say, not that we're going to say 'Gee, that's an intractable problem. I don't quite know. What do you think?' "[21] Of course, there is a middle ground between dogmatism and agnosticism, though one wouldn't know it from watching most of the talk shows. They incline toward dogmatism, and Donaldson fits right in.

Donaldson describes his approach to the *Brinkley* roundtable as "using basic reasoning, sometimes, emotion and always, I hope, verve." He adds that his method "seems to work. I probably get as many letters telling me what a jerk this writer thinks Will is as he gets saying the same thing about me."[22] Tellingly, Donaldson's idea of his tactics "working" is not that they enlighten the audience or arrive at truth, but that they induce hate mail. Donaldson does display an impressive knowledge of history and government, thinks quickly, and holds his own with the intellectually formidable Will on some serious subjects. Unfortunately, he often uses his impressive mind less in pursuit of truth than pursuit of a good fight.

To be sure, confrontation is not built into the script on *Brinkley* the way it is on other shows, and Donaldson is sometimes entirely reasonable and agreeable. In fact, because he has earned a reputation for candor, he should be taken at his word when he says, "I do not take positions in which I do not sincerely believe simply to stir things up."[23] Nevertheless, when Donaldson feels ornery, bizarre things happen. He resorts to willful mischaracterization of someone else's views, overzealous confrontation, sophistry, and gross overstatement.

Jack Germond says, "It always strikes me that Sam is getting under George Will's skin."[24] Indeed, Donaldson frequently explicates Will's remarks ("George is essentially saying that . . .") without fidelity to Will's meaning. Consider the following exchange about an alleged financial impropriety involving Attorney General Meese:[25]

WILL: We have trivialized the idea of ethics. Ethics used to be about war and peace and equity and how you treat the poor and how you deal with dictators. Now ethics is about a $15,000 loan. But is there a spectacle more—

DONALDSON: You mean, that money isn't large enough to worry about? . . . Only you and the *Wall Street Journal* talk about $15,000 as a trivialization of ethics. I think most Americans would think of it as a substantial amount of money.

Right or wrong, Will was making an important point and it had little to do with the amount of money involved. But Donaldson chose to make it sound as if Will's main point was that $15,000 is a small sum. Such tactics provide entertainment, but not enlightenment. Television critic Tom Shales says that Donaldson "makes some idiotic remarks, but he and Will have something going there and it's good television."[26]

Understandably, Will sometimes seems less pleased with Donaldson's tactics. Donaldson's mischaracterization of Will's position was especially blatant on the subject of what vice presidential candidate Dan Quayle had to do to improve his campaign:[27]

WILL: I've followed his record in the Senate and it has complicated aspects to it. They have to get him away from the Ohio State Fairgrounds where he stands on a platform and shouts. They have to get him in front of the Chicago Economic Club and the Los Angeles Foreign Affairs Council, quiet reflective audiences where he can give serious, reflective speeches.

DONALDSON: In other words, George, you say that the PR masters can come in and do a crash course . . .

WILL: If I wanted to say that, I would have said it.

In fact, Will was saying just the opposite of what Donaldson imputed to him; he was arguing that the PR approach was precisely what got Quayle into trouble, and that substance had to take precedence over imagery.

Once during a discussion about arms control, Donaldson put words into Will's mouth even more promiscuously:[28]

DONALDSON: [When] you make your argument, as you do frequently, it seems to me the end is simply that we're going to have a war [with the Soviet Union], that we're really going to have a war.

WILL: No. Perfect rubbish. We're going to have more stable deterrents than we get under arms control regimes.

DONALDSON: Yes, but your stable deterrence is superiority. Your stable deterrence is [a] United States which is simply much more strong and forceful than the Soviet Union.

WILL: I am so much a better presenter of my position than you are, Sam.

DONALDSON: Are you for equality?

WILL: I am for a central equivalence, which we had, everyone agreed, in '72, and if we had it then we cannot have it now because everyone knows the correlation of force has shifted against us.

DONALDSON: But the President said he could go back to Geneva because he had built up America's defenses and we do now have it.

WILL: The President is—and there is precedent for this—wrong.

DONALDSON: Well, only when it suits your purpose.

Here, exposed in his efforts at gross mischaracterization, Donaldson resorted to the silly remark about Will finding Reagan wrong only when it suits his purpose. Must Will agree with Reagan either always or never?

It is common for debaters to misrepresent a position that they disagree with in order to shoot it down more easily. Donaldson sometimes goes further, expressing outrage with a viewpoint that he evidently shares. This occurred when roundtable guest Tom Wicker criticized Attorney General Meese for saying that no suspects of crimes are innocent:[29]

WICKER: He's a man who should know better because he himself was suspected of crime. In fact, they had a special prosecutor investigate him, and it was declared that he was innocent. So he should know better than that statement.

DONALDSON: What do you mean he should know better, Tom? He

said it, he's a grown man. He doesn't have a speechwriter put those words in his mouth. That's his mind.

WICKER: Well, I repeat, he should know better out of his own experience. . . .

DONALDSON: He's the Attorney General of the United States.

Wicker was understandably flustered by Donaldson's heated agreement.

Another time, Will expressed the view that Donald Regan was a dishonest bully whose performance as White House chief of staff was deplorable. Donaldson countered, "I fundamentally disagree with you about Donald Regan," and then gave a long statement, pointing out that: Regan had pledged to "Let Reagan be Reagan" just as conservatives wanted; he did let Reagan be Reagan; Regan was less to blame than Reagan for most of the White House's failures; and replacing him with a better chief of staff would not solve the administration's problems.[30] That was all fine as far as it went, but none of it contradicted anything Will had said—notwithstanding Donaldson's claim that he was in fundamental disagreement with Will.

Donaldson will also go to great lengths to win an argument where the disagreement is real. This sometimes involves not only mischaracterizing what someone has said, but also blatant sophistry or overstatement. When Will argued that nuclear arms control would make the world less safe by leaving deterrence to conventional weapons (which most nations would be far more willing to use), Donaldson responded, "It seems to me like you're frightened that peace might break out." Will countered that, in fact, nuclear weapons had kept the peace for forty years. Donaldson scoffed, "Talk about an oxymoron."[31] Whatever one thinks of Will's views about nuclear weapons and arms control, it is not oxymoronic to assert that nuclear weapons have preserved peace.

A similar exchange ensued when Donaldson claimed that Supreme Court nominee Anthony Scalia would do damage to freedom of the press by making it easier for plaintiffs to prevail in libel suits. Will suggested that this would not be disastrous; it would simply make journalists more careful. Donaldson responded, "We want to be careful, but we ought to have a right to say something. This isn't South Africa."[32] The notion that broader libel liability would deny the "right to say something" and convert America into an authoritarian regime is not acceptable hyperbole; it is nonsense. Such silliness was also Donaldson's tack when Will argued that Ronald Reagan, notwithstanding his antigovernment rhetoric, used government aggressively:[33]

WILL: He wanted to change the values of the country. He wanted to change, inspirit us, energize us. Part of it was deregulation, that is, taking away bits of government, but still that's a use of government. He had a very ambitious program for government.

DONALDSON: Yeah, but you just said it, George. He wanted to use government to destroy government.

WILL: No, I didn't say that at all. He—

DONALDSON: Well, you said little pieces, taking away.

WILL: That's right, but he—

DONALDSON: He wanted to abolish two departments. He didn't get his way. In fact, he created a third.

WILL: He didn't even try.

DONALDSON: Well, he tried in his first term.

WILL: Oh, well.

DONALDSON: Are you accusing Ronald Reagan of not really trying on a campaign promise, George?

Donaldson may annoy Will but he is a producer's delight: glib, articulate, never bashful about mixing it up. By including him in the *Brinkley* roundtable, ABC took a risk. The networks have long insisted that their news reporters are unbiased, yet ABC put Donaldson in the position of having to reveal his views on substantive issues. Its willingness to do so is understandable, though, because Donaldson is a perfect roundtable participant. He would also be perfect on *The McLaughlin Group* or *Crossfire*. (He has appeared as a guest on *Crossfire* and easily withstood the badgering.)

*   *   *

Like Pat Buchanan, Donaldson is tough as nails and seems to prefer a good fight to a genuine search for truth. To be sure, the two arrive at their similar styles through wholly different routes. Buchanan's combativeness is in service of causes to which he clings tenaciously; for Donaldson, whose attachment to causes is comparatively slight, the combativeness is an end in itself. Buchanan tries to stamp out liberals, while Donaldson seeks to shake down whoever is in front of him.

On the television roundtables, substance often takes a backseat to style. However different their aims and views, Buchanan and Donaldson have similar, successful styles. Both the ideological Buchanan and his nonideological soulmate Donaldson are made for today's political talk shows.

FIVE

Celebrity Journalists

The traditional picture of a journalist is one who toils for low pay and with a low profile to bring truth to the masses. Until the 1950s, few reporters acquired much wealth or name recognition. Television changed this state of affairs by bringing reporters into our living rooms (far more vividly than radio ever had), quickly making the network anchors into celebrities. But because television was slow to provide the equivalent of a newspaper op-ed page, fame and wealth continued to elude opinion columnists. This situation changed as a result of various political talk shows that emerged primarily in the late 1960s and early 1980s. On these programs, journalists were not colorless interviewers or reporters; they were the drawing card.

The proliferation of the journalistic roundtable programs coincided with the growth of a lucrative lecture business in America. College campuses had always booked politicians, athletes, and entertainers to speak, but increasingly corporations and trade associations—with far more money to spare—were getting into the act. More people began making a living, or supplementing their living handsomely, on the lecture circuit.

The development of a whopping market for lecturers was serendiptious for the score of journalists who became public figures by virtue of the television roundtables. These Washington insiders were perfect draws for the corporations and trade associations: they could regale the businessmen with tales of real power and intrigue (and, cynics suggested, could sell their influence).

Soon, columnists aspiring to a little fame and a lot of money recognized a reliable formula. First, they had to establish a reputation as a distinguished or at least up-and-coming columnist; that was the hard part. That reputation would lead to exposure on one of the political talk shows which, in turn, would make them a hot item on the lecture circuit. Before long, they would be well known, their pockets well lined, their egos massaged, and their telephones kept ringing by politicians who know that people with access to a television audience make valuable allies.

For several years, little was said about the new journalist-as-celebrity phenomenon; it took time for observers to recognize its ramifications. After a while, some journalists became disturbed by the trend. In the span of six months, two writers expressed their concerns in influential journals.

A piece by Jacob Weisberg in January 1986 issue of *The New Republic,* titled "Buckrakers," outlined and complained about the new path from columnist to celebrity. Despite the title, Weisberg argued that "the problem isn't that buckrakers are overpaid. It's the effect that buckraking may be having on the craft of journalism."[1] Weisberg maintained that the celebrity path induces talented journalists to squander precious time and energy that could be put to good use:[2]

> Even giving the same speech again and again can be draining if it involves flying across the country, changing planes at O'Hare, making conversation for several hours with your hosts, and so on. Then there is the mental corruption of rewarming and serving up the same or similar material again and again, which may seep into your writing.

Several months later, James Fallows wrote a long piece in the *New York Review of Books,* entitled "The New Celebrities of Washington," which arrived at similar conclusions.[3] He emphasized that today's media celebrity spends so much time on the lecture circuit that he has insufficient time to reconsider old ideas.*

Both Weisberg and Fallows pointed out that the lecture circuit generally does not provide a fruitful give-and-take that proves instructive to the lecturer. One can imagine college tours where the speaker spends time both before and after the lecture talking to students to get a feel for what is on the minds of today's youth. However, the celebrity journalists rarely spend much time in the lecture setting; they usually zip in and out of town. And their lectures are not primarily at campuses or other educational environments (where the fees are relatively low), but to groups whose primary interest is neither learning nor teaching. Lecture Agent Joe Cosby says that the business groups[4]

> like somebody with a Washington Insider perspective. I recently booked David Brinkley for one of these organizations. "What's he going to talk about?" they said. "What do you want him to talk about?" I answered. They couldn't care less. We called his speech Inside Washington Today. They loved it.

These groups seek the small thrill of seeing a television star in the flesh, especially one who can take them behind the scenes. ABC's Jeff Greenfield explains that the lectures give the audience "the delicious sense of insiderness."[5] As Fallows observes, the lectures do *not* give either the audience or the speaker "a stimulating rethought-out message."[6] Indeed, the journalists generally give the same basic lecture wherever they go. Most of them admit that the lectures are mercenary in nature, rather than undertaken to learn or disseminate ideas.

*Fallows and Weisberg, and numerous journalists since, also expressed concern that the lure of lucrative lecture fees may cause columnists—perhaps subconsciously—to shade their views. The fear is either that they will tilt rightward generally, knowing that the highest paying groups prefer conservative commentators or, more likely, will avoid offending particular groups. A columnist about to make a lucrative speech to General Dynamics may be disinclined to write a column about corruption in the defense contracting industry. A healthy consensus is emerging that journalists should disclose their speaking engagements so that the public can judge for itself whether they might be improperly influenced.

Today's celebrity journalists also spend a lot of time in the television studio. Fallows recounted observing Robert Novak, while on the set of *The McLaughlin Group,* whip out his portable computer and begin pounding out his newspaper column, explaining that "I was losing too much damn time"[7] on the television shows. Times have clearly changed when newspaper reporters must squeeze their writing into the interstices of their television appearances.

In addition to time spent on the lecture circuit and in the television studio, journalists must prepare for the talk shows. It might seem that no preparation is needed for the level of discourse common to most of the shows, and a few of the more secure regulars don't bother preparing. But most of the television pundits will not risk seeming out of the swim and must stay current on the latest statistics, stories, and political gossip. They prepare by becoming more acquainted with the minutiae of the moment, since the shows focus on transient events. Charlie Peters observes that the cramming "amounts to protecting yourself, just to avoid seeming like an idiot."[8] Like the lecture circuit, it does not involve serious reading or reflection that contributes to the commentator's message or intellectual development.

Fallows, Weisberg, and others persuasively argue that the wear and tear of the celebrity path diminishes the work product of top journalists. An equally important but neglected point is that celebrity status negatively affects the way a commentator's work is received; people often respond to certain commentators as celebrities, refusing to take their ideas seriously and questioning their motives. Thus if William F. Buckley or George Will had written *The Closing of the American Mind,* in many circles it would have been dismissed as a self-aggrandizing, self-promoting tome by a celebrity, rather than debated seriously on its merits.

The best way to illustrate the problems of the journalist-as-celebrity phenomenon is to consider the careers of eminent journalists who have been hampered by celebrity status. The following profiles of Buckley and Will suggest that as a result of the demands of celebrity status, these commentators have not fulfilled their enormous potential—as intellectuals with access to a mass audience—to contribute to public insight and discourse.

WILLIAM F. BUCKLEY, JR.

William F. Buckley, Jr. has always shown incredible resourcefulness and devotion to improving thought and politics in America. However, he also possesses traits that made celebrity status inevitable, and that status has interfered with his contribution.

Buckley's father, a successful oil speculator, was militantly Catholic, anticommunist, and patriotic. He instilled these commitments in his children, along with a powerful urge to crusade on their behalf. While it was predictable that the offspring of William Buckley senior would fight full-throttle against communism and atheism, no one could have been prepared for the style that William F. Buckley, Jr. brought to the crusade.

Buckley junior was born to be a celebrity. He possessed an instinct and fondness for thrusting himself into the middle of things. At the age of six, he wrote the King of England a letter demanding that the mother country repay her war debts. Several years later, he showed up at a faculty meeting at his private school to complain about the abridgement of his right to free speech in the classroom. While at the meeting, he took the opportunity to lecture the faculty about theological doctrines.

As noted earlier, Buckley's brashness was complemented by a thoroughly theatrical manner. His childhood was so itinerant—he spent much time in Mexico and Europe as well as the United States—that he picked up a unique, captivating accent. In addition, his tongue and eyebrows sometimes dart about in unusual ways. From an early age, Buckley was handsome, witty, and charming. But while his personality and manner made celebrity inevitable, Buckley was more interested in empire-building, and he was well suited for that too.

He was educated at elite preparatory schools in America and Britain, and after serving several years in the army during World War II, was admitted to Yale in 1946. During his college years

Buckley made his presence felt as few undergraduates do. As both chairman of the *Yale Daily News* and an activist in the Yale Political Union, Buckley ferociously criticized his school's seeming addiction to liberal dogma.

His mission to set Yale right continued beyond his student days. Shortly after graduating, he wrote a controversial book attacking his alma mater. Although he was just twenty-five and taking on a revered institution, he displayed no diffidence. He titled the book *God and Man at Yale,* prompting the joke that the book was intended as an autobiography by the deity, Buckley. The book's central thesis is that Yale indoctrinates its students in socialism and atheism. Buckley's prescription is for alumni to take command and insist that capitalism and Christianity be preached instead. The book is hyperbolic (orthodox economic texts are declared "collectivist" or "egalitarian" because of modest deviations from laissez faire doctrine), but it displays a combination of courage and wit rare for one so young.

After a short time as an associate editor at the conservative publication *American Mercury,* Buckley undertook projects as bold as his first book: a stint in the CIA and another book, *McCarthy and His Enemies,* coauthored with his brother-in-law, Brent Bozell. Buckley's second book, which defended Senator Joseph McCarthy while condemning his excesses, resembles his first in displaying more verve than cogency. Although the book attracted less attention than *God and Man at Yale,* it furthered Buckley's position as an up-and-coming conservative intellectual. But these early exercises in zealotry are hardly what Buckley will be remembered for; what he did next, to a greater extent, is.

Buckley recognized that America lacked a serious conservative journal to compete with *The Nation* and *The New Republic.* The conservative "movement" was in a sorry state in the 1950s. There was no shortage of conservative icons and ideals—McCarthy, Edmund Burke, Ayn Rand, anticommunism, the free market, segregation, and Christian orthodoxy all inspired devotion in some circles—but no leadership existed to unite the scattered fragments or to make conservatism intellectually respectable in the country at large. Buckley responded by creating the magazine *National Review* and successfully recruiting the country's top conservative intellectuals, including James Burnham, Russell Kirk, and eventually Whittaker Chambers, to work for his publication.

National Review was a serious intellectual enterprise with weekly columns on foreign affairs, constitutional law, campus politics, the media, labor, liberal heresies, and more. It also possessed a scorching polemical wit, most evident in the short, acerbic comments on current events that ran in the front of each issue. *National Review* played a direct role in American politics, becoming the one conservative publication that had influence outside narrow conservative circles. But the magazine's historical significance stems less from winning converts than from galvanizing conservatives nationwide. Pat Buchanan's description of *National Review*'s effect on his own life and career is typical:[1]

It is difficult to exaggerate the debt conservatives of my generation owe *National Review* and Bill Buckley. Before I read NR, there was virtually nothing I read that supported or reinforced what I was coming to believe. We young conservatives were truly wandering around in a political wilderness, wondering if there was anyone of intelligence and wit, any men of words, who thought and felt and believed as we did. Other than that one magazine, young conservatives had almost nowhere to turn for intellectual and political sustenance. For us, what *National Review* did was take the word *conservatism,* then a synonym for stuffy orthodoxy, Republican stand-pat-ism and economic self-interest, and convert it into the snapping pennant of a fighting faith.

Through the magazine, personal tutelage, and his inspiring example, Buckley midwifed an entire generation of conservative commentators and activists. As one commentator observes, "Had there been no Buckley, there would be no George Will, no *American Spectator,* no *Policy Review,* no National Conservative Political Action Committee, no ringing Reagan speeches written by Tony Dolan."[2] Buckley also continued to advance the conservative cause through books. In 1959 he wrote his third book, *Up from Liberal-ism,* setting forth some core conservative ideas and assailing the intellectual incoherence of liberalism.

Before long, Buckley also took on a thrice-weekly syndicated news-paper column. The column was colorful and hard-hitting. Next to the staid editorial drone that dominated most op-ed pages at the time, Buckley's column practically flew off the page. It provided him a larger platform from which to preach in favor of religion and in opposition to communism and the welfare state.

The column was launched at a time when few conservatives graced newspaper op-ed pages. With the column, the magazine, and his television show *Firing Line,* begun in 1966, Buckley became a crucial conservative figure during the 1960s and 1970s. Some believe that only Ronald Reagan deserves more credit for the conservative revolution that culminated in Reagan's presidency from 1980 to 1988. Buckley has undeniably played a major role in American history and made a contribution to the nation's political discourse. However, in the 1960s a process accelerated that sharply mitigated his contribution to society: the evolution of Buckley as a celebrity.

William F. Buckley, Jr. was primarily a writer and editor for only a short time: a larger stardom lay just over the horizon. A huge step in that direction came during his quixotic campaign for Mayor of New York City in 1965. Running as the Conservative party candi-date, Buckley challenged liberal Republican John Lindsay and moderate Democrat Abraham Beame. He did so to spread the conservative gospel, not to become either mayor or famous. But famous he did become.

Armed with his formidable wit and unconcerned about victory, Buckley injected a breath of fresh air into New York City politics. Asked what he would do if elected, he said, "Demand a recount."[3] During a debate with Lindsay and Beame, Buckley was asked if he would be flabbergasted if he were elected. "After hearing Mr. Beame and Mr. Lindsay, I would be flabbergasted if I weren't elected," he responded.[4]

In fact, he wasn't elected, finishing a distant third. However, it was remarkable for a nonpolitician to receive 13.4 percent of the vote as a third-party candidate—by far the highest total ever received by a candidate of New York's Conservative party. Buckley's candidacy set the stage for his brother James, running as the candidate of the Conservative party, to win a United States Senate seat five years later. It also set Buckley himself well on the path to becoming a major celebrity.

The decisive factor, as usual, was television. Even before the mayoral campaign, Buckley and others were coming to realize that his magazine and newspaper column were not the only, nor even the best, way for him to reach the general public. His theatrical manner was clearly conducive to a sizable television audience; indeed his television appearances during the 1950s and early 1960s (on Hardy Burt's *Answers for Americans,* the *Jack Paar Show,* and other shows) tended to produce a hearty response.

He had been approached in early 1965 by a television entrepreneur who proposed a regular political talk show in which Buckley would face off against prominent liberals on controversial issues. The project was not immediately pursued because Buckley was about to launch his mayoral candidacy. As it turned out, the political campaign improved the prospects for the television series by making Buckley better known. It also confirmed his appeal as a television personality.

During the campaign, Buckley proved himself a true master of the medium. The *New York Daily News* wrote, "Love him or hate him, TV fans found it difficult to turn off a master political showman,"[5] and the *New York Journal American* declared that Buckley "wowed New York on television. He is more fun to listen to than most professional comedians."[6] Writing in the *Village Voice,* Norman Mailer went further: "No other actor on Earth can project simultaneous hints that he is in the act of playing Commodore of the Yacht club, Joseph Goebbels, Robert Mitchum, Maverick, Savonarola, the naive prep-school kid next door, and the snows of yesteryear."[7] New Yorkers were not the only ones to learn about the new kid in town. Theodore White wrote in *Life* that "on television Buckley is a star."[8]

Shortly after the campaign, Buckley's *Firing Line* commenced on a trial basis on an independent New York station and before long was adopted as a regular show and syndicated to dozens of cities. Buckley's stylish go-for-the-jugular manner caught the nation's attention. *Time* noted that "before he delivers a cruncher, his tongue licks from the corner of his mouth. . . . Similarly, the elevation of his eyebrows telegraphs the drop of a guillotine blade."[9]

Firing Line drastically accelerated Buckley's ascendance to celebrity. He had been in demand as a television performer and lecturer, but now the requests increased substantially. In a short time he graced the covers of *Time* and the *Wall Street Journal* and was featured in *Esquire* and *Harper's.* By 1967, writer Larry L. King wrote that Buckley was "a legend in his time" and (paraphrasing Mailer) "the greatest spectacle on Earth."[10]

To a point, Bill Buckley's celebrity status increased his influence by expanding his audience, but in two important ways it diminished his contribution to society. First, the overwhelming peripheral demands on his time greatly reduced his chance to develop and disseminate serious ideas, which he had shown definite potential for doing. Second, people gradually took him less seriously, responding to Buckley as a personality, not as a thinker.

A literary critic has written of the Faustian bargain facing serious thinkers who become celebrities: "the choice between careful, qualified, well-argued scholarship or submission to the popular demand for simplified, sloganized ideas, unburdened by footnotes."[11] But Walter Lippmann had demonstrated that it is possible to be both a popular journalist and a philosopher, and in his younger days, Buckley aspired to be both—indeed, for a time his single greatest ambition was to make an original contribution to political science. No less an authority than Russell Kirk, a leading conservative intellectual, believed Buckley had the potential to do so.[12] The burdens of celebrity, as much as anything else, doomed this aspiration.

In 1962 Buckley decided to write a "big book" setting forth a sustained political philosophy. The book, tentatively titled *Revolt*

Against the Masses, was intended to adapt the political philosophy of Jose Ortega Gasset to modern America. However, Buckley abandoned the project in 1965. His biographer, John Judis, suggests that the demands of celebrity left Buckley insufficient time to write the book. In reality, Buckley had yet to become a major celebrity and dropped the project primarily because contemporary events in America called into question his central thesis. Nevertheless, Judis may be right that the abandonment of the big book marked the beginning of the end of Buckley's development as a political theoretician.

The mayoral race and *Firing Line* followed shortly, and major celebrity status overtook Buckley almost immediately thereafter. For the duration of the 1960s and the following two decades, he wrote over twenty books but almost all were either collections of his columns or light entertainment. The two exceptions, *The Unmaking of a Mayor* (1966) and *Four Reforms* (1973), were welcome additions to the marketplace of ideas but hardly represented the fulfillment of Buckley's potential as a thinker. *The Unmaking of a Mayor,* an engaging account of the mayoral campaign, did include some serious reflections about the corruption of the major parties, the inadequacy of the press, and the role of race and religion in politics. But *Four Reforms,* his only full-length, idea-oriented book of the period, was recognized even by Buckley's supporters as "too brief to be meant as a [major] theoretical contribution."[13] The other books were spy novels, accounts of his sailing adventures, and two autobiographical journals each chronicling a week in his life of celebrityhood.

While Buckley may have been content with that output, some of his admirers felt cheated. The celebrity lifestyle depicted in his autobiographical journal *Cruising Speed* "seemed fuller to him than to those who remembered his early promise."[14] Many never forgot the early promise. Over twenty years after Buckley abandoned the magnum opus, some were still hoping for it. Thus Morton Kondracke, reviewing a collection of Buckley columns published in 1986 (the year Buckley turned sixty, *National Review* turned thirty, and *Firing Line* twenty), wrote:[15]

It would have been exciting if Mr. Buckley's various anniversaries had been commemorated by publication of a different book from this one. . . . Is the West too weak to prevail? Are the liberals really still ahead? Is William F. Buckley really a pessimist? These are subjects for a serious book.

Cruising Speed, which described a week in Buckley's life in 1970, helped clarify why he produced few of the books of the sort Kondracke desired. His incredibly heavy schedule went far beyond his column, magazine, and television show to include countless lectures, extensive socializing, and a personal response to most of the 600 letters he received each week. He admitted in the book that the lectures were designed to provide the audience with theater, not intellectual stimulus. Similarly, the letters and responses were generally not discourses on ideas, but the distractions celebrities routinely face: requests for appearances and favors, fan mail, and so forth. Today Buckley says that 40 percent of his time is spent answering mail. He continues to lecture extensively and acknowledges that "you don't learn much by lecturing and most of the time it's pretty damn exhausting."[16]

One reviewer of *Cruising Speed* suggested that Buckley's schedule called into question "the depth of his search for ideological truth."[17] At the end of the book, he directly broached the subject of whether his talents were being, at least in part, misspent. Reflecting on his friend John Kenneth Galbraith's suggestion that he devote himself to writing major books ("Then—only then—you will discover the means to give a theoretical depth to your ideological positions"), Buckley conceded that he had "not myself dug deeper the foundations of American conservatism," and gave an unconvincing explanation of why it was unnecessary for him to dig deeper:[18]

How can I hope to do better against positivism than Voegelin has done? Improve on Oakeshott's analysis of rationalism? (How does one illuminate a sunburst?) Rediscover orthodoxy more engrossingly than Chesterton did?

Buckley pleaded that he could be satisfied only by a "sense of social usefulness," but he failed to explain how the road show and celebrity beat were more useful than deep, scholarly reflections. (*The Washington Monthly* fittingly subtitled its review of Judis's biography of Buckley, "He Could Be A Great Thinker, But He's Too Busy Running to the Airport."[19]) Buckley made it sound as if he faced the choice between his newspaper column and magazine or books on politics and philosophy. But as noted, Walter Lippmann had established that day-to-day journalism and serious works of philosophy could coexist; in fact, they could be mutually reinforcing. As Lippmann put it:[20]

> I have lived two lives. One of books and one of newspapers. Each helps the other. The philosophy is the context in which I write my columns. The column is the laboratory or clinic in which I test the philosophy and keep it from becoming too abstract.

Lippmann was able to fulfill his constant journalistic responsibilities while writing major philosophical books because he zealously guarded his time, putting aside huge blocks solely for scholarly reflections and writing. His colleague James Reston remarked that Lippmann was just about the only thoughtful man in Washington who never complained that he couldn't find time to think.[21]

In discussing his own choice to eschew more scholarly efforts, Buckley neglected to discuss the superfluous demands that had resulted from his celebrity status. Compared to some of the distractions, the parties, correspondence, and lectures were downright productive. For Buckley became embroiled in a half-dozen lawsuits or extended threats of lawsuits, including a squalid affair stemming from his joint television appearances with Gore Vidal during the 1968 Democratic convention. After the two exchanged scandalous remarks on television (Vidal called him a "crypto-nazi"; Buckley threatened to punch out the "queer"), Buckley spent more than a month writing his version of the encounter for *Esquire*. When Vidal countered in *Esquire* with his own side of the controversy, Buckley had to be talked out of writing yet another piece about the matter.

*   *   *

Buckley's work suffered as a result of such nonsense. His newspaper
column remained engaging, but it rarely probed far beneath the
surface or explored new ground over the years. As Morton Kondracke wrote in a favorable review of a collection of Buckley's
columns:[22]

> He reportedly knocks out his column in twenty minutes flat.
> . . . That is too little time for serious contemplation of difficult
> subjects. Often he picks targets that are like fish in a barrel—
> human rights hypocrisy at the United Nations . . . advocacy of
> pederasty by a homosexual-rights leader and, of course, evil
> doings of the men who run the Soviet Union.

> He hits these every time, but it would be more interesting to
> see him analyze why so many people in the world are hostile
> to the American system, what we ought to do about dictators
> friendly to us who get in trouble with their own people, how
> to cope with poverty.

Kondracke registered this concern in 1986 but as early as the late
1960s Buckley had become first and foremost a personality whose
lifestyle reduced his capacity to articulate political ideas. John Judis
writes that by 1971, when *Cruising Speed* appeared, Buckley was
"falling into the routine of what critic Joseph Epstein called the life
of the 'celebrity intellectual.' "[23] In fact, by that point Buckley was
no longer falling into such a routine; *Cruising Speed* suggests that
he had already done a free fall. (Ironically, as the descent from
serious commentator to celebrity continued throughout the 1970s,
Buckley's television show *Firing Line* became more serious and less
theatrical.)

The plunge into celebrity waters was deeper still in the 1970s and
1980s as suggested by a comparison of *Cruising Speed* with Buckley's second "one week in the life of" journal, *Overdrive,* published
twelve years later, in 1983. Like the earlier journal, *Overdrive* documented the life of a celebrity: the overwhelming correspondence,

lectures, socializing. But something was missing. *Cruising Speed* had also been the occasion for at least some wrestling with the major issues of the day, especially the civil rights movement and the Vietnam War. Indeed, it devoted over twenty pages to an uncommonly substantive lecture about the limits of free speech in a democracy. *Overdrive,* by contrast, went into far more detail about Buckley's personal life—the indoor swimming pool, customized limousine, servants—with virtually no reflections on public issues.

The adjective "happy" is often and rightly pinned on Buckley, but Judis's account of his life and career in the 1980s suggests a somewhat sad and unwilling metamorphosis:[24]

> Buckley had become the victim of his own celebrity. . . . He was swept up—and away—in that luminous world of entertainers, actors and actresses, and wealthy partygoers feted by gossip columnists for their style. . . . In the month spanning his birthday and *National Review*'s December birthday celebration, Buckley himself received even more attention from the press than he had five years earlier, but the kind of attention he received revealed the extent to which he had entered the pantheon of American celebritydom, in which he was valued not for what he said, but for the way he talked, dressed, and lived.

Judis, himself a fervent leftist, laments that Buckley lost his edge and became an establishment celebrity rather than the old fire-in-the-belly radical rightist. A more telling point is made by Harvard historian Alan Brinkley who, in a review of the Judis book, suggested that the bigger loss was Buckley's ideas, not his axe:[25]

> [Buckley's] problem is not that he has shed his militancy but that he has failed to articulate carefully or thoughtfully a mature political outlook. . . . This appealing, intelligent, and increasingly generous man seems to be sacrificing his considerable gifts to the blandishments of celebrity.

Completely apart from the ways in which Buckley's celebrity status affects the quality and nature of his work, it mars the way his ideas are received. For when Buckley does put his considerable gifts to good use, people often fail to notice. During the mayoral campaign in 1965, columnist Murray Kempton wrote that people "almost forget . . . how serious a man Buckley wants to be."[26] As he became a consummate celebrity, it became easier to forget.

Indeed, in some intellectual circles Buckley is not taken seriously. Thus writer Wilfrid Sheed, unlike Kondracke, does not yearn for Buckley's magnum opus; he cynically writes that the big book "would have come at the cost of too many good sideshows, of a sort that no one else could possibly have staged. . . . The action may not even be in the main tent anyway: simply sit back and enjoy the circus."[27]

This tendency of some intellectuals to dismiss Buckley was evident in the reaction to one of his few full-length, idea-oriented books, *Four Reforms*. While not intended as a major work of political philosophy, the book was useful on its own terms. It set forth several proposals involving welfare programs, tax reform, and constitutional amendments to prevent criminals from escaping on technicalities and to permit government aid to religious schools. These ideas were serious (a decade later, Congress enacted tax reform similar to Buckley's proposal; his arguments that the wall between church and state is too rigid and that criminal procedural protections should be relaxed have been widely repeated) and he presented them forcefully and intelligently. Yet the book was treated with condescension by the very people—liberals—who had the most to lose by not taking it seriously.

A review by Robert Lekachman in *Commonweal* illustrates how Buckley had come to be regarded as a character rather than a thinker. Lekachman was a well-respected liberal economist who might have been expected to wrestle mightily with Buckley's ideas. But the opening paragraph of his review finds him reacting to the author as celebrity:[28]

On the wine-bibber's 0–7 vintage rating scale, this is an indifferent offering, at most a 3. Swirled and sniffed in the glass of contemplation, the words lack bouquet. On tasting, this conservative fermentation gives unmistakable signs of aging poorly in the bottle. Fair is fair. From time to time flashes of the old Buckley insolence light the page. The baroque vocabulary does not cease to amaze. Where save in the writings of our hero is one regaled with words like prescind, etiolated, decoct, anfractuosity, eristic, and thaumaturgic?

Then, after a dismissive and condescending discussion of Buckley's proposed reforms ("Buckley is manifestly uncomfortable with the masses of data he offers in evidence"; "This dreamy account . . ."), Lekachman concludes by returning to the subject that seems to interest him most where Buckley is concerned: personality.[29]

I have no doubt said enough to convey my judgment that *Four Reforms* is the mixture as many times before. Is the comparatively temperate tone of Buckley's polemic a sign that its author is aging? Is the equally mild nature of my own reaction an indication that the reviewer is also mellowing with age? He who reads may judge.

Lekachman's unwillingness to take Buckley seriously as a thinker became even more manifest by his reply to Buckley's letter to the editor. Buckley protested, with documentation, that Lekachman had misrepresented his argument about welfare. Lekachman, not usually one to avoid a challenge, deemed it beneath himself to respond to the charge, instead writing that "Mr. Buckley's communique presents the judicious with a choice: either this reviewer is a careless, prejudiced reader or Mr. Buckley, gifted polemicist though he is, writes amateurish, opague, expository prose."[30] And thus Buckley was written off as a polysyllabic "gifted polemicist," not one capable of contributing seriously to the debate on welfare reform or constitutional law.

The review of *Four Reforms* in the *Nation* was similar in tone. The *Nation* did not assign the review to an economist or constitutional lawyer but to critic and translator Charles Lam Markmann, who had just completed an unflattering book about the Buckley family. Markmann's discussion of Buckley's proposed reforms drips with sarcasm and condescension ("Law and order has always been dear to Buckley; it brings this newest little tract to its hell-fire conclusion").[31] The review provides little notion of Buckley's proposed reforms, and no idea how Buckley supports them; it instead communicates contempt for the man.

This tendency to react to Buckley as personality while paying his ideas short shrift is one of the costs of his celebrity. The phenomenon has become commonplace. In his book *Confessions of a Conservative,* Buckley's protege-turned-adversary, Garry Wills, puts it bluntly: "He has become unwillingly a dandy. . . . Striving for objective results, he *seems* only interested in theatrical effects. . . . Intending to strike blows, he is applauded for striking poses" (emphasis in original).[32]

Some of Buckley's supporters understandably blame his critics for this phenomenon. In attacking the ad hominem responses to *Overdrive,* James Nuechterlein argued in *Commentary* that it is senseless to ignore Buckley's thought while focusing on his lifestyle.[33] This complaint overlooks the fact that in *Overdrive* Buckley invited such a reaction; the book was about his celebrity, not his philosophy. Nevertheless, Nuechterlein was entirely correct to lament the general phenomenon of people responding to Buckley's persona and ignoring his ideas.

The culmination of this unfortunate development occurred when, at a banquet hosted by the Ethics and Public Policy Center in November 1986, Buckley gave what many regarded as a tremendous, substantive speech about all that ails America. Judis describes the fallout:[34]

> Buckley received a thunderous ovation. [His son] Christopher Buckley believed that "he never spoke better." But to Buckley's disappointment, no reporter asked him for a copy of his speech afterwards. And while the event and Buckley's speech were mentioned in several gossip columns, the contents of the speech were not discussed.

Thus, ironically, even as the election of his friend Ronald Reagan as president crystallized the mission he had begun twenty-five years earlier, Buckley himself was largely removed from the battle of ideas in the 1980s. He continued to be a visible presence—*Overdrive,* the spy novels, and the sailing books sold well, and his latest ventures were chronicled in the repositories for gossip—but newspapers looking for a conservative column tended to opt for someone else.

To be sure, there were occasions in the 1980s when Buckley's ideas were much discussed, but usually when he said something outrageous, for example, criticizing a blind man for sailing the Atlantic, or proposing that AIDS victims be tatooed on their rear ends. On these occasions *Nightline* eagerly trotted him out. He was advancing ideas that virtually no one took seriously, except those seriously offended. He was brought on *Nightline* not to debate a burning issue but as a spectacle: a celebrity saying something outrageous rather than a commentator saying something challenging.

In some obvious respects the career of William F. Buckley, Jr. poses an excellent illustration of the perils in store for a journalist who succumbs to the temptations of celebrity. But there are several reasons why he may be thought at best an imperfect exemplar of this growing trend. First, he is unique. His fame preceded the new journalist-as-celebrity phenomenon and did not follow the usual path. Although television played a crucial role in his ascent to celebrity, as it does with today's new class of celebrity journalists, his fame also resulted from things—the early books, his mayoral campaign, his theatricality—that are less common. Quite likely, Bill Buckley would have become a national figure regardless of the direction of his career; thus his career may not seem instructive about today's growing industry of journalist celebrities.

However, a discussion of Buckley is indispensable to a consideration of the new celebrity journalism because he has always represented an alternative to the anonymous, sober work that has traditionally characterized the journalistic profession. Jacob Weisberg's "Buckrakers" article in *The New Republic* describes the vision of today's celebrity journalists:[35]

That ideal is . . . like the lifestyle of a celebrity journalist that William F. Buckley, Jr. portrays so vividly in *Overdrive*—zip-

ping in his limousine from cavorting with the president, to
making speeches, to taping "Firing Line." And he always saves
a few minutes to dash off his column.

But there is a second way in which Buckley's uniqueness may
render him an imperfect case study of the effects of celebrity journalism; his celebrity played an important role in launching the conservative movement, and conservatives will be forgiven if they think this
accomplishment worth some sacrifices. Thus Christopher Simonds,
reviewing the Judis biography in *National Review,* sniffed at the
notion that Buckley's celebrity interfered with more meaningful
accomplishments:[36]

> In fact, Buckley has from his position as a "celebrity" done far
> more to advance, if not to articulate, conservatism than he
> might have done as an academic or as the leader of a small,
> perfectionist cult. Cluckings that, but for the television camera
> and the popular press, he might have been the next Eric Voege-
> lin seem trivial coming from the Right: coming from the Left,
> they are disingenuous. Yes, wouldn't it be dandy if Buckley
> had, back in whenever, chucked it all and gone off to the college
> of St. Dymphna to write the *Revolt Against the Masses.* Mean-
> while, Walter Mondale, President for Life. . . .

Simonds has a point, but he simplifies the matter too much.
Couldn't Buckley have exploited a limited degree of celebrity without taking the full plunge? After all, by the 1980s his celebrityhood
was superfluous to his role as a conservative advocate or evangelist.
Not only had the conservative revolution occurred, but he was
already famous and the celebrity-related distractions of the 1980s
did nothing to strengthen the base from which he launched his
conservative missiles. Moreover, if Buckley had produced major
scholarship it would have had an audience well beyond the academy
precisely because he was a celebrity at an early age. There was never
a simple either/or choice between Buckley as obscure theoretician
or Buckley as empire builder.

Nevertheless, Simonds rightly reminds us of the man's uniqueness; his ascent to celebrity status did, especially in the early years, result in much more than lining his pockets. The various political commentators who have become minicelebrities in the 1980s have not and cannot use their more limited celebrity as launching pads for revolutions.

One other qualification is in order. There are those who, pointing to Buckley's mediocre academic record at Yale, speculate that he was *not* a potential theoretician waylaid by the demands of celebrity; rather, they maintain, he lacked the depth and patience to make a major contribution to American's intellectual life. If these people are correct that Buckley was cut out to be a popularizer rather than a serious thinker, he may have found the perfect milieu to maximize his contribution.

The contention is unverifiable, precisely because at a young age Buckley was swept onto the celebrity path. But it is true that his protege, George Will, not Buckley himself, has most often been pegged as the natural successor to Walter Lippmann as the nation's premier philosopher/journalist.

Thus, for several reasons it is even more difficult with Buckley than with most to calculate the penalty exacted by the onset of celebrity. But beyond doubt, there were some opportunity costs involved in William F. Buckley, Jr.'s dazzling trip down celebrity lane.

GEORGE WILL

In some ways George F. Will offers a better illustration than Buckley of the journalist-as-celebrity phenomenon. Unlike Buckley, Will traveled the standard path to journalistic celebrity. In addition, Will has not launched a political movement, and thus his fame cannot be seen as a means to that end. Finally, Will more demonstrably possesses the depth and temperament to be a public philosopher. It is no accident that, at least earlier in his career, he was frequently compared to Walter Lippmann.

For several decades, Lippmann dominated political commentary. His depth, originality, and learning—he studied under William James and George Santayana at Harvard—placed him head and shoulders above his colleagues. Millions of Americans would not formulate an opinion on an issue until they had read Lippmann's column, and far more people read his books on philosophy and government than read the works of accomplished academicians.

In the 1970s and early 1980s, numerous people declared Will the natural successor to Lippmann's exalted position as America's public philosopher/commentator. Will's detractors, however, find the comparison distasteful. Lippmann's biographer Ronald Steel insists that Will is less like the impartial philosopher Lippmann than the vituperative slasher H.L. Mencken.[1] Sidney Blumenthal scoffs that Will's friendship with Nancy Reagan "do[es] not certify him as a Lippmann. . . . [Lippmann] towers over his pretenders."[2]

Both sides are correct. Will is perhaps the closest we have to a contemporary Lippmann: someone with a first-rate mind and extensive training in philosophy who also has access to a mass audience and thus enormous potential to elevate public discourse and understanding. However, Will's contribution does not approach Lippmann's. This may stem, in large part, from the times: Will's contribution might have been more akin to Lippmann's but for the impediments of his celebrity.

Like Lippmann's, Will's background and education distinguish him from his peers. Will has written that his happy life derived from his "shrewd choice of parents."[3] Certainly his choice of parents got him off to a good start as a thinker: his father was a respected philosopher at the University of Illinois. In a moving tribute to his father upon the latter's retirement, Will wrote that his dinner conversations later in life never improved upon the ones he had while growing up.[4]

But George was not a child prodigy. At an elite high school for professors' children, he was a B student. The grades, coupled with Will's extracurricular activities, earned him a scholarship to Trinity

College in Hartford, Connecticut. It might seem surprising that Will's college years were not spent nearer ivy, but as a youth he was more interested in Henry Aaron than Henry James. While Will's baseball fanaticism never faded, his attachment to a life of the mind developed in college and beyond. He earned excellent grades at Trinity and, upon graduation, he enrolled in Magdalen College at Oxford. There he studied politics, economics, and philosophy, the latter under the distinguished philosopher Geoffrey Warnock.

Upon receiving his degree at Oxford, he was admitted to the selective philosophy graduate program at Princeton University. After one year he shifted to the political science department, from which he eventually received a Ph.D. Will's doctoral dissertation, "Beyond the Reach of Majorities: Closed Questions in the Open Society," argues that tolerance, far from an absolute value in a democracy, must have parameters. The final chapter argues in favor of laws banning totalitarian and racist parties. (The dissertation proves that Will's penchant for erudite quotations was acquired early in life. It quotes Goethe, Conrad, Swift, Ogden Nash, E.B. White, and Marshall McLuhan.)

In 1967 Will finished his work at Princeton and landed a teaching position at Michigan State University. After one year there, he moved on to teach at the University of Toronto, but soon left the teaching profession for good. His next move helped determine the course of his adult life. Colorado Senator Gordon Allott was looking for a speechwriter with an academic background. A friend recommended Will, who became Allott's main speechwriter and jack-of-all-trades.

Most congressional staffers labor in anonymity, but Will attracted much attention. During his three years as a Senate aide, he was offered a job as an editorial writer by the *Wall Street Journal* and a job at the White House by the chief of staff, Alexander Haig. He ended up without either job, in part because of his respective aversions to New York City and Richard Nixon. Will turned down the *Journal*'s offer and sent word to Haig that he should look at the anti-Nixon piece by Will that was about to be published in the *Washington Post*; he didn't hear from Haig again.

Will's work for Allott also caught the eye of conservative activists who, unlike the *Journal* and Haig, were unimpressed. The right-wing publication *Human Events* called Will a major obstacle to conservative legislation. While this claim exaggerated Will's influence, it further suggests that he was no ordinary legislative aide.

One conservative who was not down on Will was William F. Buckley, Jr. In 1972, while still working for Allott, Will wrote pieces for Buckley's *National Review* under the pseudonym Cato. After Allott's defeat in 1972, Will went to work for the magazine full-time, editing the book review page and writing a "Capitol Issues" column.

This was at the time of Watergate, and most of Will's columns revolved around the same theme: Nixon was in quicksand and deservedly so. Will rarely asserted these conclusions directly and crudely. Instead, he patiently spelled out the facts and left the reader just enough room to draw his own conclusion. One effective column simply quoted from the most revealing aspects of the Watergate tapes without Will saying a word. While most of the "Capitol Issues" columns lacked the full flair and erudition of the later Will, they consistently contained the best prose in the magazine: snappy, confident, convincing.

Will left *National Review* in January 1976, a career move made possible by his emergence as a successful newspaper columnist. Back in 1972, Will had met Meg Greenfield, deputy editor of the *Washington Post*'s op-ed page, at a political science conference. Greenfield saw the thirty-one year old Will in action, speaking in various workshops, and was impressed. She asked Will to submit pieces to the *Post*.

He did so periodically during 1973, and before long the paper accompanied his columns with a statement that "the author is Washington Editor of *National Review* and a frequent contributor to the *Post* editorial page." By year's end, he usually contributed two columns a week. On January 1, 1974, Will's piece in the *Post* was accompanied by the announcement that beginning that day his column would appear regularly twice weekly in the *Post* and be syndicated nationally by the *Washington Post* Writer's Group.

Before long the column was increased to three times a week, but was reduced back to two when Will was hired by *Newsweek* to write a biweekly column. Will received rave reviews from the beginning, and fellow conservative columnist James Kilpatrick correctly predicted that he would sail to the top of his profession: "He is going to be *the* conservative columnist in the country."[5] Will's love of writing shone through the columns, and was confirmed in Buckley's book *Overdrive;* Buckley related Will's comment that he rose a happy man on those days when he had to write a column.[6] Will has said that he wished he wrote three newspaper columns a week and a weekly column for *Newsweek.*

Such a schedule became impossible when Will became a television commentator. This occurred in 1976 when he became a regular participant on *Agronsky and Company.* The show increased Will's visibility and perhaps helped bring about the event that marked his arrival and spurred his further ascent: his receipt of the Pulitzer Prize for commentary in 1977. The award was well deserved. During the 1970s, Will was in a different league from most of his colleagues.

First, his range of subjects far exceeded that of his peers. Will often wrote on nonpolitical matters, regularly offering meditations about child-rearing, baseball, books, movies, and science. In addition, he wrote engagingly on subjects that can be categorized only as "miscellaneous," such as bells, bicycles, clocks, Nebraska, male perspiration, toys, trading cards, telephone solicitation, hotel lobbies, souvenirs, and countless other things that few people think about, much less write about. These columns often succeeded because Will used his neglected subject as a metaphor for something poignant and more familiar: "A chiming clock with a swinging pendulum powered by slowly descending weights is a constant reminder that nothing stands still, and that suns and civilizations and men run down and cannot be rewound."[7]

Will's columns about politics were less distinguishable from those of his colleagues; it is not easy to write with great depth about public issues in 800 words. Nevertheless, Will often presented a political issue in a broader context than did other commentators, and served up penetrating insights. His analysis of the Iran hostage crisis in 1979 was such an instance:[8]

The crisis that began because of weakness, and was prolonged by confusion, and ended in extortion, has been followed by a national hysteria of self-deception symbolized by a sign carried by a celebrator: "America 52, Iran 0." When calamity is translated into the idiom of sport and christened a victory, when victims are called heroes and turned into props for telegenic celebrations of triumph, then it is time to recall George Orwell's axiom that the great enemy of clear language is sincerity.

The hostages were used by Iran for the humiliation of America and the consolidation of Iran's revolution, and now the former hostages have been used by America in a pageant, the effect of which is to prevent the country from thinking about how it allowed Iran to succeed.

Some Americans even say that the crisis was "a good thing" because it "brought the country together." But so did Pearl Harbor, which was not a good thing and would have been worse if America's response had been vigils and ribbons.

In the 1960s, professors noticed the growing trend of students to answer questions with statements like "Well, my feeling about Hamlet is . . ." and "my reaction to the Renaissance is. . . ." The language of "emotion" and "feeling" was evidence of a culture losing interest in reason, celebrating sentiment, obsessed with "authenticity" and defining it in terms of strong emotions, warm feelings. Descartes' "cogito, ergo sum"—I think, therefore I am—became "I feel, therefore, I am."

In an acute dissection of the nation's recent mood, Thomas Bray of the *Wall Street Journal* notes that "How does it feel?" was the emblematic question of the hostage crisis, asked of everybody; about everything. The celebrating will end when the thinking begins.

While Will was not alone in recognizing America's reaction to the hostages' return as bizarre, no one else so eloquently explained what hidden purpose the celebration served. Will conveys the point that the reaction to the hostages' return was massive self-deception in several ways. First, he characterizes the hostage crisis in stark but reasonable terms: "begun because of weakness, prolonged by confusion, ended in extortion." Next, he notices little things, such as the not so innocent sign that he plausibly cites as reflecting a "national hysteria." Third, he avails himself of a powerful analogy. Is the hostage-taking good because it brings people together? Pearl Harbor was not a good thing, Will reminds us, effortlessly deflating the wishful thinking to which the crisis gave rise. For most columnists, digging beneath the surface of the hostage situation would be task enough. Will, in the last two paragraphs, ties it to larger societal trends. Along the way, he brings in an appropriate Orwell quote and a clever twist on Descartes' *cogito.* With regard to this column, no one has to ask, "Where's the beef?"

In 1978, a collection of roughly one-fourth of Will's *Washington Post* and *Newsweek* columns was published as a book, *The Pursuit of Happiness and Other Sobering Thoughts.* The anthology received glowing reviews, such as the assessment of the *Virginia Quarterly Review:* "If Alexis de Toqueville was right that newspapers are essential to 'maintain civilization,' it just may be that America's best hope flows from the pen of George Will."[9]

Soon thereafter came Will's big career move, as he established a relationship with ABC television, which initially hired him to make frequent appearances as a contributing analyst on *World News Tonight.* In November 1981, he became a regular on a new ABC Sunday morning show, *This Week with David Brinkley.* For the next two years he was on two weekly roundtable shows, *Brinkley* and *Agronsky.* In 1984, ABC forced him to choose between the two and he chose *Brinkley,* where the income and audience are far greater.

Brinkley attracts an audience of several million viewers, and helped establish Will as a commentator with unmatched exposure. His columns appear in roughly 500 newspapers with a total circulation of over 30 million. Will's *Newsweek* column and various ABC appearances—as a commentator at the political conventions and guest on *Nightline,* for example—reach millions more. Eventually

Will became more associated in the public eye with television than print. He projected a vivid television persona and the medium turned him into a minicelebrity.

1983 brought forth Will's first "real" book, *Statecraft as Soulcraft.* (A year earlier, a second collection of Will's columns had been published under the title *The Pursuit of Virtue and Other Tory Notions.*) True to his billing as Lippmann's successor, Will took on a subject far more ambitious than specific issues of the day or the political scene. Tackling deep and enduring issues of political theory and government, the book set forth a coherent political philosophy: a "strong government conservatism" that would proudly concern itself with the inner lives of its citizens.

Statecraft as Soulcraft advances several important theses. First, Will argues, from its founding America has unwisely exalted the notion that government's role is to maximize the happiness and interests of discrete individuals. Will attacked the nation's very premise, urging its replacement by the ancient tradition that sees society as an organic whole and expects government to cultivate the *virtue* of its citizens, not simply to promote their interests.

In the book, Will endorsed the welfare state, though for conservative reasons—less out of compassion or a sense of justice than because it strengthens community ties by expressing an "ethic of common provision." The book also made the case for another lost tradition, what might be called "Burkean prudence": the need to conserve society's traditional values and the danger of precipitous change. Will argued that both liberals who seek constant and major progress, and conservatives who seek to dismantle the welfare state and add a horde of constitutional amendments, ignore the wise counsel of Edmund Burke that society is a carefully woven fabric that cannot be tugged at rashly without severe consequences. Change must be slow and interstitial.

The book's major theses sailed against contemporary winds. For these reasons, and because it intelligently discussed critical issues, *Statecraft as Soulcraft* was important. And it was so received by several philosophers and political theorists. Reviewing Will's book in the *New York Times,* eminent Harvard political theorist Michael Sandel noted with approval Will's effort "to change the character and tone of the debate."[10] William Kristol of the Kennedy School of Government found the book an important contribution.[11] In *The American Scholar,* philosopher Charles Griswold, Jr. warned his colleagues against dismissing the book as the work of a popular commentator, noting that Will is a rare popular figure in a position to interest and educate the public on major questions of political theory. He maintained that the book was a useful step in that direction.[12]

As it turns out, Griswold had the wrong worry. Philosophers treated Will's book with respect; popular journals and newspapers, on the other hand, were largely dismissive. Considering the fact that this was the first full-length work by someone with a reputation as a serious thinker, it was greeted with little sense of importance. Some critics pointed out legitimate flaws, including Will's failure to define "soul" and explicate the nature of "soulcraft," and his promiscuous use of aphorisms from sundry philosophers. But the book's problems do not fully explain its reception. Rather, the reaction to Will's book resembles what had happened to Buckley: critics were reacting to Will the celebrity, and refusing to take seriously Will the philosopher.

Indeed, several critics openly went beyond what Will had written, criticizing his character or television personality. The *Atlantic*'s review referred to the "harrumphing persona of [Will's] television appearances."[13] More significantly, in the *National Review* Joseph Sobran charged that the book was designed for self-promotion rather than promotion of ideas. Sobran argued that the ostensibly conservative Will expressed views that would ingratiate him in useful liberal circles. After quoting Will as saying that conservatism, "properly understood," approves of government's role in creating wealth and endorses a welfare state, Sobran added tartly that "Conservatism, properly understood, makes you welcome at the *Washington Post, The New Republic,* and Harvard." Sobran renewed the charge of pandering in his harsh conclusion about Will's book: "a toothless, coffee-table Toryism, nicely calculated for liberal consumption."[14]

This tendency of reviewers to engage in ad hominems was more noticeable in the reaction to Will's next anthology of columns, *The Morning After,* and his second "real" book, *The New Season.* Increasingly, reviewers discussed Will's pomposity on television and his friendship with Nancy Reagan, and gave short shrift to his ideas. *The Morning After,* published in 1986, was received far less favorably than the two previous collections. In a review for the *Los Angeles Times,* Lippmann biographer Ronald Steel suggested that Will was not a bona fide intellectual but "a product of the age of *People* magazine—he wants people to react to his personality."[15] The review in *The New Republic* went so far as to cast aspersion on Will's intellect.[16] The quality of Will's column did fall off in the 1980s but not so dramatically as to explain the radical difference from the reaction to his previous anthologies. This resulted at least in part from his emerging celebrity status.

The reaction to Will's next book, published a year later, manifested this same phenomenon. *The New Season* described the political climate in which the 1988 presidential election would occur. The book offered perceptive if not earth-shattering analysis, poking fun both at liberals for failing to learn from landslide defeats and at conservatives for failing to make good on campaign promises. The witty, well-written piece of relatively unambitious fun was coldly received. One reviewer wrote that "above all his book celebrates George Will."[17] A *Washington Monthly* review titled "The Lightweight Philosopher" called into question both Will's intellect and integrity.[18]

If reviewers were reacting to George Will the celebrity, there was a lot to react to. Will pulled down roughly $15,000 for a lecture and his annual income reportedly reached one million dollars. In the 1980s he was featured in *Esquire, People,* and *Sports Illustrated,* as well as lampooned in the comic strip *Doonesbury.* Many newspapers—including the *Washington Post, Wall Street Journal, Los Angeles Times,* and *Christian Science Monitor*—ran features on Will the celebrity. *Washingtonian* magazine saw fit to report about his personal life several times, even offering a detailed chronology of his divorce.

Critics maintain that all the attention went to Will's head. He sometimes sees himself as above the ethics of his profession, on at least two occasions blatantly violating them. His troubles in this regard and his celebrity status are difficult to disentangle: both stemmed in part from a friendship he developed with President and Nancy Reagan.

Shortly after Ronald Reagan's election in 1980, signs emerged that George Will would occupy a special position during the upcoming administration. While the president-elect was in Washington to meet with congressional leaders, he accepted an invitation to dinner at the Wills' Chevy Chase home. There, the Reagans and Bushes dined with the capital's elite, including *Washington Post* owner Katherine Graham and Democratic party chairman Robert Strauss.

Many reporters criticized Will for socializing with the president-elect, arguing that friendship with politicians interferes with the press's adversarial posture. The *Washington Post* quoted Will as responding that "I am not an intimate of the Reagans. And I'm not an adviser. I'm just a fella. I sit out here and write columns."[19]

If that explanation did not satisfy everyone, neither did a column Will wrote soon thereafter arguing that friendships with politicians are compatible with a journalist's duty.[20] In a heated op-ed piece in the *Post,* William Shawcross accused Will of failing to grasp the basic function of journalism to keep vigil over the powerful.[21] Such somber criticism attracted less attention than Gary Trudeau's *Doonesbury* cartoons about Will's relationship with the Reagans. In one strip, reporter Rick Redfern calls Will to ask about the controversial dinner. "Look Rick," Will responds, "I'm not an intimate of the president. I'm not even an adviser. I'm just a guy from Chevy Chase who likes to chow down with the president-elect."

Will was unchastened by criticism of his relationship with the Reagans. The first couple dined at the Wills' home several times in ensuing years, and the Wills were guests at small White House gatherings. But friendship did not transform Will into a yes man. In print and on television he frequently maintained that Reagan was insufficiently vigilant in the face of the Soviet threat. After Reagan served one year, Will gave him a grade of B— (though in the same column he gave Nixon, Ford, and Carter F, C—, and D—, respectively).[22]

Regardless of how the president felt about his report card, the administration obviously regarded Will as an ally. In 1982, Will was sent a draft of a speech Reagan was to give before Britain's Parliament, and asked for suggestions. Instead, he wrote a separate speech and sent it to the president, who combined aspects of the two speeches. When Will's contribution came to light he was criticized for moonlighting as a presidential aide. The harshest attack came from *Chicago Daily News* columnist Mike Royko, who wrote: "[In Chicago] newspapermen try to act like watchdogs. In Washington, it appears, some are more like lapdogs."[23]

Royko and others overlooked the distinction between objective reporters and opinion commentators like Will. In light of his well-known position as a conservative partisan, and his function to offer opinions rather than news, Will's friendship with and assistance to the president were arguably defensible. But one thing Will did for Reagan was not.

In 1983, it was revealed that prior to the decisive 1980 presidential debate the Reagan team studied from a purloined Carter briefing book. Investigators explored who had been aware of the Reagan team's possession of the book, and the answer included Will. One disclosure led to another, and it was eventually revealed that Will had helped prepare Reagan for the debate with Carter. (In *New York* magazine two years earlier, Will admitted that he had helped coach Reagan; no one seemed to notice or care at the time.[24]) The plot thickened, for after the 1980 presidential debate, Will had appeared on ABC as a commentator and, without disclosing his role in preparing Reagan, praised the latter's performance.

When this was brought to light in the summer of 1983, Will came under fire. Some criticized his failure to report the stolen briefing book and others his coaching Reagan, though many people found these actions benign. There was, however, nearly universal criticism of Will's failure to disclose his participation prior to praising Reagan on national television. The consensus was that even openly partisan commentators should disclose their personal interests so their audience can take into account any potential bias.

There is no need to rehearse the chorus of condemnation of Will's actions. For present purposes, the most incisive assessment came from columnist Joseph Sobran. What was most disturbing about Will's involvement, Sobran wrote perceptively, was that it showed Will to be an "operator" rather than the "pure observer" he was thought to be.[25]

Amidst the fuss over "Debategate," Will wrote a long column confessing some misgivings about his actions.[26] However, subsequent events revealed that Will still does not hold himself to high standards of disclosure. In 1987 he wrote several columns passionately advocating the confirmation of Robert Bork to the Supreme Court. Eventually *Washington Post* ombudsman Joseph Laitlin reported receiving information that Will was the best man at Bork's wedding a few years earlier.[27] In fact, Will was only an usher, not the best man. Nevertheless, Will had again chosen not to inform his audience of his strong personal involvement in the matter on which he was commenting.

On one other occasion in the 1980s, Will displayed a shaky regard for journalistic ethics. This time the issue concerned not preferential treatment of Will's friends, but dubious conduct toward an adversary. Will has never made any bones about his feelings for Jesse Jackson. Throughout the 1984 presidential campaign, Will maintained that the failure of the press and Democratic candidates to criticize Jackson was condescending to blacks: "It says that blacks are not expected not to talk rot."[28] Because Jackson's candidacy was more serious in 1988, Will seemed to take even more seriously his duty to speak the truth about it. However, he adopted improper means in his effort to expose Jackson.

On January 10, 1988, Jackson appeared on *This Week with David Brinkley* and faced an ornery Will. Will's first two questions were tough but fair, and Jackson handled them routinely. Will's third query to Jackson, however, was obscure: "As president, would you support measures like the G-7 measures in the Louvre Accord?" Jackson replied, "Explain that." Will retorted, "You're the one running for president."

When columnist William Raspberry asked him about the Louvre Accord question, Will virtually admitted that he was trying to reveal Jackson's ignorance. "That's information too," he told Raspberry, ignoring the fact that he had done precisely what he had long accused others of doing: giving Jackson special (though unfavorable) treatment. As Raspberry wrote, Will's question was illegitimate because it was designed "to embarrass the candidate rather than to flesh out his policy position."[29]

Will's celebrity status, his relationship with Reagan, his nondisclosures, and his improper treatment of Jackson are part of the same ball of wax. The association with Reagan was a case of what has been called "insider journalism." Insider journalism preceded celebrity journalism—presidents have always courted influential members of the press—but the two overlap. Politicians regard journalists with a television following as especially important allies. Thus, a reporter's getting a slot on one of the roundtable shows leads not only to wealth and fame, but to breakfasts with the president. And if celebrity status leads to insider status, the latter also reinforces the former. Jeff Greenfield claims that far from diminishing Will's standing, the Debategate flap "brought him into outer space. . . . It added the insider magic."[30]

The package of fame, wealth, and power can distort one's perspective. Both the Debategate flap and the Jackson affair reflect a distorted perspective on Will's part. Political reporter Ken Auletta warns of the dangers of a journalist becoming a celebrity, saying it "robs you of the humility you need to do your job as a journalist. . . . You start thinking, 'Why should I go interview some thirty-year-old kid who thinks he can run a campaign for president?' Or perhaps you start thinking, 'Why should I "interview" an overrated charlatan who thinks he can be president? I'll trap him instead.' "[31]

It is hard to imagine a reporter asking a Louvre Accord-type

question on an edition of *Meet the Press* in the 1950s. The question
shows us a 1980s journalist, seeing himself not just as a journalist
but as a major player, taking it upon himself to do something—
sandbagging a candidate—that, if it should be done at all, should
be left to political opponents rather than reporters. Hugh Sidey has
aptly warned about the "Mick Jaggers of journalism, so highly paid,
so powerful, and self-important that they feel no personal re-
straints."[32] Sidey was referring primarily to network correspon-
dents, but more and more, columnists like Will are acquiring
formidable wealth and power of their own. The celebrity trail, the
Debategate mess, and the Jackson affair all reflect a phenomenon
that seems increasingly problematic for journalists: Will was pulled
away from the role he seemed most suited for—the pure philosophical observer—and turned in less fruitful directions.

The ways in which celebrity status has hindered Will's contribution are illuminated if we return to the Lippmann comparison. The
fact that Will, like Lippmann, is by training more a philosopher
than a journalist led to several other similarities. According to their
critics, Will's and Lippmann's failure to climb the traditional journalistic ladder—small town newspaper, wire service, and so on—
resulted in a deficiency of journalistic ethics. Certainly, both had
little compunction about their proximity to political power.

More significantly and more positively, their backgrounds are
reflected in their aspirations as columnists. In the introduction to
his first collection of columns, Will wrote, "I have made it an aim
in my life to die without ever having written a column about which
presidential advisers are ascending and which are descending." He
explained that he sees his task as exploring "the kernel of principle
and other significance that exists, recognized or not, inside events,
actions, policies and manners."[33] These aspirations were Lippmann's too. David Halberstam notes that Lippmann "did not write
of the minutia[e] of government, of the daily swirling Washington
rumors or the small factional fights within the bureaucracy, which
at the moment often loomed so large to his peers." For Lippmann,
journalism "was not just facts and bulletins, journalism must explain things, journalism must embrace ideas."[34]

The most important similarity between Will and Lippmann is

their status as rare philosophers with access to mass audiences. Public philosophers have a unique opportunity to educate the public on matters of philosophical importance. Lippmann's admirers emphasize his importance in serving this function.[35]

ARTHUR SCHLESINGER: As a thinker deeply responsive to the complex equilibrium of intellectual forces around him, he chose the role of helping produce public sense in the community rather than pursuing private truth in individual solitude [in the academy].

RAYMOND ARON: The commentator, especially one who writes about international politics, is able to point up the significance of current events, even the most fleeting, only by reporting the event in connection with the whole background. . . . Philosopher of history by necessity, the commentator becomes inevitably a teacher. . . . Walter Lippmann is a political teacher, inspired by a certain philosophy of diplomatic history.

SENATOR PAUL SIMON: Perhaps it is simply that the years have gilded the memory of reading Walter Lippmann, but I want to read the thoughts of those who have some sense of history and what life is all about. . . . In an age of television with its sense of the immediacy of everything, perspective is needed even more than at the height of Lippmann's influence. I yearn for the column that seems to come from someone with a cabin in the woods, who has read Plato this morning as well as the morning newspapers.

While Simon goes on to cite Will as one who provides a broader perspective than most columnists, he rightly maintains that no contemporary commentator has approached Lippmann's contribution as a public philosopher. Several of Lippmann's books about government and philosophy achieved far larger readerships than the works of leading philosophers in the academy, and some became seminal works there. Some of his books were influential among journalists and politicians who themselves had access to mass audiences.

Sidney Blumenthal compares Will's output to Lippmann's:[36]

[Will] has written no original work of moral philosophy recognized by moral philosophers, as Lippmann did in *A Preface to*

Morals. Will has made no original contributions to the study of public opinion or foreign affairs. He has written no book based on actual events, as Lippmann did in the case of the Scopes trial. Nor has Will helped promote the ideas of a more interesting mind, as Lippmann did with Keynes's in *The Method of Freedom.*

Will's contribution to American thought has come almost exclusively through his newspaper and magazine columns and his television appearances. Obviously, in such venues one cannot achieve the depth attainable in books. As one reviewer of *Statecraft as Soulcraft* remarked, that book was Will's single "attempt to push closer to first principles than would ordinarily be possible in an appearance on *Agronsky and Company* or in his columns in the *Washington Post* or *Newsweek.* "[37]

Lippmann's biographer Ronald Steel charges that Will, rather than a deep and sustained thinker of Lippmann's ilk, is "to a large degree a creation of television, where his contribution is that of the ten-second take." Steel maintains that in his column Will draws blood like a picador, then "scamper[s] away to safety, saved by the 800 word limit of his column from making a coherent argument."[38] This charge is unfair. A limit of 800 words does not preclude a coherent argument, and Will has made plenty of those. But 800 words does tend to preclude a deep and sustained argument. *Statecraft as Soulcraft* suggests that Will does not need the safety of an 800-word limit. Have the demands of celebrity status held him back?

Although Will dismisses the notion that he has spread himself too thin,[39] his schedule suggests otherwise. In addition to writing his newspaper and *Newsweek* columns, he has been a major player on the lecture and television circuits, as well as a member of various boards and commissions. Such a schedule does not leave a great deal of time for scholarly reflection, research, and writing. Even before the onset of celebrity status, journalists were a notoriously busy lot. But, as noted, Lippmann zealously guarded his time to ensure adequate opportunity for thinking and major writing endeavors.

The difference between Will's and Lippmann's contributions

transcends the fact that the latter produced various important books. The books provided Lippmann with a broad framework and context within which his columns operated.

One area in which Will sometimes seems to lack an adequate framework is the law. He obviously has a deep interest and acquaintance with legal issues, yet in both his column and on television he takes a willfully simplistic view of some complex legal issues. Thus Will has mocked the Supreme Court for protecting a constitutional right to privacy that "the framers neglected to mention."[40] Will neglects to mention that the Ninth Amendment suggests the existence of constitutional rights other than those explicitly named. The intricate question of unenumerated rights divides constitutional scholars, but Will makes the issue seem entirely one-sided. His columns assailing the Court's abortion decisions or defending the constitutionality of antisodomy statutes avoid the serious foundational issues, or "resolve" them with a conclusory sentence.

Similarly, Will repeatedly assails affirmative action, insisting that the whole issue comes down to the bedrock principle that rights inhere in individuals rather than groups. He has stated this principle often, but never considered that a contrary position may be defensible. Legal scholar Owen Fiss argues that the history of the Fourteenth Amendment dictates interpreting it as a device for protecting disadvantaged groups rather than individuals;[41] Michael Kinsley has offered moral and policy arguments for a similar approach.[42] Will's pronouncements on the subject ignore these perspectives. The public would benefit from his making a sustained and lengthy analysis of such issues. (We recall Galbraith's advice to Buckley that book writing would provide "theoretical depth to your ideological positions.")

The effect of celebrity on Will's work concerns not just what he hasn't written, but the quality of his later writing. In the 1970s and early 1980s, Will was by far the best political columnist in the country. But most memorable Will columns, including several about space exploration and the dignity of handicapped persons, stem from this period, with a comparative drought in recent years. Today many of his columns offer fairly routine criticisms of our government's fiscal irresponsibility and ruminations about the crumbling of the communist bloc and the aimlessness of the Democratic party. In both subject matter and degree of insight, they are similar to what many columnists write.

Veteran Will-watchers readily attribute his decline to the demands of celebrity status. Eleanor Randolph, who pored over Will's old columns in researching an article about him, says, "They were fabulous. Every once in a while he'll still do one of those, but so much of his energy is dissipated in giving speeches and doing television that his writing has gone downhill."[43] Jude Wanniski's *Mediaguide of 1987* states that because of his constant appearances on television and the lecture circuit Will "no longer has time to think."[44]

Will once said that he never writes grade-B columns, and it wasn't an empty boast.[45] He is such a fine craftsman that even his mediocre efforts surpass most op-ed commentary. But Will is no longer the country's best contemporary columnist, much less Walter Lippmann's equal. Both Michael Kinsley and Charles Krauthammer produce more grade-A columns. Neither is as gifted a stylist as Will, but their columns show more originality and trenchancy.

Ronald Steel summarizes the difference between Lippmann and Will by suggesting that Lippmann is a man of letters, Will a man of television.[46] This is unfair to Will, a skilled writer. But more importantly, it is a mistake to write off television as a medium for the public's education. Lippmann himself appeared on television and the nature of those appearances further establishes that his contribution was greater than Will's partly because of the times; his one-hour solo interviews underscore the failure of today's political talk shows to provide useful forums for journalists like Will.

In the interviews on CBS, Lippmann discussed the nuances of the Vietnam War at length. The public, accustomed to either jingoism or antiwar slogans, couldn't help but be educated by his patient, multifacted analysis. He also discussed at length more enduring subjects, such as America's role abroad and the qualities that make great statesmen.*

Today there is no Fred Friendly at the networks to arrange for George Will to do lengthy analyses of public issues and ideas. Instead, he spars in fifteen-second bursts with Sam Donaldson, who seems only marginally interested in probing his ideas. The *Brinkley* roundtable is not the setting to examine Will's notion of statecraft as soulcraft, as illustrated by what happened on a rare occasion when Will did introduce the concept. The immediate issue was proposed drug-testing of government employees:[48]

WILL: Government employment is not a right, it is a privilege and it can be conditioned in various ways and a law like this, conditioning employment, is fulfilling an expressive function of the law, which is to try and teach and express certain values. And it accords with something I heartily approve of, which is a general attempt to stigmatize drug use.

DONALDSON: Well, by your definition, all employment then would be a privilege.

WILL: No. No.

DONALDSON: In other words, I have a right to be employed by ABC News but not by the federal government. Is that your view?

WILL: I'm saying—

DONALDSON: Are you listening, Roone [Arledge, head of ABC News]?

Instead of questioning or fleshing out Will's notion of statecraft as soulcraft, Donaldson embarked on a misguided interrogation culminating in an inside joke.

More often than not, Will makes little effort to develop a profound point on *Brinkley*. Rather, every Sunday morning this sophis-

---

*When the interviewers pressed for predictions, labels, and instant assessments, Lippmann steadfastly resisted. Asked which potential vice presidential candidate would help Lyndon Johnson most, Lippmann replied: "That's not a good question . . . because I'm not that kind of a political dopester." Asked to assess the presidency of the recently assassinated John F. Kennedy, he declared that "any genuine historical judgment is quite impossible" at that time. Steering the questioners away from such *McLaughlin*-like queries, Lippmann insisted on a more penetrating exploration.[47]

ticated thinker solves major issues in twenty seconds or less. Why did Egypt make a historic peace with Israel? "Because Jimmy Carter terrified Sadat into flying to Jerusalem because he talked about bringing the Russians back into the mess."[49] Is Mikhail Gorbachev different from previous Soviet leaders? "Not a bit. I think he's the most Leninist Leninist I've ever seen."[50] It is cause for concern that today's would-be Lippmann is best known for his appearances in forums where in a single sentence he explains the achievements or flaws of Anwar Sadat or Mikhail Gorbachev.

As we have seen with both Buckley and Will, celebrity status diminishes a commentator's contribution not only by hindering his work but by affecting the way the work is received. Thus, Will's important book *Statecraft as Soulcraft* was insufficiently appreciated because reviewers, and presumably other readers as well, were suspicious of Will's motives or were predisposed to dislike it because of his television persona. In fact, much of Will's work is not taken at face value because of his celebrity status.

Some of Will's critics have depicted his success as a public relations coup. Writing in the *Nation,* Ben DeMott argued that Will's television style created the misleading impression that he is a deep and original thinker. Demott argued that Will's new conservatism is different only "as a style and posture . . . as a winning personality rather than as a summons to a certain height. . . . The bottom line . . . is self-presentation." DeMott went so far as to suggest that Will is a phony:[51]

> There's reason to ask earnest questions about our ability to distinguish the fake from the real. . . . We need a real Right and a real Left. But equally profoundly, in the end, we need to hang on to clarity about the difference between challenge and charm, conscience and its counterfeits—the pursuit of virtue and the pursuit of something else.

One might dismiss DeMott's diatribe as politically motivated were it not echoed by conservative Joseph Sobran, who was once a fan of Will's. Sobran too charges that self-promotion is Will's game.

As noted, Sobran called *Statecraft as Soulcraft* "nicely calculated for liberal consumption." In a subsequent piece in *American Spectator,* Sobran disclosed that Will had responded to his book review with a short note suggesting that Sobran should have "ascribed my bad ideas to my bad thinking rather than my bad motives." But Sobran was not apologetic. He responded: "I could have, yes. But I didn't see bad thinking as the real problem."[52] Sobran saw the problem as Will's desire to please liberals in order to advance his career.

These charges are made more plausible and tempting by Will's ascent to celebrity status. Unfortunately, the accusations deflect attention from Will's ideas. When he is dismissed as someone in search of fame, fortune, and power, his formidable thought is taken less seriously.

One final way in which celebrity status has hurt Will suggests that there is something to the charge that he is too concerned with self-presentation. While there is insufficient evidence to justify the charge that Will tailors his ideas to win acceptance, there *is* evidence that his commentary is sometimes affected by a desire to project his personality. This tendency is clearest in Will's writings about baseball, where he sells himself as a cultured fanatic. To say that his writings on the subject are overstated is an understatement.

For a while, he seemed to consider the American League's designated hitter rule the second focus of evil in the world. He has called the rule "the worst American scandal since slavery,"[53] and informed readers that "I have warned Ronald Reagan that he will be judged by whether he rids the nation of the DH."[54] To his credit, Will later wrote a column admitting second thoughts about the designated hitter rule. But he has continued his hyberbolic hysteria concerning our national pastime. The following is just a small sample:

> [*Baseball Research Journal* is] the world's most learned periodical.[55]

> [*Elias Baseball Analyst* is the] most important book since Gutenberg [Bible].[56] [It] contains all the information citizens ought to be required to master before being allowed to vote.[57]

Between April and October, real Americans think about politics, if at all, only in baseball categories.[58]

That is how March makes proper Americans feel. Life is void, the world is a moral void, the universe is an empty shell. Then proper Americans look toward April, the horizon where the sun will rise. The sun is baseball.[59]

It has been said that baseball is to the United States what revolutions are to Latin America. . . . I think baseball is more serious than any Latin American revolution.[60]

Since winter began—since the last out of the World Series . . . there has been nothing to do but pout about the rottenness of a universe in which the regular season is just 162 games long.[61]

Bull Durham [the movie] is about baseball and love, and what else is there?[62]

It has been said that baseball is only a game. Yes, and the Grand Canyon is only a hole in the ground.[63]

"Bill James Baseball Abstract" is the most important scientific treatise since Newton's *Principia.* [64]

There have been serious arguments, not to mention wars, over what God wills. But no one can doubt what he wills for Americans in summer: 26 teams playing 162 games.[65]

It may be harmless amusement to declare that people who don't like baseball are not real or proper Americans, but baseball is too good a game to need promiscuous overpraising and Will is too good a writer to continue to produce such claptrap.

Some detect contrivance behind Will's baseball fanaticism. Ronald Steel writes that it is "designed for those who congratulate themselves on their love of the game."[66] In fact, Will's love of baseball is undeniable: it is a big part of his life, not just of his column. But however sincere his love for the game, Will's writings about baseball do seem infused with a desire to sell George Will. It is perhaps no coincidence that in the 1970s Will's writings about baseball were generally mature; the silliness emerged as his celebrity status grew (though he fortunately avoided the silliness in his recent book about baseball, *Men at Work*).

Television, of course, encourages such excesses. Thus, on *Brinkley,* Will has remarked that "the national anthem should be 'Take Me Out to the Ballgame' "[67] and the idea of baseballs being doctored to increase their liveliness is "Soviet disinformation" that is "striking at the essence of America."[68] When there was talk of a baseball players' strike, Will stated that "the president, if necessary, should conscript the devils and make them play baseball."[69] When Sam Donaldson, unwittingly playing the straight man, mentioned Harry Truman's seizure of steel mills, Will pounced: "This is much more important. The country can live without steel."[70]

Caricatures

The careers of James Kilpatrick and Robert Novak provide additional evidence of the high price exacted by television stardom. They too have spent a good deal of time in the television studio and on the lecture circuit, diverted from their finer work. However, the following profiles focus on a slightly different problem. Kilpatrick, a fine columnist, and Novak, a worthy historian, are best known for their unflattering television personas. They illustrate how today's political talk shows can convert serious thinkers and writers into cartoon figures.

JAMES KILPATRICK

It is risky to speculate about someone's writing based on his television demeanor. Seeing James Jackson Kilpatrick hurl poisonous verbal darts or grumble unpleasantly on television, one expects his newspaper column to be more vehement and cocksure than literate. In fact, Kilpatrick is a gifted stylist who writes sweetly and skeptically. On television, Kilpatrick seems to think that the shortest distance between two points is an epithet or a grunt. Muttering disgustedly out of the side of his mouth, he gives the impression of someone who spends more time arguing about football in bars than analyzing the finer points of Supreme Court decisions. The many people who know only his television persona will be surprised to learn that Kilpatrick is a cultured country sage.

One might picture a young James Kilpatrick as the toughest kid in reform school. In fact he was a child prodigy, whose first publication, a poem about Lindbergh's flight to Paris, came at the ripe young age of six. After that, it was one fast step after another up the journalistic ladder: copyboy for the *Oklahoma City Times* at thirteen, editor of the student newspaper in high school, journalism school at the University of Missouri, freelance writer, photographer, and public relations staffer at Stephens College, and reporter for the *Richmond News Leader*. Kilpatrick rose swiftly at the *Leader* while simultaneously covering the United States Patent Office for the *New York Times*. In 1949, at the age of twenty-eight, he was designated the *Leader*'s chief editorial writer, and two years later became the editor in chief, the youngest person in the country to hold that position at a major newspaper.

Kilpatrick is not, however, altogether proud of the uses to which he put his considerable skills during those early years. Although born and raised in Oklahoma, he was a southerner at heart and by blood—his grandfather was a captain in the Confederate army and generations of Kilpatricks lived in New Orleans—and a very unreconstructed southerner at that. In the 1950s, he devoted much of his intellectual firepower and his newspaper's editorial page to defending racial segregation.

Kilpatrick's book *The Sovereign States,* published in 1957, urged the southern states to disobey the Supreme Court's ruling in *Brown v. Board of Education* requiring school desegregation. Although the tract consisted primarily of a plausible constitutional argument for states' rights—a revival of James C. Calhoun's doctrine of nullification—it was tinged with racism. Kilpatrick argued that segregation was necessary because the "Negro race, as a race, has palpably different social, moral, and behavioral standards"—to wit, illegitimacy, promiscuity, and crime, which could not be attributed to blacks' historical oppression or ongoing poverty.[1] Kilpatrick concluded that "white and black cannot come together, as equals, in any relationship that is *intimate,* personal and prolonged." Integration would cause "debasement of the society as a whole."[2]

Because Kilpatrick was an influential southern editor, and because his segregationist appeal was couched in coherent constitutional arguments, civil rights activists worried that *The Sovereign States* would become a bible of southern resistance to desegregation. While the book did not have the feared impact, it did play a role in making massive resistance respectable. Kilpatrick wrote so well that even the book's harshest critics acknowledged his graceful and lively narrative style. Over the next few decades he solidified a reputation as a craftsman. Southern author J. Harvie Wilkinson rightly called Kilpatrick "easily one of the most gifted phrasemakers of the national press."[3]

It was some time before Kilpatrick stopped applying his gifts to the unworthy cause of segregation. His 1962 book *The Southern Case for School Segregation* conceded that the segregation battle was legally lost but further fanned the flames of white supremacy. The *National Review* described how Kilpatrick threw down the gauntlet to blacks to prove their equality: "From now on white leaders will take seats in the grandstand—a 'retreat to neutrality' Kilpatrick calls it— and see what the Negro can do for himself. . . . The Negro wants equality? Let him earn it."[4] More problematically, Kilpatrick discussed in depth the claim that the Negro race was innately inferior, concluding that the evidence justified such a presumption.

Eventually Kilpatrick recanted his view of white superiority and turned his talents toward more reasonable battles. He fought effectively enough to establish himself as one of the leading conservative commentators in the country.

His big break came in 1964. At the time, there were no southern conservatives writing for the op-ed pages of the country's major newspapers. Long Island's *Newsday,* trying to establish a prominent national syndicate, had plenty of liberal columnists but no conservatives in its stable; it signed on Kilpatrick, and he was on his way. A year later, the *Washington Star* syndicate snapped him up, and it was only a matter of time before Kilpatrick became one of the most widely syndicated opinion columnists in America.

Kilpatrick's writing is characterized by a terse eloquence; his columns are rarely flashy but always solid and well executed. In contrast to *The Sovereign States* (which he openly admits in the introduction to be a partisan tract—a "brief" for states' rights), his column projects an appealing skepticism. Kilpatrick recalls that in his earlier days "I saw everything in the nicest, crispest blacks and whites," but today, "I'm in my seventieth year and I see that many things are gray."[5] In fact, Kilpatrick learned this lesson well in advance of turning seventy. Back in 1975 he explained that he tried to "avoid the Olympian attitude to pronounce on things definitively. I have bent over backwards in my column to say there is another side to a situation, to show no pretensions toward infallibility."[6]

Kilpatrick's fairness and open-mindedness sometimes manifest themselves in surprises. Although a staunch conservative generally, he has disappointed fellow conservatives on numerous major issues: he favored legalized abortion, the establishment of the Legal Services Corporation, and a nuclear freeze, and opposed constitutional amendments requiring prayer in school and a balanced budget.

Kilpatrick's unpredictability and fine prose are two reasons why his column is among the best to grace the op-ed pages. In addition, he often offers astute political analysis that is well ahead of the conventional wisdom. Long before most of the media were paying attention to George McGovern's 1972 presidential campaign, Kilpatrick wrote a superb piece for *National Review* capturing the campaign's tone and essence, its potential and obstacles. In the following passage Kilpatrick so adroitly serves up several metaphors that a mere two paragraphs convey a good feel for McGovern and the context of his campaign:[7]

> McGovern is neither as handsome as Lindsay or as happy as Humphrey; he offers the cartoonist none of Muskie's rockbound crags. In the game of guess the stranger's occupation, you might hazard a guess not far from the mark: He is the new minister in town, the one who wants the congregation to try a couple of different hymns.
>
> . . . On every issue from aircraft and amnesty down the alphabet to warship and welfare, McGovern takes a position cal-

culated to make every particular conservative hair stand on
end. Yet he advances these positions as placidly as if he were
grandma reading instructions on how to knit: knit two, purl
six, share the wealth, soak the rich.

Such low-key gracefulness and sharp analysis characterize much
that Kilpatrick writes.

He has written several fine pieces, for example, about the controversy surrounding the Vietnam War Memorial. These columns convey appreciation for veterans' objections while nevertheless insisting
that the critics of the memorial misunderstand its purpose. When
he finally saw the memorial, Kilpatrick outdid himself in a piece
that is stunningly powerful and perceptive. The kind of heartfelt but
controlled sentiment that he expressed would shock those familiar
only with the fuming curmudgeon of television:[8]

> We walked through the usual litter of a construction site, and
> gradually the long walls of the memorial came into view. Noth-
> ing I had heard or written prepared me for the moment. I could
> not speak. I wept.
>
> This memorial has a pile driver's impact. No politics. No re-
> criminations. Nothing of vainglory or of glory either. . . . This
> memorial carries a message for all ages: this is what war is all
> about.
> It is about Howard Owens, Michael R. Page, Leveret R.
> Prosky, Ronald R. Reil, Leonard S. Skoniecki, Jr., Donny Ray
> Stewart, Ronald R. Stroschein, Thomas S. Sudlesky, Donald L.
> Templeton, Thermall Thompson. . . . They died on this day in
> 1968.
>
> On this sunny Friday morning, the black walls mirrored the
> clouds of a summer's ending and reflected the leaves of an
> autumn's beginning, and the names—the names!—were etched
> enduringly upon the sky.

Unlike people on both ends of the political spectrum, Kilpatrick
resisted the temptation to see the memorial as a pointed political

statement about the Vietnam War. Rather, he recognized it as a statement about war in general and the nothingness of death that war produces for so many. The memorial was not a comment on the particular cause, but a requiem for the deceased. It was about the names, about the people who were reduced to names. Kilpatrick hauntingly captures the power of the memorial by writing with equal power, and with understanding and nuance.

There are certain subjects on which Kilpatrick has developed an expertise and which he unfailingly presents with balance and precision. He writes often and well, for example, about judicial decisions. His ability to cut through a maze of complexities to the heart of legal issues, and to show appreciation of both sides of the argument, makes him the perfect columnist for laypersons interested in constitutional law.

When in 1988 a United States Court of Appeals ruled that the army could not dismiss a soldier because of "homosexual tendencies," Kilpatrick weaved his way through a complicated fact pattern to capture precisely the essence of the dispute:[9]

> The Watkins case provides a classic example, as old as Antigone and Creon, of the conflict between the rights of an individual and the powers of the state.
>
> The government's view is that the armed services are special. The Constitution gives Congress power "to make rules for the government and regulation of the land and naval forces." As the Supreme Court many times has said, that power is entitled to unusual deference. . . .
>
> The army defended its regulation against homosexuality as one of compelling importance. Many straight soldiers despise homosexuals; their presence in a barracks creates—or could create—tensions that would undermine discipline and morale; their admitted orientation clearly implies a desire for sexual gratification through sodomy. . . . Some of these same arguments were once used to justify the segregation of blacks. A vague "desire" to engage in sodomy is not enough. It is only

the criminal act that could justify dismissal among the armed services.

In the 800-word column, Kilpatrick managed to give a sufficient factual matrix of the case (omitted here), to place the matter in its largest theoretical context (state powers versus individual rights), to describe succinctly and fairly the government's position in military cases generally and in the case at hand, and to explain his reason for rejecting it. One can disagree with his conclusion, but it is hard to disagree that this column served the highest aspirations of an op-ed piece: advancing understanding and provoking thought on an important issue.

More often than not, Kilpatrick's views on constitutional law fall on the conservative side; either way, the columns are balanced and well argued. When John W. Hinckley, Jr., was acquitted by reason of insanity, Kilpatrick was angered, but not so much that he couldn't see straight—he saw straight to the fundamental issues involved and advanced his own view with restrained verve:[10]

Any man who sets out to assassinate a president, under the delusion that his action will favorably impress a young actress, is plainly irrational. We reasonably would say that such a person would be "out of his mind," and that it was an "insane" thing for him to do.

But such words as "irrational" and "deranged" and "insane" are cotton words. Their meaning pulls apart at the touch. The terms are matters of degree. All of us might agree, at one extreme, that it would be cruel and inhumane to imprison the obvious lunatic—the pathetic creature who stabs an infant thinking that he is cutting a watermelon. . . . John Hinckley suffered no such delusion.

The heart of the matter [is]: what did the defendant intend to do? . . . A jury does not require psychobabble to get at a question of intent. When Hinckley acquired his arsenal of weapons, what did he intend to do? When Hinckley engaged in handgun practice against simulated human targets, what was in his mind? The evidence of intention was overwhelming.

Kilpatrick's position—that the insanity defense has been interpreted far too broadly—is strengthened considerably by his restraint. He doesn't call for smashing all wrongdoers; indeed he acknowledges cases where it would be "cruel and inhumane" to punish, and patiently explains why Hinckley did not present such a case. Again, regardless of whether one agrees with Kilpatrick's conclusion, he undeniably presents his argument fairly, intelligently, and provocatively.

In addition to writing about government, Kilpatrick writes periodic pieces, datelined Scrabble, Virginia, (his hometown), that reflect lovingly about life in the country. His masterly little book *The Foxes' Union* includes many such pieces, other reminiscences, and tender descriptions of nature. He also writes a weekly language column that calls attention to abuses of language and underscores Kilpatrick's love of the written word.

But all of his fine craftsmanship is not what made Kilpatrick famous. His writing was overshadowed, even undermined, by his very different television persona. Kilpatrick's credentials as a writer and thinker earned him two regular television slots in the late 1960s. In 1969 he was hired as one of four regular participants on the roundtable political discussion program *Agronsky and Company.* What made Kilpatrick famous, however, was not thirty minutes a week on public television but ninety seconds a week on network prime time.

In 1970, when CBS hired him and Nicholas Von Hoffman to exchange barbs in a weekly "Point/Counterpoint" segment on *60 Minutes,* Kilpatrick was en route to stardom. It didn't hurt when Von Hoffman was replaced by Shana Alexander in 1975; the feisty segment was made more titillating by the addition of an underlying battle-of-the-sexes motif. By 1979, when "Point/Counterpoint" was discontinued, Kilpatrick was recognized wherever he went.

Kilpatrick's television persona bore no resemblance to his eloquent, balanced, and skeptical writings. On *60 Minutes* every pro-
nouncement was made with total certitude and often contempt for
his interlocutor. He spoke quickly, furiously, and sometimes nastily.
In 1974, television critic Edith Efron summarized the Kilpatrick/
Hoffman phenomenon:[11]

> Both men have converted themselves into cartoons—living
> flesh-and-blood cartoons produced for Sunday display on CBS-
> TV.
> Weirdly enough, neither of these men resembles the stereotype
> he is enacting. Both are unusually complex and interesting men
> with intellectual virtues worthy of national display. But the
> viewer contemplating their TV "images" would never know it.
>
> The two gentemen do psychosurgery on themselves . . . . And
> in the process, their IQs drop like stones and they seem to
> become one-dimensional and vaguely mad.

It got even worse when Von Hoffman was replaced by Alexander
the next year. For while Kilpatrick never allowed himself to be
bullied by Von Hoffman, he was rarely the aggressor. Efron sur-
mized that his vituperation was "vitiated by some inner compulson
to respectability."[12] With Alexander as his opponent, any compul-
sion to respectability went out the door. Eyes bulging with fury, lips
twitching rapidly, bald head bobbing, Kilpatrick became a vivid
cartoon character. The anger and certitude were present on
Agronsky too, but delivered in a calmer, world-weary way. On
Agronsky Kilpatrick wore a scowl and was petulant, but he didn't
resemble a Volkswagen caught between gears as he did on *60 Minutes.*

Kilpatrick's persona on *Agronsky/Inside Washington* does reflect
a side of his real-life personality: the stout, colorful, country curmudgeon. His colleague Strobe Talbott remarks fondly that "Jack
is the only person I know who uses words like 'bosh' and 'balderdash' in ordinary conversation."[13] But the television persona is one-
sided and exaggerated. Upon meeting Kilpatrick, one is struck by

his warmth and charming good nature, and his colleagues confirm that he is pleasant and engaging generally, his smiles far outnumbering his scowls. But that is a James Kilpatrick television audiences rarely see.

Some people's behavior undergoes a spontaneous change when the television camera's red light stares at them, but conscious role-playing takes place too. Kilpatrick acknowledges that he and Von Hoffman actually agreed on many issues,[14] and his off-screen disagreements with Von Hoffman and Alexander were civil. On *60 Minutes,* Kilpatrick rarely found anything either of them said remotely plausible, and expressed his disagreement ungraciously. This was the network's expectation and the performers played along. As Edith Efron put it:[15]

> What would happen if James Kilpatrick decided to reveal his poetic, literary streak—to talk eloquently, let's say, of his love of nature, as he often does in print? . . . It would wreck CBS's neat little Right-Left arrangement.

Kilpatrick himself says, "Shana and I have great affection for each other. It didn't show. I guess that was show business."[16]

Unlike *60 Minutes, Agronsky* was not a prime time network show, and its dramatic requirements were less blatant. But it too had unwritten rules of engagement, which Kilpatrick knew well: speak tersely and assertively and don't hesitate to get involved in spunky exchanges. Asked whether he deliberately adopted a schtick on *Agronsky,* Kilpatrick says, "Not consciously." He does, however, recognize the radical difference between his television style and print style. "On television, if you're going to make any impact at all you have to say things emphatically. There's just not time for qualifiers, nuances, and flourishes."[17]

Indeed, Kilpatrick's performance on *Agronsky/Inside Washington* is devoid of subtlety. He is best known for lowbred skirmishes rather than refined commentary. Jack Germond fondly remembers the days on *Agronsky* when Peter Lisagor would "stick these little needles into Jack and all the air would come out of him."[18] Kilpatrick's fans, by contrast, relish his doing the same to Carl Rowan.

Kilpatrick and Rowan often lock horns on racial matters. Kilpatrick has confessed the errors of his earlier racist thinking, but he remains opposed to affirmative action and at odds with Rowan on most civil rights issues. Unfortunately, their television clashes rarely probe beneath the surface and consist largely of Kilpatrick, who projects a distinct unhappiness, seemingly trying to make Rowan equally miserable. On a recent show, Rowan, lamenting several Supreme Court decisions about civil rights, made the mistake of characterizing the decisions as judicial activism. The following exchange ensued:[19]

KILPATRICK: Where were you on the subject of activism in May 1954?
ROWAN: I like—
KILPATRICK: Come on, you liked that act—
ROWAN: Oh, I like activism—
KILPATRICK: Sure, you loved that activism—
ROWAN: . . . But let me tell you this, we've got enough division and enough racial strife . . . . But my concern goes beyond that. I think I smell a lot of trouble down the road brought on by the new Justice Kennedy. . . .
KILPATRICK: Don't try to predict how Supreme Court justices will vote. We did that in the case of Harry Blackmun; and it just didn't turn out that way.

Kilpatrick was eager to needle Rowan rather than probe his point, and offered a gratuitous little lecture condescendingly dismissing Rowan's concern about the direction of the Court.

A recent *Inside Washington* discussion on the state of American education further illustrates Kilpatrick's gruff, screechy and intolerant television style. He expressed a clear position, but not in a manner conducive to useful exploration:[20]

TALBOTT: The president has endorsed the idea of these national performance standards or goals. It will be within the life of the [Bush] presidency that we will see clearly whether these goals can be met without more federal spending. I'm quite sure it will require more federal spending and then he will be called to account for it.

KILPATRICK: Money, money, money, money, money, money, money, money, money, money, money, money, money. That's all you guys talked about and that's not where the answer lies. It lies in attitudes, among other things.

ROWAN: That's what we're drowning in . . . clichés about how money doesn't solve anything. You don't solve anything in America without money.

KILPATRICK: Teachers' salaries have gone up and up and up, Carl.

TALBOTT: And they're still egregiously underpaid as a sector of our economy.

KILPATRICK: Taxes, taxes, taxes, taxes, taxes, taxes.

Such antics created a vivid television persona that inspired several parodists. On *Saturday Night Live,* Dan Aykroyd, playing Kilpatrick to Jane Curtin's Alexander, called Curtin an "ignorant slut." In his parody of *Agronsky and Company* for the *The New Republic,* Michael Kinsley had "Jack Curmudgeon" bark, "Harrumph. Balderdash. Poppycock. Horsefeathers. Et cetera."[21] A parody of *Agronsky* by Arthur Haupt in the *Washington Post* involved a discussion of terrorism. When it was suggested that America be prudent about military action against terrorists, the parodied Kilpatrick responded: "No way. Whuhhhh—this sort of terrorist business has got to be nipped in the bud. PDQ. Guerrillas, gorillas, what's the difference? (subsides into grumbles)."[22] The caricatures were right on pitch; on *60 Minutes* Kilpatrick was nasty, on *Agronsky* just bitter. On neither show did he offer anything resembling the graceful, insightful commentary that characterizes his writing.

Indeed, the parodies were barely parodies at all; they were all too realistic. Consider Kilpatrick's contribution to an actual discussion of Oliver North's activities in soliciting funds for the Nicaraguan contras from foreign nations:[23]

SIDEY: What is wrong in this process of trying to get friends to help you carry out your policy?

KILPATRICK: Nothing wrong with it at all.

DREW: What's wrong is if you are violating the law.

ROWAN: Elizabeth is right, they were violating the law and they knew it or they would not have gone to such devious means to try to do it. But Gordon, you raised the—
KILPATRICK: Nonsense. Horsefeathers.
ROWAN: . . . I think that document listed yesterday indicates [that] to a great degree Oliver North was a guided missile. And one of the things the jury is going to have to decide is even though he was doing what Bill Casey wanted him to do—
KILPATRICK: Yeah, yeah.

This kind of pithy boorishness was also on display during another discussion about Colonel North:[24]

PETERSON: Senator Hatch says we ought to pardon him, the president should pardon him.
KILPATRICK: I'm for that; damn right.

PETERSON: There's a huge defense fund, and it's ongoing, as I understand it—
KILPATRICK: I've contributed to it.
PETERSON: You have contributed to it?
KILPATRICK: Darn right.

On some occasions, this style interferes with a participant's effort to get a discussion off the ground. When New York Mayor Ed Koch was accused of inflaming racial tensions, Kilpatrick defended him with silliness, not syllogisms.[25]

SIDEY: Carl, what is so awful about this? We've had little demagogues in politics—
KILPATRICK: Big demagogues, little demagogues.
SIDEY: Medium-sized demagogues.
DREW: I think what sets this one apart is that Koch is inflammatory, and he knows it. This is quite consistent with the way he has behaved much of the time that he has been mayor. New York is a tinder box of racial tensions, and he certainly doesn't help the state or the country by pouring gasoline on it.
ROWAN: I agree.

KILPATRICK: He sounds like Frank Purdue [the chicken salesman].
SIDEY: Well, this is big state politics, though. Let's be honest about
it.
KILPATRICK: It's hard-ball politics.

ROWAN: Well, there's hard-ball politics and there is this business
of being irresponsibly inflammatory. And that's what Koch is.
KILPATRICK: Oh, I don't think he's been that.

These are just a few examples of Kilpatrick's television style,
which often amuses or annoys but rarely educates. His television
viewers do not get the benefit of the perceptive mind that Kilpatrick's faithful readers know him to possess.

Kilpatrick's career, like Buckley's and Will's illustrates how celebrity can take its toll on a commentator's work. As a result of *60
Minutes,* Kilpatrick was an early traveler down the celebrity journalist trail, doing the lecture circuit throughout the 1970s. During
this time he was constantly on the road, giving as many as forty-five
speeches a year. He isn't exaggerating when he says that this activity
"drove me to a heart attack."[26]
    Like Buckley and Will, he combined the syndicated column,
television appearances, and lecture trail with other activities, such
as thrice-weekly radio commentaries, sporadic contributions to *National Review,* and a monthly column for *Nation's Business* magazine. In his final column for *Nation's Business,* explaining why he
was leaving, he acknowledged that he had been spread awfully thin:
"At sixty-five, I intend to shed professional responsibilities one by
one until at seventy I may be able to do the reading and thinking
and writing that an overcrowded schedule prevents."[27] This was a
notable concession from someone who makes his living reading,
writing, and thinking.
    Because Kilpatrick rightly prides himself on being a serious
writer, it is all the sadder that his writing is diminished by huge
chunks of time spent on television and the lecture trail. Between the
two, some of our best columnists are expending a huge amount of
time and energy on the spoken word.

*　　*　　*

Completely apart from the effects of celebrity status on his serious
work, Kilpatrick epitomizes an unfortunate effect that television has
on some print journalists; it turned him into a cartoon figure, known
far less for his column than his buffoonish television persona. The
conversion of a serious, talented writer into a cartoon figure does
neither himself, journalism, nor democracy much good. In discussing Kilpatrick's and Von Hoffman's performances on *60 Minutes,*
critic Edith Efron nicely summarized the phenomenon and its
costs:[28]

> James Kilpatrick just happens to be one of the finest reporters
> and most lucid writers at work today. . . . A thoughtful man,
> a reasoning man, he too is the embodiment of civilized political
> discourse. . . . Now what on earth are [he and Von Hoffman]
> doing up there on the screen—turning themselves into simplis-
> tic, even scary caricatures?

> Messers. Kilpatrick and Von Hoffman really shouldn't make
> caricatures of themselves—for their own sakes and for ours. If
> America is suffering from anything, it is from a surfeit of
> low-grade political stereotypes, slogans, and oversimplifica-
> tions.

Kilpatrick doesn't dispute Efron's description but shrugs off her
conclusion: "Caricature is an art in itself" he says.[29] This defense
is, to put it mildly, less convincing than the indictment.

It may be that Kilpatrick's television fame, albeit unflattering,
increased the audience for his column. Certainly, newspapers are
more likely to add a columnist to their op-ed page if he is well-
known. However, there may be many people who note Kilpatrick's
name on the op-ed page but don't bother to read the column out of
the belief that they already see the live article on television or that
the individual on their screens doesn't seem likely to be much of a
writer. Liberals are especially apt to eschew reading what they may
presume to be angry conservative grunts; if so, they miss an engaging, skeptical, and independent conservative voice.

Other readers may read Kilpatrick columns while actually hearing the Kilpatrick they see on television. We are not ideal readers who see only the words in front of us. We bring preconceptions to what we read and the wrong preconception about the author can interfere with a sensitive reading. Indeed, some people report that it took them quite a while to recognize Kilpatrick's piquancy as a writer; who knows how many gave Kilpatrick too little chance or no chance at all? *Agronsky* and *60 Minutes* conditioned people to expect from Kilpatrick neither eloquence nor insight.

Moreover, television may be contributing to the gradual demise of the op-ed page. There is a steep downward trend in the number of new columnists newspapers are picking up, which indicates a decline in the number of people who read political commentary. Kilpatrick agrees that such a decline is taking place and doubts whether there will be an audience for serious op-ed commentary twenty years from now. "Television has a lot to do with that," he says.[30]

Shows of the sort that made Kilpatrick famous may be especially responsible for the demise of the op-ed page. Much has been made of the fact that television news has displaced the front page as the source of most people's information, and caused hundreds of newspapers around the country to fold. So too the rise of opinion commentary on television may directly result in less attention to the op-ed page. Asked whether the proliferation of talk shows is to blame for the decline of the op-ed page, media critic Barbara Matusow responded, "No question. They're overexposed on TV and there's so much opinion coming at people."[31]

The supplanting of the newspaper op-ed page by the television version may be inevitable but it would be somewhat less problematic if the political talk programs displayed commentators at or near their best; in Kilpatrick's case, they emphatically do not. Jacob Weisberg's comments in *The New Republic,* focused on George Will, apply even more to Kilpatrick:[32]

The more popular programs like *McLaughlin* become, the more they supersede careful writing as the preferred way for journalists to inform and persuade. Although George Will says that "everything else takes a backseat to writing," his basic vocation has suffered from his audience's paying more attention to his televised output on ABC.

Like Will, Kilpatrick's first and greatest love is writing. More than Will, his television work has overshadowed his writing. And also more than Will, he offers a style of commentary on television that bears almost no relation to his written work and contributes little to the exposition of ideas.

Instead of being remembered as a country sage and fine stylist who brought lucid, balanced opinions about law and other subjects to the op-ed pages, Kilpatrick will probably be remembered for barking at Shana Alexander and sparring with Carl Rowan. (It is over a decade since Kilpatrick left *60 Minutes,* yet he is still approached by strangers who nudge him and say, "Jane, you ignorant slut!"[33]) Mary McGrory summarizes the Kilpatrick phenomenon: "He writes charmingly about life in Virginia and human problems. But he has created a [television] persona and he humphs and grunts every Saturday night."[34]

To be sure, Kilpatrick does not bewail his television stardom and the effect it has had on his career and image. But regardless of his own feelings about the matter, he poses a somber example of the effect of television on journalists and journalism. James Jackson Kilpatrick has reason to be proud of his accomplishments as a writer. Others have reason to be displeased that the public knows one of our finest columnists less for his contribution to democracy than as fodder for *Saturday Night Live.*

ROBERT NOVAK

On the roundtable programs that have secured him infamy, Robert D. Novak frequently chides his colleagues for failing to understand how average Americans live and think. By implication, Novak depicts himself as having a finger on the pulse of life outside the Washington Beltway. This may seem odd since Novak and partner Rowland Evans write the ultimate Washington insider's column, "Inside Report." However, by both birthright and upbringing, Novak can indeed claim a link to middle America.

Novak grew up in a middle-class family in Joliet, Illinois. By his own account, his childhood was unremarkable, resembling Beaver Cleaver's more than Pat Buchanan's. Like Kilpatrick, he showed an early interest in journalism, covering sports for both his high school and hometown newspapers.

Novak remained a midwesterner through college and beyond, attending the University of Illinois and then working for two small Illinois newspapers. After a stateside tour of duty during the Korean War, he worked for the Associated Press in several midwest locales. In 1957, AP transferred him to the nation's capital to cover Congress. Four years later he joined the Washington bureau of the *Wall Street Journal,* where he covered the Senate, especially the Finance Committee. Novak wasted no time in establishing a reputation as a superb reporter.

In the army, Novak had come under the influence of Whittaker Chambers's book *Witness.* The book (for which he wrote an introduction to a later edition) helped convince him that anticommunism should be a major part of his life's mission. Novak determined that his career as a journalist afforded ample opportunity to carry out that mission, and he did indeed come to be associated with a fervent brand of cold warriorism. He also came to be associated with Rowland Evans, a less predictable development.

Evans, a reporter in the Washington bureau of the *New York Herald Tribune* while Novak worked for the *Journal,* wished to write a regular column but was told by his employer that the column would have to appear six days a week. He sought a partner and was referred to Novak, who also harbored the ambition to be a columnist. In May 1963, when Novak was only thirty-two, he and Evans were signed by the *Chicago Sun Times* syndicate to write a syndicated political column jointly.

The Evans/Novak column became a must-read for those interested in behind-the-scenes government maneuvering. One read it to find out who wrote the last presidential speech, who had the president's ear, who was infighting with whom and who was prevailing. It wasn't all gossip; the columnists told the inside story about policy battles as well as turf fights. At its peak, the column ran in well over two hundred newspapers.

Occasionally, Evans and Novak were misled by a source and stuck their necks out prematurely. Their grossest miscues (including an erroneous report that the Carter administration was on the brink of an arms-for-hostages deal with Iran that would result in the release of America's hostages prior to the 1980 election) prompted critics to call them "Errors and No Facts" and led some newspapers to drop their column. Nevertheless, it remained many people's window on government intrigue. Evans and Novak had a multitude of highly placed sources, and their track record as insiders was estimable. They broke the story of the Soviet Union building the Krasnoyarsk radar detector in violation of the ABM treaty; years later, the Soviet government pleaded guilty to the charge.

Novak's life is full of incongruities. He is a consummate insider who lambasts the "inside the Washington Beltway" mentality; a serious writer and thinker who has come to be known primarily for television buffoonery; a Jew who is more harshly critical of Israel than virtually any other columnist; and a wealthy man who sees himself as a populist and enemy of the elite. By far the greatest anomaly in Novak's life, however, is his partnership with Rowland Evans. The two have been compared to Mutt and Jeff, Oscar and Felix, and other odd couples. In contrast to his short, swarthy, aggressive, Jewish, middle-American partner, Rowland Evans is a lanky, waspish, relaxed, eastern patrician.

Of course, much links the two as well, especially talent and conservative politics. On the latter point there is some confusion. It is widely believed that Novak and Evans are lapsed liberals. Novak admits having voted for John F. Kennedy in 1960 and as late as 1971 *National Review* lamented Evans and Novak's "liberal bias."[1]

In fact, Novak insists that he was always a fierce anticommunist (and voted for Kennedy thinking him a more effective anticommunist than Richard Nixon) and fairly conservative generally. He has moved from right to far right, not from left to right.

There are good reasons, though, why many people think Evans and Novak's conservatism a fairly recent development. Throughout the 1960s and most of the 1970s, their column was as close to objective as a column can be, indeed generally no less objective than the news pages. As noted, their subject matter was usually the inside scoop in Washington, and was of limited interest to those who read the op-ed pages for provocative opinions. Their writing was reportorial: even, clear, drawing little attention to itself and certainly not espousing any party line. (This started to change in the late 1970s, and now the authors make no effort to conceal their conservative perspective.)

A second reason for confusion over Evans's and Novak's ideology during the 1960s and 1970s stems from several books written by one or both. Novak's book, *The Agony of the GOP 1964*, offered a penetrating look at the schism in the Republican party between the conservative Goldwater and liberal Rockefeller forces, with no indication of the author's affinities.

His next book, *Lyndon B. Johnson: The Exercise of Power*, published in the middle of Johnson's presidency, was coauthored with Evans. The Johnson book clearly established Evans and Novak as gifted journalist-historians, and if they had any ideological axe to grind, they concealed it remarkably well. Prominent writers Larry L. King and Arthur Schlesinger, Jr., and various other reviewers, stressed the book's impressive objectivity: the authors seemed sympathetic to Johnson but critical as well. Just as Evans and Novak's mid-term assessment of a moderate-liberal Democratic president was balanced, so too was their mid-term assessment of a moderate-conservative Republican. Their book *Nixon in the White House: The Frustration of Power*, published in 1971, was also widely praised for its objectivity.

Objectivity was only one of Evans and Novak's virtues as authors. The Johnson and Nixon books provided piercing insights into extraordinarily complex leaders, as well as dogged reporting about the mood and events of the day.

The Johnson book combined voluminous detail and astute analysis with a wealth of revealing anecdotes. Although books written in the middle of a presidency obviously lack historical perspective, they offer immediacy. Schlesinger, a major historian, noted that the Johnson book would be indispensable to future historians. Indeed, two decades later it remains one of the best portraits of Johnson. The authors were shrewd and prescient, forcefully depicting how Lyndon Johnson, notable for his brilliant use of power, was being brought down by forces almost uniquely impervious to skillful political maneuvering. Their closing sentence summarized the situation adroitly: "The future and shape of Lyndon Baines Johnson's presidency rested with events singularly intransigent, taking place 10,000 miles away in a war that month after month refused to respond to the mastery and exercise of presidential power."[2]

Their mid-term Nixon book captured traits—paranoia, isolation and aloofness—that presaged the president's later troubles. The book earned high marks across the political spectrum; several reviewers suggested that it was essential reading for anyone desiring insight into the mysterious administration of a deeply complex president.

In his three books, Novak established himself as an impressive journalist-historian, capable of shedding light on the most opaque political figures. But he did not continue in the direction of becoming a sophisticated chronicler of American politics.

He and partner Evans took on dozens of peripheral professional responsibilities. They not only churned out their column four times a week, but also wrote occasional pieces for *Reader's Digest, Forbes,* and *American Spectator,* sent out frequent tax and political newsletters, and appeared often as questioners on *Meet the Press.* Eventually, Novak became a constant television presence: a regular participant on *The McLaughlin Group* and a frequent substitute host on *Crossfire.* (Indeed, he took Pat Buchanan's seat during

Buchanan's two-year stint in the White House.) In addition, he and Evans had a weekly interview show as well as minicommentaries on CNN. All of this exposure made Novak a top draw on the time-consuming lecture circuit as well.

In the late 1980s his already hectic schedule intensified. He became a regular panelist on yet another show, ABC's *Money Politics,* a discussion roundtable devoted exclusively to economic issues. In addition, he left *The McLaughlin Group* to form his own show, *Capital Gang.* Running one's own show requires far more work than being a participant on someone else's.

Unsurprisingly, given his schedule, Novak has not fulfilled his promise as a historian. His only subsequent book, *The Reagan Revolution,* also written with Evans, was far slimmer and less impressive than their previous works. The book was primarily a gushing and unenlightening brief on behalf of supply-side economics and Ronald Reagan. While the earlier books provided deep insight into complex men, the Reagan book revealed little new about a less difficult figure.

Although Novak's first three books displayed a style quite different from Theodore White's *Making of the Presidency* series, they were of a similar genre and arguably as good. Had he continued in that vein, Novak might have garnered a reputation as a journalist-historian in a league with White. However, he became a television celebrity, which led to a radically different reputation.

Signing on with the *The McLaughlin Group,* in 1982, in itself risked diverting him from his better work. But it was the way he chose to play his part that enshrined Novak in the Cartoon Journalists Hall of Fame. Novak played the consummate villain, so hateful that even many viewers who recognized the contrived nature of his performance could not help but despise him.

It was clearly not Novak's staunch conservativism that infuriated many in the television audience; the equally conservative Pat Buchanan did not rile liberal viewers nearly as much. Rather, it was Novak's unpleasant persona, that of *enfant terrible,* that drove many to distraction. *Esquire* wrote that his "sallow complexion, Brezhnevian brows, and 'Two Ton' Tony Galento conversational style provide Novak with a reputation for darkest evil."[3]

Indeed, Novak is known as the "Prince of Darkness." The nickname is widely used in Washington, though it is not well known that it was bestowed back in the 1960s as a reference to Novak's gloomy view of the prospects of western civilization, not as a comment on his personality. The nickname spread in the 1980s because on television Novak's manner is dark indeed. At a recent dinner roast for Novak, Senator Robert Dole joked that on Halloween Novak masqueraded as a human being, and the monster from the *Nightmare on Elm Street* movies went disguised as Novak.[4]

On a show where five men constantly interrupted and insulted one another, it seems surprising that a silver-haired, intelligent historian stood out as the evil one. It took some work. Novak's *McLaughlin Group* adversary Jack Germond explains that "Bob takes no prisoners. He's much more willing than anyone else to use ad hominems. He's more willing to use anything!"[5] *Life* magazine's Loudon Wainwright nicely depicts Novak's obnoxiousness: "When the rest of the pack turns and howls at Novak, he sits back and smirks with intense delight, a gray-haired cherub in a bright red necktie who is thrilled because he has just thrown his dinner on his sister."[6]

The part of Novak's sister was often played by Morton Kondracke, who occasionally let Novak's assaults get under his skin. This suggests the ferocity and unpleasantness of the attacks because, as most Washington insiders and certainly Kondracke in unprovoked moments knew, Novak was play-acting. As a questioner on *Meet the Press* and *Evans and Novak,* Novak is tough but dignified and professional. On *The McLaughlin Group* and *Crossfire,* he checked his dignity and professionalism at the door. Michael Kinsley, who has sparred with Novak on both shows, says Novak "is a total self-creation on TV."[7] Novak's *Capital Gang* colleague and friend Mark Shields adds that Novak wasn't the first to cultivate a villainous television persona, "but he perfected it."[8]

But around the country, countless viewers assumed they were

seeing a genuine beast, not an actor. Shields explains that he is greeted enthusiastically at airports all over the country by people who know only one thing about him: he takes on the beastly Novak. Shields notes that while Novak is actually a nice guy it's almost impossible to convince viewers of that fact, for they don't see what happens off-camera. Mark Green, an occasional *Crossfire* adversary, says Novak is "calm and charming before and after the show, but when the red light is on he acts as though you just murdered a member of his family."[9] Green adds that although they disagree about most issues, off-screen Novak treats him with respect. The television audience, however, sees only contempt as Novak attacks "you and your ilk, Mark."

Like Kilpatrick on *Inside Washington,* Novak's behavior on *The McLaughlin Group* is grist for the parodist's mill. A parody of *McLaughlin* in *Washingtonian* magazine had Novak answer one question, "Let's cut the crap and get on with it," and scold Kondracke, "Aside from being hopelessly pro-Israel, Kondracke, you're also absymally ignorant."[10] In fact, it is almost impossible to parody Novak's performance on *McLaughlin* successfully because it was an extravagant exercise in self-parody. On one typical show,[11] Novak insulted Richard Cohen ("What a surprise, Richard! A blend of pacifism and Israelism, all in one little package"), Germond ("Foreign policy is not your long suit, Jack"), and Kondracke ("Read the Constitution sometime"), and also engaged in the following interrogation of Germond after the latter said that Raymond Donovan was a weak Secretary of Labor:

NOVAK: What do you know about it?
GERMOND: He had no—
NOVAK: What do you know about it?

On another show,[12] Novak's very first remark, a response to a comment by Eleanor Clift, was "Eleanor, you didn't disappoint me. That is a ridiculous position." Before the show was over, he called Congressman Jack Brooks "one of the big jerks in Washington," and told McLaughlin that one of his queries was "a simple-minded question because you don't understand what's going on." Columnist Colman McCarthy characterizes Novak's style as, "Speak loudly and carry a big schtick."[13]

Novak's capacity for insults was inexhaustible. He once told McLaughlin, "I hope you're being the devil's advocate, because I don't think you're that stupid."[14] On another show he said, "Let me just tell you, John—you talk a lot but you don't have much information."[15] Whenever Shields, a former political consultant appeared, Novak attacked his friend as a "former hack."

Novak's pet bugaboo was communism. Any mention of the Soviet Union was enough to launch him on a lecture of the failure of his colleagues to appreciate the red menace. The lectures tended to be apocalyptic. When Eleanor Clift mentioned various discrepancies in Oliver North's testimony before Congress, Novak pounced: "We're talking about really the fate of the struggle between the West and Communism, and you're talking about little discrepancies."[16] Another time Richard Cohen suggested that the outcome of the Soviet invasion of Afghanistan might be "a kind of Finland." Novak responded as if someone had called his mother a whore: "I can't let pass the obscenity of comparing Afghanistan with Finland. I mean, that is outrageous, Mr. Cohen. And the whole idea that these people from the—the Finns, who fought with the Nazis and have accepted their punishment for it—that you compare them to these freedom fighters in Afghanistan, I think that is just something that shouldn't go without passing."[17]

Sometimes Novak's anticommunist ravings bore an idiosyncratic relationship to reality. In discussing a tax reform proposal, he told McLaughlin that "your favorite Marxist, Alexander Cockburn, . . . told the truth, that this has really done a body blow to the graduated tax system."[18] The following exchange ensued:

GERMOND: If you don't like this bill you're a Marxist? Is that it now?
NOVAK: Yes.

Novak's anticommunism was the major source of his insults. The conservative McLaughlin was a dupe of the Soviet Union and "luckily most people in the country are not like [Michael] Kinsley, so sympathetic to anything the Soviet Union might do."[19] ("That's me," Kinsley responded with a laugh.) When Germond accused both Sandinista and contra supporters of obsessiveness, Novak informed him that "some people are obsessed with freedom, Germond. You wouldn't understand."[20]

One can be every bit as cold a warrior as Novak without becoming a caricature. But the way Novak expressed his anticommunism on *The McLaughlin Group,* and his demeanor generally, certainly converted him into a cartoon character. The following exchange shows him willingly playing the role, with help from Mark Shields:[21]

NOVAK: One quick question. There is a communist offensive about to be launched against the Miskito Indians. I'm interested, Mark, whose side are you on in that offensive? The Communists or the Miskito Indians?

SHIELDS: Bob, I want to be on your side in any offensive. You're about as offensive as anybody I know.

NOVAK: That's a good joke, but I'd like to know whose side you're on.

SHIELDS: No, Bob—you think I'm for the slaughter of people?

NOVAK: Whose side are you on?

The powers at Cable News Network are not turned off by such shenanigans. They recognize true villainous talent, and use Novak as a frequent substitute for Buchanan on *Crossfire.* When Buchanan left for the White House in 1985, Novak stepped in full-time. With Novak in place of Buchanan, the show, if it is possible, picked up in intensity and suffered in decorum. Novak smelled a communist rat whenever a left-of-center guest appeared on the show. And he drove Tom Braden to distraction, especially in the closing "Braden vs. Novak" segment. He remarked chillingly that when events in the Philippines unfolded, Braden would have blood on his hands. He blamed "people like you, Tom," for creating the climate that led to a brutal Central Park rape. Braden responded (or nonresponded), "I'm so mad I can't say anything."

Away from the television studio, Novak is anything but a creep. As *Conservative Digest* suggests, most viewers don't realize that

Novak "doesn't strangle bunnies named for Eleanor Roosevelt, and has never tried to push Eleanor Clift in front of a metro train. The terrible truth is that Bob Novak is a very nice guy."[22] Indeed, Novak is cultured and learned, loves sports and the arts, and has many friends across the political spectrum. Asked on *Capital Gang* for his New Year's wish, Al Hunt expressed the hope that the public would get to know the real Bob Novak, not the synthetic television villain. A good wish, although Novak has only himself to blame for being misunderstood. No one forced him to cultivate the image that he did.

On *Capital Gang* Novak is actually a much tamer creature than the monster who stalked *The McLaughlin Group*. He delivers and receives insults with a smile, and both he and the rest of the cast are clearly on friendly terms. Nevertheless, a very high percentage of his remarks are outlandish insults. On one show when his friend Al Hunt came out for gun control, Novak remarked, "You're just like Hitler."[23]

As his former *McLaughlin Group* adversary Eleanor Clift puts it, "Novak is brilliant. He's a brilliant historian. But on television he's kind of a caricature."[24] Clift might have added that Novak is much better known for his crazed television persona than as a brilliant historian. Novak has expressed displeasure about the overshadowing of his serious work: "It is a little depressing in some ways that I have spent thirty-one years in this town, twenty-five as a columnist, and when I'm recognized now it is as a television celebrity. Not even as a television commentator!"[25]

Although Novak finds this state of affairs a bit depressing, he does not express doubts about his decision to opt for fame and fortune over respectability and better works. But his satisfaction with this Faustian bargain doesn't make the conversion of journalists into cartoon figures, diverted from their best work, a happy one. This phenomenon is not restricted to Kilpatrick and Novak, although they are currently the prime exemplars. Michael Kinsley, a supremely talented wordsmith, recently gave up his post as editor of *The New Republic* to sign on as host of *Crossfire*. *The New Republic* will survive without Kinsley's editing, and he will go on writing his column. (In fact, he took the *Crossfire* job in part because jettisoning his duties as an editor gives him more time to write.) But it is only a matter of time before Kinsley is less known for his incisive writing than for his less flattering television style—replete with bulging veins, shouting, interrupting, and tendentiousness. Charlie Peters, Kinsley's old boss at *Washington Monthly*, puts it bluntly: "I'm worried about my good and trusted friend becoming involved in this game. I worry that he'll become the cartoon liberal."[26]

The diverse careers of Buckley, Will, Kilpatrick, and Novak share a subplot. Four highly talented writers and thinkers were, largely because of television, pulled away from their best work and taken less seriously than they deserve to be. They will be remembered, in varying degrees, for the wrong things. The analyses of their careers raises an important question: whether the journalist-as-celebrity slide is unstoppable, especially since success breeds imitation and so many top commentators now travel the celebrity path. Are subsequent generations of top-flight commentators destined to have their contribution diminished by becoming celebrities and caricatures?

The lure can be resisted. Mary McGrory, a prominent columnist who eschews television fame and the lecture circuit, says, "I don't want to be a celebrity. I don't have time for that."[27] But her perspective is rare. More and more top columnists engage in spats on television and entertain trade associations in exchange for the perks of celebrity.

As this trend increases, we are far less likely to be blessed with a valuable national asset: the public philosopher or historian. It is rare for someone from the academy—such as Garry Wills and Mortimer Adler—to achieve a sizable enough following to elevate the public's understanding of important and enduring issues. The deepest thinkers in the pundit community are in an ideal position to make such a contribution. (Indeed, Wills achieved an initial following through his syndicated newspaper column.) Television helps give them this opportunity, but what television gives with one hand it takes away with the other; while providing commentators with nationwide exposure, it also yields temptations that diminish their contribution.

At a minimum, commentators should be encouraged to think hard about the costs of their quest for fame and wealth. Jack Germond, himself a traveler on the celebrity trail (though he limits his lectures to twelve to fifteen a year, a fourth of what some of his colleagues do), concedes that "you can't let the speeches and television drive your schedule. Celebrity impinging on your ability to do your job well is a genuinely serious concern and it requires people to be damned careful."[28]

III

Between the Forty Yardlines

Most Americans agree that a healthy public debate requires a broad dissemination of views from diverse sources. Yet few Americans who have given the matter much thought believe that our major media offer a truly broad range of ideas. Indeed, both conservatives and liberals charge that the media are one-sided or narrow in the presentation of news and opinions, although they disagree about where the bias lies.

William Rusher's book *The Coming Battle for the Media* makes the most recent comprehensive complaint about liberal domination of the media. The crux of the argument is that most of the major players in the media—the editors and reporters at the *Washington Post, New York Times, Wall Street Journal, Time* and *Newsweek,* and the producers and reporters at ABC, CBS, and NBC—are liberal. The conservative media watchdog group "Accuracy in Media" (AIM) works full-time to expose the liberal bias that emanates from these sources, and Jesse Helms's bid to take over CBS was designed to eliminate precisely such bias. It is a crucial article of faith among conservatives that the major media are stacked against them.

On the other side of the fence, leftists believe that the media offer a narrow range of views, excluding any voices left of the safe, respectable liberal establishment. Three recent books articulate this viewpoint: Mark Hertsgaard's *On Bended Knee,* Edward Herman and Noam Chomsky's *Manufacturing Consent,* and Michael

Parenti's *Inventing Reality*. Their precise emphases differ: Hertsgaard focuses on the media's deferential treatment of the Reagan
administration; Chomsky and Herman emphasize biased right-wing
coverage of various foreign policy issues; Parenti touches on numerous areas. But they all concur that the major media pay short shrift
to leftist perspectives.

Thus, a seemingly contradictory symmetry exists: both the left
and the right complain about bias in the major media. The media
view this phenomenon as confirming their neutrality and objectivity: if both liberals and conservatives complain of bias, the media
must be fair and balanced. Ironically, the truth is just the opposite:
both conservatives and liberals are correct in their charges of media
bias.

It is well documented that the political views of a majority of
reporters at the major media outlets are left of center. The majority
is less substantial than it once was, but remains a majority. And
conservatives are on safe ground in asserting that journalists' political leanings affect their work. To think otherwise is to assume that
reporters and editors have an incredible capacity for objectivity.
Most reporters try to be impartial but their world view necessarily
intrudes into some of the myriad decisions they must make—about
what is and isn't newsworthy, for example.

While the right-wing media critics are correct about a liberal bias,
the leftist critics are also correct. For although the major media
outlets shade left of center, they offer a narrow range of opinions
that excludes anyone who challenges certain basic assumptions. As
it happens, it is mostly—although not exclusively—the far left that
is today denied significant access to the major media, especially
television.

We shall primarily address the leftist rather than rightist critique
for two reasons. First, the Right's complaint concerns primarily the
presentation of news, whereas this book deals with opinion commentary. In the latter category, conservatives have no cause for
complaint. They are better represented than liberals on newspaper
op-ed pages and television's political talk shows: the most widely
syndicated columnists are George Will and James Kilpatrick, and

no liberal commentator gets as much television exposure as John McLaughlin, Pat Buchanan, or Robert Novak. Second, the media's tilt to the left side of the fifty yardline in the battle between conservatives and liberals is less significant than the fact that whole areas of the playing field are excluded. Indeed, as we shall see, the leftist complaint, properly framed, recognizes that the far right is also largely excluded from the major media.

America's founders committed the republic to few specific assumptions. The Declaration of Independence enumerated only a handful of self-evident truths and, as legal codes go, the Constitution is slim; it establishes a form of government but to a very great extent leaves particulars to be filled in through the democratic processes. Yet, for largely historical reasons Americans have always shared or acquiesced in many assumptions above and beyond the truths set down in the Declaration and the system of government established by the Constitution. Our national debates are narrower than those of many democracies.

To a certain extent, of course, a national consensus is necessary; a society cannot function unless most if not all of its members share certain assumptions. Thus, America cannot be expected to embark on continual scrutiny of the value of constitutional democracy or the self-evident truths that are inseparable from it (although we are secure enough to permit even those ideas to be challenged without punishment or censor). But beyond a commitment to its defining national charter, a healthy democracy encourages a broad spectrum of views. While people will disagree as to the precise bounds of America's elemental charter, the current spectrum of debate undeniably excludes many ideas that pose no challenge to that charter.

Indeed, while substantial consensus existed among Americans in 1789, over the years consensus about a greatly widened range of issues emerged and the area of national debate narrowed. Today, what has been called America's "national religion"—a set of assumptions virtually unchallenged in the political arena and the mass media—includes (but is not limited to) the sanctity of the two-party system; the desirability of a capitalist system with a developed welfare state; the acceptability of corporate capitalism; the value of nationalism as opposed to internationalism; and the general benevolence or at least good intentions of American foreign policy.

Because of the breadth of American consensus, it is said that our politics is centrist, taking place "within the forty yardlines." On balance, it is probably healthy that American politics involves a large consensus and few radical shifts (although it may reach unhealthy proportions when presidential candidates disagree about little besides the pledge of allegiance and whether taxes are a last resort or no resort at all). But assuming that a high level of consensus is desirable, it is purchased at too high a price when citizens never even question important assumptions that are far from self-evident, when not only our government but our discourse stays between the forty yardlines. America's democracy would be richer if our political debates included challenges to the current national consenses.

Public debate should not be viewed simply as a tool to achieve one's agenda, but as a vehicle for robust self-government. Commentators should not be seen as proselytizers but as thought-provokers. As Bill Moyers says, the best commentator states his views "not because you're trying to tell people what to think, but because you hope the viewer will find a new way of framing his thoughts about a particular subject."[1] Citizens should open their arms and minds to commentary that helps them frame their views in new ways, regardless of whether they initially approve of the commentator's general orientation.

Thus, one need not disagree with all or even any elements of the national religion to feel cheated by the narrowness of American discourse. Aside from the obvious fact that we should be open to enlarging our circles of consensus and adjusting our paradigms of thought, attacks from outside our circles help us hone and refine our existing paradigms. People who generally trust America's foreign policy motives are unlikely to change their perspective if they hear arguments that a major goal is promoting a climate for corporate investment; they may, however, at least question their perceptions of particular situations. Similarly, arguments that the Democratic and Republican parties are equally corrupt and unresponsive may not convince people to opt for other parties or even to disapprove of the two-party system; some may, however, become conscious of the decay of the two parties and the need for reform.

The emergence of a broad national religion is unhealthy if the consensus is based on inertia and conditioning rather than examination and conviction. Today in America, the major media continually reinforce our predilections and rarely expose us to serious challenges. Thus, while the commentators on the political talk shows have vigorous disagreements within the forty yardlines, they reliably endorse the national religion. Columnist Colman McCarthy observes that, for example, "You don't see people on television who would tell the audience that America has a war economy."[2]

Hodding Carter, himself a frequent participant on the *Brinkley* roundtable, says, "We need a lot more skeptics who will question the whole exercise, who are going to say 'It's not the policies that are wrong, but the mindset.' I'm willing to say only that the policies are wrong."[3] Carter and Carl Rowan prefer more social programs for the poor than do James Kilpatrick and Robert Novak, but they do not attack corporate capitalism generally. Some of the commentators harshly criticize the two major parties, and disapprove of many American foreign policy initiatives, but none question the sanctity of the two-party system or the basic benevolence of America's international role.

The debate over the recent Supreme Court decision on flag-burning provides a perfect illustration of how television keeps our debate within the forty yardlines. The many regular participants on the roundtables, as well as the guests on *Nightline* and *MacNeil/Lehrer,* disagreed about the Court's decision but shared two premises: that the flag is a sacred symbol and that only a degenerate would burn it. On the op-ed pages, a few iconoclastic commentators from the right and the left questioned these assumptions. John Lofton, a spiky spokesman for the religious right, argued that the flag is merely a national symbol and does not deserve the sacred status reserved for religious texts.[4] Lofton argued that the reaction to the case showed how the country has dangerously lost its Christian moorings. Colman McCarthy found it offensive that the flag-burner was reflexively dismissed as a low-life ("a maggot" said James Kilpatrick on *Inside Washington*; "a scumbag" offered Al Hunt on *Capital Gang*), rather than someone with a justifiably passionate opposition to Reagan's foreign policy.[5] Few Americans were exposed to these views, for McCarthy and Lofton are rarely seen on television; their positions evidently take them beyond the pale.

As the exclusion of Lofton suggests, the narrowness of political debate on television is not simply a case of the absence of leftists. Hodding Carter says, "I don't care if it's center to left or center to right, the trouble is the narrow range. It has nothing to do with the fact that it tilts to the right now. I didn't like it when it was to the left." Carter rightly observes that while the media shades right or left in different eras, it never veers sufficiently far from the center. On his scale, "If A is hard left and Z is hard right, our commentary ranges from L to S."[6] Conservative political analyst Kevin Phillips agrees that the major media shy away from serious challenges to the conventional wisdom.[7] William F. Buckley, Jr. echoes this sentiment, noting that, for example, "If someone believes very strongly in a flat tax, the chances are he won't be invited to participate" in a discussion of fiscal policy.[8]

The networks would not have to look hard to find serious commentators, from both the Right and the Left, who oppose aspects of the national religion. Alexander Cockburn, Christopher Hitchens, and Robert Scheer are just a few left-wing voices whose inclusion would broaden our debate. We are likewise generally deprived of the vigorous right-wing views of Lofton, Cal Thomas, and others who are often as contemptuous of the Republican party as the Democratic party and sometimes harshly critical of corporations. Columnist Georgie Anne Geyer observes that the talk shows "seem to have a 'don't touch them' attitude towards the *Washington Times*."[9] We are missing action at both ends of the playing field.

Today, the far left is especially underrepresented. The exclusion of the far right is less pronounced because Pat Buchanan and Robert Novak receive a great deal of exposure and there is only a little room to their right. By contrast, there is considerable room on the political spectrum to the left of Jack Germond and Carl Rowan. Carter points out the absurdity of "what passes for the identification of the left. It's ludicrous that I would be considered to the left."[10] McCarthy complains that "Kinsley would build fewer B-2 bombers, so *Crossfire* says he's on the left. It's a joke."[11] Carter adds that "at a minimum we should have on a regular basis the Hitchens and the Cockburns."[12] To do so, however, would require the networks to expand the range of what they consider acceptable views.*

The ascent of George Will at ABC was a function of his talent, but also required his fitting within the boundaries of acceptability. William Rusher explains that the network hired Will to do commentaries on the news because it "know[s] Will as a professional who can be depended on to enunciate moderately conservative views without ever going too far."[13]

In addition to their boundaries of acceptability, the media evince a proestablishment bias. Thus it is no accident that Buchanan has more extreme views than most regular roundtable commentators and, in addition to appearing on his own shows, has been a guest on *Nightline* a number of times: he is a member of the Washington club, having served in the White House under two administrations. The preference for establishment figures, like the boundaries of acceptability, reflects television's natural caution. Television critic Tom Shales puts his finger on the prevailing approach: "People are certified. They go through a certain process and they become certifiable television personalities."[14]

Thus at a certain point a person's opinions or even effectiveness become insignificant because he is in the club. Robert Novak's views, like Buchanan's, are on the far end of the acceptability spectrum. However, Novak was not always extreme. By the time he became known as an ultra right-winger, he was already an estab-

*The situation is only a little better in the major print media. The *New York Times* op-ed page ranges no further left than Anthony Lewis, a mainstream Mondale-type Democrat. Cockburn and McCarthy have access to the *Wall Street Journal* and *Washington Post,* respectively. However, Cockburn's column appears only monthly; McCarthy's is semiweekly, relegated to the Style section half the time. Similarly, the far right is barely represented in the major print media.

lished television presence. Most commentators who are as far right as Novak and Buchanan receive limited mass media exposure. Shales notes that television management likes things "as mainstream as possible but once you're accepted into this society, then you're fine. Novak and Buchanan have proven themselves on that score."[15]

The acceptability factor and the celebrity status achieved by some commentators create a situation where certain journalists become ubiquitous while others never receive public exposure. Even within the forty yardlines, we would benefit from more player substitution. Not only do the political roundtables trot out the same commentators each week, but often the same commentators appear on several shows or are highly visible in the print medium as well. Pat Buchanan, himself a ubiquitous television presence, has correctly observed that "the essence of press power lies in the authority to select, elevate, and promote one set of ideas, issues, and personalities—and to ignore others."[16]

The tendency of the networks to rely almost exclusively on certified television personages, and more often than not mainstream ones, is by no means limited to the selection of commentators for the round-table shows. On the hybrid news/commentary shows *MacNeil/Lehrer* and *Nightline,* the regulars are neutral interviewers and the key to broad, challenging discussion is the selection of guests. These shows turn out to be the gravest offenders when it comes to keeping discourse between the forty yardlines.

When Ted Koppel was denounced by conservatives for allowing officials of the Soviet government to spread their country's propaganda on *Nightline,* he responded eloquently:[17]

One of the things that makes America great is that we are willing to run the risk of letting our population listen to ideas that are alien to us. . . . What are we afraid of . . . that their ideas are better than ours, their spokesman more eloquent? I'm not worried.

Ironically, to judge from *Nightline*'s guests, Koppel and the producers may not be worried about exposing the American people to Soviet propagandists but they don't want us exposed to *Americans* with unorthodox pedigrees or positions. *Nightline* parades white, male establishment guests, a high percentage of whom did or do serve in government and a low percentage of whom hold left-of-center views.

Fairness and Accuracy in Reporting, the liberal counterpart of Accuracy in Media, recently tabulated the guests on *Nightline* over a four-year period. Henry Kissinger and Alexander Haig led the group with fourteen appearances each, followed by Jerry Falwell and Eliot Abrams with twelve. In fairness to Koppel, he is not out to exclude the left; Jesse Jackson has made frequent appearances. Rather, *Nightline*'s ideological tilt is a function of conservatives being in power and reflects *Nightline*'s obsession with insiders and players—people who do or recently did play a role in formulating policy. When *Nightline* opts for commentators instead of government officials, it generally rounds up "the usual suspects": familiar Washington pundits and think-tank experts.

Since Koppel himself proclaims the virtue of exposing Americans to alien perspectives, it is difficult to justify *Nightline*'s heavy reliance on those in or near to power. *Nightline*'s failure to offer a truly broad range of perspectives is especially harmful because the show is widely watched and could afford to branch out; its popularity is based largely on the excellence and credibility of Koppel, not the familiarity of the guests. Still, Jack Germond rightly cautions that *Nightline* shouldn't be singled out for trotting out the same old faces. "That's true of all the talk shows, true of the whole ghetto of political discourse," Germond says.[18]

It is certainly true of public television's *MacNeil/Lehrer Newshour.* Like *Nightline,* many of its guests are past or present government officials* and few of its guests step more than an inch outside the yardlines of conventional wisdom. It is not surprising that the radical Alexander Cockburn finds the ideological range on *Mac-Neil/Lehrer* excessively narrow, but he exaggerates not a whit in describing the show, and his assessment should disturb people of all political persuasions.[20]

> The hardy reader [of program transcripts] will soon observe how extraordinarily narrow is the range of opinion canvassed by a show dedicated to dispassionate examination of the issues of the day. . . . [It] ranges from the corporate right to cautious center-liberal.

Colman McCarthy exaggerates, but only a little, when he says, "The idea of a debate on these shows is whether to build the M-X or the B-2."[21] Someone like McCarthy, who believes the United States should dismantle most of its military machine, doesn't receive many invitations.

In addition to its nightly discussions, *MacNeil/Lehrer* calls on two in-house analysts, mainstream Republican David Gergen and mainstream Democrat Mark Shields, for weekly political analysis. These two establishment figures agree as much as they disagree, and their quarrels are usually along the margins. Of course, it is to *MacNeil/Lehrer*'s credit that Gergen and Shields feel free to agree so readily; this is one show that does not thrive on synthetic conflict. However, the audience would benefit from some *real* conflict, that is, from the introduction of commentators with different assumptions and perspectives.

There are several possible explanations for the major media's failure to present a wider debate. One obvious explanation is suggested by the famous aphorism that freedom of the press exists only for those who own one. At least to some extent, the ownership of

---

Progressive magazine notes that "putting power on display and airing its message is [*Macneil/Lehrer*'s] ultimate purpose," which tends to entrench the status quo: "The Left's failure to appear contributes, of course, to the very powerlessness that caused its exclusion."[19] Again, the media's tendency to entrench the status quo is not a complaint for the left only: in the 1960s and 1970s, the scale tipped the other way.

the media determines what ideas are disseminated. In his book *Four Arguments for the Elimination of Television,* Jerry Mander observes that "there are still no poor people running television, no Indians, no ecologists, no political radicals, no Zen Buddhists, no factory workers, no revolutionaries, no artists, no communists, no Luddhites, no hippies, no botanists, to name only a few excluded groups."[22] While some of these groups (such as the poor) are at least championed by commentators who have regular media access, other groups have viewpoints that rarely receive expression. Such groups and persons are not the only losers; the rest of us are too because robust self-government suffers.*

Mander observes that "to have only businessmen in charge of the most powerful mind-implanting instrument in history naturally creates a boundary to what is selected for dissemination to nearly 250 million people."[23] But the real problem may be less that the media is run by businessmen than that it is run by businesses—entities with distinct financial interests. There is a leftist school of thought that attributes the narrow range of American discourse to the control of the media by for-profit corporations, which have political agendas and are responsive to the demands of advertisers with agendas of their own.

These critics point out that the communication corporations obviously have an enormous stake in what information and opinions will be purveyed to the public; their status depends on the outcome of the American political process, which in turn depends on the attitudes of the American people. No one doubts that such attitudes are profoundly affected by the information and opinions people receive. The media's owners, therefore, have great incentive to control the flow of information and opinions to Americans.

The critics recognize that the major media have some commitment to the First Amendment, and thus do not stifle a healthy

---

*The one show that gave a regular voice to the excluded groups cited by Mander, as well as to radical feminists, militant blacks, avowed atheists, pacifists, and libertarians (among others), was the *Morton Downey, Jr. Show.* However, *Downey* trotted out such people as freaks for crowds to gape and shout at, not as people with serious and usually neglected viewpoints. It thus typified, rather than resisted, the media's contempt for viewpoints outside the forty yardlines.

debate as long as it stays within unthreatening parameters; they will not, however, permit their resources to be used in a way that seriously jeopardizes their direct interests. The critics further maintain that the moneyed class is largely united as to what serves its interests. Thus, while robust debates occur on some issues, the corporate forces, according to Noam Chomsky, "keep . . . the debate within the bounds of acceptable premises,"[24] acceptable meaning not threatening to corporate health and well-being.

The leading voice assailing corporate control of the media is Ben Bagdikian, whose book *The Media Monopoly,* originally published in 1983, revealed that the vast majority of America's media outlets are owned by a handful of corporate powers. Bagdikian documented an unsettling situation:[25]

By the beginning of the 1980s most major American media— newspapers, magazines, radio, television, books, and movies— were controlled by fifty corporations.

Twenty corporations control more than half the 61 million newspapers sold every day; twenty corporations control more than half the revenues of the country's 11,000 magazines; three corporations control most of the revenue and audience in television; ten corporations in radio; eleven corporations in all kinds of books; and four corporations in motion pictures.

The trend is toward increased concentration. The updated version of Bagdikian's book, published in 1987, revealed that the number of controlling corporations had shrunk considerably: today, twenty-nine rather than fifty corporations control the major media, and a mere fifteen produce over half the daily newspapers sold.

Bagdikian draws a sinister inference from the existence of this information oligopoly: that the media are critical instruments used by major corporations to maintain their wealth and power and that they amount to a private ministry of information and truth. He argues that the major media's implicit taboo against criticism of corporate capitalism, for example, is almost as sweeping as the explicit prohibition of criticism of communism in the (pre-*glasnost*) Soviet Union.

Defenders of the media respond that day-to-day operations are generally left to media professionals, not corporate executives. Bagdikian counters that the owners hire and fire the people who actually run the show, and that the power to hire and fire is the power to control. Bagdikian, a former national editor of the *Washington Post,* insists that in the regular process of hiring and firing of reporters, editors, writers, and producers, the corporate owners ensure an environment relatively conducive to corporate interests.

In this view, overt censorship is rarely needed: the initial determinations of access are made by people with similar outlooks and agendas. Thus, no one maintains that corporate management interferes with the daily operations of most shows or that Robert Novak and John McLaughlin fear losing their talk shows if they include more leftist commentators. Rather, Bagdikian would argue, General Electric would not have sponsored *The McLaughlin Group* in the first place, or CNN slotted *Capital Gang,* if they thought McLaughlin and Novak likely to produce shows threatening to their interests, i.e., shows where leftist, and especially anticorporate views were well represented.

Occasionally the media owners find their expectations so thwarted that they directly stifle the dissemination of ideas. It is difficult to assess the extent to which this takes place because it occurs behind closed doors and by forces not eager to publicize it. But in the 1950s and 1960s, CBS alienated enough of its own employees that it became exposed on this front. It became public knowledge, for example, that the network reined in the independent-minded Edward R. Murrow and Howard K. Smith. CBS wanted Murrow's *See It Now* to stick to relatively safe subjects, and refused to advertise the most controversial shows. And the network came to regret that it had given Murrow as much independence as it did. A decade after the cancellation of *See It Now,* Fred Friendly observed that no production team or reporter was again given the degree of control Murrow had over program content and expression of opinion.[26]

Howard K. Smith suffered as a result. Smith's comparison of Southern bigots to Nazi storm troopers was actually blipped out. On another occasion, Smith wished to end a show on racism by quoting

Edmund Burke's observation that "all that is needed for the triumph of evil is for good men to do nothing." CBS, fearing a hostile reaction in the South, refused to permit the quote. As a result of Smith's persistence on the subject, the network forced him to resign.

A recent example of corporate interests stifling threatening discourse was the *New York Times*'s dismissal of maverick columnist Sidney Schanberg. Schanberg, who received a Pulitzer Prize for his coverage of Cambodia, wrote a regular urban affairs column on the op-ed page. His column stood out on the *Times*'s staid op-ed page because he railed against the Westway highway project in Manhattan, greedy banks, corporations, and real estate agents. Schanberg ridiculed the *Times* for devoting more space to the problems of rich suburban homeowners than to New York City's decaying infrastructure. The management came to view him as a direct threat to the corporate interests of the New York Times Company. Westway, for example, was ardently supported by the real estate developers whose advertising is important to the paper. Moreover, Westway would have revitalized much of Manhattan's West Side, including the *Times*'s own building.

Schanberg refused to pull his punches. As a result, he lost his job and *Times* readers lost his unique column. On August 20, 1985, the *Times* printed a two-paragraph insert, buried in an obscure location, stating that Schanberg was asked to accept another assignment. Schanberg was not permitted a final column, and the *Times* never discussed his firing. But the explanation was no secret. As *New York* media critic Edwin Diamond put it, Schanberg made excursions "outside the boundaries of the acceptable."[27] While the dismissal was hotly debated in the journalistic milieu, the heat was well contained. Anyone who pursued the story ran into a brick wall at the *Times.* Alexander Cockburn wrote that "it would be interesting to hear [Anthony] Lewis and the rest of his op-ed cellmates [at the *Times*]" discuss Schanberg's dismissal.[28] The challenge went unheeded.

Thus, the *Times* stilled the voice of a gadfly and chilled anyone at the paper disposed to criticize its actions. The paper didn't need to threaten anyone. Rather, the firing itself spoke volumes, and the reverberations may be felt for a long time. As Bagdikian says, "The worst damage is not in one particular incident but in the long-lasting aftermath in which working professionals . . . behave as though under orders from above, although no explicit orders have been given."[29] Bagdikian would argue that Schanberg's dismissal was an unusual case only because the likes of Schanberg are usually not given major media access in the first place. The result, he says, is[30]

the self-serving censorship of political and social ideas. . . . Most of the screening is subtle, some not even occurring at a conscious level, as when subordinates learn by habit to conform to owners' ideas. But subtle or not, the ultimate result is distorted reality and impoverished ideas.

As noted, the leftist critics claim that the problem is exacerbated by the fact that the major media have *common* interests: none of them wishes to scrutinize alternatives to corporate capitalism, for example, or to do anything that engenders too great a threat to the status quo under which they flourish.* Bagdikian's summary, if true, is exceedingly troubling: "We now have a small group of powerful owners with remarkably similar political and social views. As a result, our major media probably offer the narrowest range of ideas available in any developed democracy."[33]

Public television was expected to be immune from the commercial forces that constrain television programming but, according to some critics, it has failed to expand the spectrum of political debate

---

*The leftist critics point out that the networks are also responsive to the demands of advertisers, themselves primarily corporate, who communicate what programming they prefer and will tolerate. In 1960 then-CBS president Frank Stanton stated what has since become common knowledge: "Since we are advertiser-supported, we must take into account the general objectives and desires of advertisers."[31] Often, the networks go further, discussing prospective shows with major advertisers, who suggest or insist upon certain changes. The advertisers' concerns are parochial. While desirous of a large audience, they often take a broader view of their financial interest. For example, the manager of corporate communications at General Electric has acknowledged that "we insist on a program environment that reinforces our corporate messages."[32]

for several reasons. The key to public television was its independence; freed from the influence of corporate owners and advertisers, it could make decisions based solely on society's needs. However, the Public Broadcasting System (PBS) never established its much-vaunted independence. From the beginning, public television was at the mercy of its primary source of funding—the federal government.

The Nixon administration's ideological assault and threats against PBS are well known. The Reagan administration did more than threaten. The administration's original proposed federal budget for 1983 included total jettisoning of PBS; it ended up settling for a damaging 25 percent decrease in an already small allocation for television. (Japan and Great Britain spend a far higher percentage of money on public television.) As a result, PBS has become heavily dependent on corporate sponsors, thus undermining the very point of its existence. Public television's fear of offending government and corporations has produced tangible and unfortunate consequences. A PBS documentary *Banks and the Poor,* accusing banks of exploiting the poor, was canceled by numerous stations, just as many PBS stations declined to run a show, *Who Invited Us?,* critical of American interventionist foreign policy. The message has been sent, and the result is a dearth of shows that dare to challenge the conventional wisdom or the status quo.

Corporations not only play a major role in determining which shows will run, but also influence those they choose to underwrite. Chevron sponsored Bill Moyers's *A Walk Through the Twentieth Century* and Moyers reports that "I should have been able to air controversial views. I wasn't."[34] S. L. Harrison, a former director of corporate communications for the Corporation of Public Broadcasting, reports that during his tenure, "Public TV producers regularly showed programs to underwriters to make sure that they would not offend sponsors."[35]

One of the major contributions of PBS to political debate is the *MacNeil/Lehrer Newshour,* funded by AT&T and other corporations. As suggested earlier, *MacNeil/Lehrer* perfectly illustrates PBS's failure to broaden the spectrum of political debate in America. Its debates generally feature a mainstream Republican view carefully balanced by a mainstream Democratic view, each delicately elicited by a polite interviewer. Television critic Marvin Kitman writes that "Kermit the Frog is more opinionated than Robin [MacNeil] the opinion-former, and that's one reason why AT&T is backing the *Newshour.*"[36] (Similarly, General Electric, the sponsor of *The McLaughlin Group,* is obviously not displeased by the show's conservative slant.) *Progressive* magazine bluntly maintains that the so-called public affairs programming on PBS "is not designed to raise public debate. . . . What corporate underwriter would pay for that?"[37]

After public television, the next great hope for a broadened spectrum of debate was offered by cable television. Cable was designed to create diversity but, according to Ben Bagdikian, "The original dream is all but lost."[38] As a result of various enactments by Congress, the cable systems have come to be owned by the very companies that own the rest of the media:[39]

> Broadcast and cable channels continue to multiply, as do videocassettes and music recordings in dozens of languages. But if this bright kaleidoscope suddenly disappeared and was replaced by the corporate colophons of those who own this output, the collage would go grey with the names of the few media multinationals that now command the field.

To be sure, the proliferation of cable outlets may yet result in a truly wide dissemination of ideas, as the lock the three major networks have on the public becomes further loosened. That remains our best hope, but it certainly has not happened to any significant extent yet.

Some dismiss complaints about corporate control of the media as crass conspiracy theories. Social critic Tom Wolfe declares the notion beneath serious discussion:[40]

> This is the old cabal theory—that somewhere there's a room with a baize-covered desk where a bunch of capitalists are

sitting around, pulling strings. These rooms don't exist! I mean, I hate to tell [Noam] Chomsky this. . . . When was the last time you heard an American capitalist give a political statement? Now of course one way to answer this is to say "They don't make statements, they control the way we think." You know, it's patent nonsense. . . . I'd love for them to give an example. I don't think they can.

There *are* examples of corporate censorship, such as Schanberg's firing. But more importantly, Wolfe misrepresents Chomsky, who makes it clear that he does not believe in a capitalist conspiracy: rather, he sees the corporate actors who control the media each pursuing their private interests. In any case, Wolfe and others can dispute the cause, but they cannot deny the phenomenon of a narrow spectrum of debate in the major media.

Whatever role corporate political interests play in sterilizing our debate is supplanted by the fact that the powers that be sometimes act to placate their superstar commentators. Charlie Peters tells what happened on his final appearance on *Agronsky* years ago. Peters tweaked George Will, saying, "Sometimes you sound like Adam Smith and sometimes you sound like Robespierre." Will was not amused. According to Peters, after the show Will ripped off his microphone and stalked out of the studio. Peters says that "the producer called me and chastised me for having upset George, who was the star of the show then. They never invited me back."[41] Peters does not believe Will vetoed his appearance, only that the producer didn't want to tamper with his star's contentment.

In a similar vein, Christopher Hitchens claims that when he was invited as a guest on *Crossfire* the producer instructed him "to go easy on 'Bob' Novak that evening or bid farewell to *Crossfire*." Hitchens went at it full throttle with Novak and maintains that "Novak thereupon vetoed my appearing on the show."[42] Novak did appear with Hitchens once in 1990, but sources at the Cable News Network confirm that he refused to do so from 1985 to 1987, when Novak was the usual host on the right. Thus Hitchens, one of the left's most eloquent and combative voices, was essentially blacklisted. Americans received less exposure to the unconventional views of Peters and Hitchens because those two annoyed the stars. Such a pecking order may make sense from the standpoint of stations' financial interests—Novak and Will are proven commodities—but it has an unhealthy effect on our debate.

Another proven commodity is Pat Buchanan, and CNN recently squandered an opportunity to broaden the debate allegedly in order to placate Buchanan. Buchanan is highly prized at CNN because he is a conservative icon, and CNN's audience is disproportionately white, well-to-do, and therefore largely conservative. In the spring of 1989, *Crossfire*'s Washington staff reportedly wished to replace Tom Braden as the liberal host with Mark Green, a progressive activist who had frequently served as a substitute host over the years. According to sources at CNN, Buchanan vehemently opposed the move, and to mollify him the network temporarily abandoned its plan to replace Braden. Later in the year the network made a firm decision to replace Braden, and narrowed the choices to Green and Michael Kinsley, whose political views are considerably closer to the center than Green's. Notwithstanding the protest of liberals that Green was a truer spokesman for the left, Kinsley was chosen.

It was well known around CNN, and reported in the *Washington Times,* that Buchanan strongly opposed the selection of Green. Some sources at CNN maintain that Green was the first choice of *Crossfire*'s Executive Producer Randy Douthit but that management in Atlanta overruled Douthit out of deference to Buchanan.[43] Douthit insists that the decision was his, and speculation to the contrary cannot be proven. But what is undeniable is that CNN lost an opportunity to provide a regular forum for a committed liberal advocate who frequently questions aspects of America's national religion. Kinsley holds up his end on *Crossfire,* but he is the first to admit that the choice of Green would have broadened the show's ideological range.

To be sure, corporate ideology and the influence of superstars are hardly the only reasons for the limited range of discourse in the major media. Another explanation emphasizes not the political or

financial interests of the media owners, but their insular elitism. As
Hodding Carter says:[44]

> The ownership, corporate and individual, essentially dines at
> the same places, comes from the same places, listens to the
> same voices as all the rest of the elite in the country. And that
> absolutely has an effect: not so much on what gets done but on
> what doesn't get done. Much of what passes for debate on all
> talk shows is simply the rehash of the conventional wisdom by
> those of us who see each other regularly and move up and down
> the corridors of other people's power, where we trade anecdote
> and viewpoint.

Charlie Peters wholeheartedly endorses Carter's notion that the talk
shows offer a rehash of conventional wisdom, but advances a more
market-oriented explanation for the phenomenon; he maintains that
the range of discourse is narrow because "challenging views make
a listener uncomfortable. Hearing something one hasn't thought of
doesn't add to one's confident grip on life."[45] An uncomfortable
listener is likely to change the channel. According to this view, a
circular effect occurs: because people are protected from jarring new
views, such views never get a chance to win acceptance, and they
continue to be excluded on the grounds that they are jarring.

However, the notion that ratings would be hurt by the inclusion
of nonmainstream participants is far from self-evident. It seems
likely that clashes between Alexander Cockburn or Christopher
Hitchens and Pat Buchanan, for example, would help ratings. People watch some of the shows to see sparks fly. When Hitchens was
a guest participant on *The McLaughlin Group,* the sparks flew faster
and more furiously than usual.

Of course, if the inclusion of radical voices would help ratings,
it seems bizarre that the networks haven't caught on. However, that
leads us back to the leftist contention that narrow discourse results
from the corporate owners' desire to avoid threats to the status quo.
The leftists have a ready reply to the claim that the owners would
do anything to increase ratings. Bagdikian says that the corporate
powers are by and large profit-maximizing, "but in pursuit of that

goal they [will] suppress or deemphasize news or entertainment that might seriously question their power."[46] That is, they will sacrifice short-term ratings for long-term security, and believe their long-term security would be threatened by a broad discourse.

Some evidence supports this surmise. Gore Vidal points out that although his wild exchanges with Bill Buckley in 1968 gave ABC its highest ratings at the political conventions, he wasn't invited back. He believes it was because he revealed himself to be "an apostate to the national religion," telling the audience that "there was no difference at all between the two parties because the same corporations paid for both . . . [who] in turn pass . . . it on to those candidates who will defend the faith."[47] As Vidal sees it, he and Buckley were expected to put on a safe Democrat versus Republican routine. To attack the two-party system, and lay the blame for its corruption at the doorsteps of corporate America, was to step outside the boundaries of the acceptable.

Of course, regardless of how the marketplace would react, it is not necessarily a good idea to include Hitchens on *The McLaughlin Group* or to square Vidal off against Buckley. Doing so would broaden the range of discourse, but it would also exacerbate the circus atmosphere. The Buckley-Vidal exchanges produced lawsuits, not enlightenment. Hitchens's appearances on *Crossfire* and *The McLaughlin Group* made Novak even crazier than usual. This leads to yet another explanation for the narrowness of our discourse: because of the format of most of the shows, discrepancy among fundamental perspectives makes an intelligible discussion impossible: As Chomsky says,[48]

The technical structure of the media virtually compels adherence to conventional thoughts; nothing else can be expressed between two commercials, or in seven hundred words, without the appearance of absurdity that is difficult to avoid when one is challenging familiar doctrine with no opportunity to develop facts or argument.

Thus, in the rapid-fire *McLaughlin Group* atmosphere it would be absurd to expect someone like Chomsky to answer every question with a fifteen-second explanation of how the other participants had fundamentally flawed perspectives: a coherent discussion would never get off the ground.

This view receives support from Richard Cohen, who has participated on the roundtables and says, "It is really hard in the conservative age to enunciate the liberal position in twenty seconds." Cohen, who is not radical by any stretch, illustrates the difficulty:[49]

> Take, for instance, the Bush drug plan. If you want to say this is a load of crap, that the United States has the highest prison population it's ever had, that there's never been a correlation between imprisonment and crime, and point out the failure of the Rockefeller drug program and various other drug programs, you have to first question people's assumptions. And you don't have the time to do that.

If a moderate liberal like Cohen has trouble developing a position in the roundtable format, radicals would face a near impossible task. What is needed is a *Firing Line* format—one hour for one subject with one guest—which would enable meaningful challenges to the national religion and conventional wisdom.*

In the final analysis, there is a wide variety of potential and overlapping explanations for the narrow range of views in the major media, especially television: corporate control, the marketplace, the old boy

---

*Indeed, *Firing Line,* far more than the other shows, has accommodated voices that challenge the national religion. The program provides a wider selection of guests for another reason as well: the choice of subjects. The roundtables emphasize Washington-oriented current events, and thus rely on Washington generalists. People like Nat Hentoff, who writes an enlightening column devoted almost exclusively to the First Amendment, is an unlikely invitee to the roundtables. They do, however, show up on *Firing Line.*

Its broad range of ideology, coupled with its search for truth, provides a marked contrast between *Firing Line* and the roundtables. On *Firing Line,* Buckley and guests like Michael Harrington offer fundamentally different visions yet search for common ground. On the roundtables there is often forced or exaggerated disagreement about small matters among participants whose perspectives on fundamental matters are not very different.

network, the formats, obeisance to the stars, and an inbred caution. It is not terribly important that people agree on which of these factors best explains the phenomenon of our narrow discourse, especially since it is likely that they all play a role. It is more important for us to recognize that, regardless of the causes, the phenomenon is harmful.

Again, it is critical that the need for a broader spectrum not be dismissed as a partisan issue. It was Spiro T. Agnew, not the leftists, who complained in the 1960s about a narrow group of elites shoving a single perspective down the throats of Americans. And Patrick J. Buchanan, who helped write Agnew's speeches attacking the media, has written that the media's monopoly on ideas and information "is as serious a matter for democracy as Arab control of the Mideast oil is for the economies of Western Europe."[50]

Of course, Buchanan and Agnew on one hand, and Bagdikian and Chomsky on the other, reach very different conclusions about exactly what ideas currently prevail in the media. But there is no reason why they cannot join forces in calling for a broad public debate in which a wide range of ideas clash aggressively to win the hearts and minds of Americans.

Of course, we need to face the vexing question of just how broad our discourse should be. Back in the 1960s, there was debate over a proposal requiring the FCC to assure a broad range of viewpoints. William F. Buckley, Jr. stated the problem with this approach succinctly:[51]

> Where does the spectrum end, and crackpottery, whether of the mischievous or harmless variety, begin? I ask that quite seriously. There are responsible people in the United States who do not believe that the John Birch society is crackpot. . . . And there is a distressingly large number of people in this country who hold that the presentation of the Communist view of things is clearly a part of the responsibilities of covering the left end of the spectrum.

Today in America there remain white supremacists and Stalinists who would love access to the airwaves to preach their hateful, violent messages. And there are a sizable number of followers of

Lyndon Larouche who insist that there is an international drug
conspiracy led by the Queen of England.

However, regardless of where one draws the line between serious
views and crackpottery, few fair-minded persons would say that the
current spectrum encompasses all serious viewpoints. People may
disagree violently with Noam Chomsky, for example, but the MIT
linguist is undeniably intelligent and creative, and has something to
add to the political debate. Almost no one would justify his exclusion from the airwaves on the grounds that he is a crackpot.

Buckley is correct that there is no value-neutral way of determining which views are serious and which are excludable, and he is also
correct that government ought not decide which viewpoints merit
a national audience. However, *someone* must make that determination. It is unobjectionable to urge the networks to provide a broader
spectrum of opinion.

Over the years television critics have castigated the networks for the
indifference to the public's need for a wide range of program matter.
There is no area where the deprivation is more important than in
the sphere of political commentary. The indisputable truth is that
Americans are deprived of a broad dissemination of political views
on the airwaves. Regardless of the explanation for it, the first step
toward a solution is clear: to voice our dissatisfaction loudly.

CONCLUSION

There are two principal problems with political commentary on television: (1) today's political talk shows contribute little, and sometimes even detract, from the robust debate needed to sustain a healthy democracy; and (2) television leads top commentators astray, making them celebrities or converting them into cartoon figures while diverting them from their finest and most socially useful pursuits.

Where the latter problem is concerned, the need is for more reflection about the opportunity costs of the pursuit of wealth and fame. The situation is not much more complicated with respect to the impoverished state of political talk shows. It is fairly clear what kinds of programs would better serve our democracy: longer, more serious shows, with fewer participants, dedicated to fewer and more enduring topics, and featuring a wider range of commentators and viewpoints. Ultimately, there are two routes, which can be undertaken simultaneously, to making that vision a reality. The first is to enlist the networks. The second is to provide truly independent and well-funded public television.

Defenders of today's political talk shows maintain that they provide political commentary in a form that people will watch. Howard K. Smith used to say that the worst sin in television news is to be dull, and Sam Donaldson is fond of telling how he used to reject that sentiment—exalting as it does style over substance—until he realized the truth at the heart of Smith's message: the most in-depth, informative programming does no good if unwatched. Those who control commercial television always make this point in justifying the dearth of quality programming.

There are, however, major problems with the "blame the viewer" excuse for the superficial fare offered. First, this attitude exalts or at least accepts the marketplace as the sole determiner of programming. While television is useless if no one watches, there is some audience for virtually any show. Indeed, there is a population of public affairs junkies who regularly watch C-SPAN's coverage of obscure political events and Bill Moyers's most esoteric public television specials. A proliferation of *Firing Line*-type shows might not attract huge audiences but would find viewers, and our democracy would benefit—especially since the increased stimulation of our most devoted citizens tends, at least to some extent, to have a trickle-down effect.

There is no reason to expect the unfettered free market to provide for an optimal public debate, a point less tendentious and debatable than the thesis that the corporate owners use the media to spread self-serving propaganda. The forces that drive a market can move it in directions unrelated to the public interest. For this reason, the hope that cable will vastly enrich television geared toward public policy may be in vain. As Tom Shales says, cable is no panacea because "it is in the same business, which is maximizing audiences."[1] Simply put, programming that serves the station best may not serve self-government well.

From the earliest days of television, the profit motive has produced programming results that are perverse in a society committed to self-government. When Edward R. Murrow's *See It Now* was canceled in 1956, *New York Herald Tribune* critic John Crosby noted the horrific fact that CBS could slot *Beat the Clock* but could not slot *See It Now.*[2] Murrow was justifiably furious about the insensitivity of the media owners to the requirements of a healthy democracy. Toward the end of his career he publicly lamented the clash between the public and corporate interests and pleaded with the networks to mitigate their obsession with the bottom line in deference to the needs of a democratic electorate.

It is a wonder that the public so easily acquiesces in the networks' obsession with ratings. Television stations are given control of the public airwaves in exchange for a pledge to operate in the public interest. Murrow rightly remarked that "nothing in the Bill of Rights or the Communications Act . . . says that [the networks] must increase their net profits each year, lest the Republic collapse."[3] America is a democracy first, a capitalist economy second. Our form of government stems from our commitment to self-evident principles; our commitment to corporate capitalism does not. One would think, then, that promoting and nourishing self-government would be worth a small reduction in network profits.

To a small extent, this has been recognized and acted upon. The Federal Communications Commission (FCC) used to require a certain amount of public affairs programming, although the networks would clearly have been more profitable without such a requirement. And even though those regulations have been lifted, the networks continue to devote Sunday mornings to civic-minded programs (perhaps solely to avoid criticism that would eventually hurt their pocketbooks). But that is close to the full extent of the networks' sacrifice for democracy. It is not asking too much for them to provide more and better shows—and at more popular viewing times—that would help Americans do their jobs as citizens, even though doing so might result in slightly reduced revenues.

But even if we accept the marketplace as the determiner of programming, and ask for no sacrifices by the networks, there is a second danger in the "blame the viewer" indulgence. This attitude is a classic self-fulfilling prophecy. If viewers are given no serious political programming, they cannot watch any; and if they are given no chance to watch it, they cannot develop the taste for it. Given the current structure of television—run by corporations answerable to shareholders and hardly answerable to a supine FCC—the networks are not about to accept losses for the sake of democracy.* But

*Significantly, this was not always the case. Tom Shales points out that "NBC used to have a show called *Wisdom,* about great thinkers and their thoughts. This was on NBC. It was on Sunday afternoon but still it was on N-B-C! One thing that died at the networks was the old idea that you did certain programming because it was the right

even if we stipulate that they should not be asked to do so, the least they could do is take *risks* on behalf of our democracy.

The networks' unwillingness to take risks and attempt to alter viewing habits is part of their larger tendency to underrate viewers. Over the years, countless quality shows have been rejected by stations before the public ever had the chance to see them. The public is always blamed when this happens, notwithstanding the absence of an opportunity to prove prevailing assumptions wrong. And on some occasions when the network showed some daring, viewers have conclusively disproved those assumptions.

Almost no one would have guessed that serious documentaries about often depressing subjects would land a show near the top of the prime-time Nielsen ratings, but *60 Minutes* has done exactly that. There are also examples of audiences showing unexpectedly elevated tastes in the realm of political commentary. When Fred Friendly conceived of bringing Walter Lippmann to television for one-hour interviews on the nuances of foreign affairs, the idea was greeted skeptically. The Lippmann interviews became huge successes, eagerly awaited around the world. Martin Agronsky reports that when he expressed his idea for a roundtable political show, the prevailing view was, "No one's going to like this show because it's just a bunch of talking heads."[5]

Because of *Agronsky and Company*'s success it was widely imitated, but now people won't take chances with more in-depth kinds of commentary shows. However, just as *Agronsky* surprised people—or, more to the point, its audiences surprised people—so too a different and better kind of format could prove successful as well. Colman McCarthy scoffs at the idea that no one would watch serious political commentary. "A lot of people would have found it fascinating to see Izzy [I.F.] Stone talk at length about problems in America."[6]

---

thing to do, a noble service to the community, and you lost money at it." Shales notes that the networks used to put aside whole blocks of time—not just Sunday mornings—for good shows, with little concern about financial consequences. Twenty years ago, he notes, the idea of all time periods, even Sunday mornings, being highly competitive would have been considered ludicrous.[4]

Television may be more a medium of heat than light, but shows like *Firing Line* and *Nightline* prove that the two need not be mutually exclusive. The first challenge is to find producers who have some commitment to providing light. It is equally important that their commitment be sufficient to drive them to take some chances. It usually isn't. In 1983 *Nightline* was expanded to a full hour, but when it took a dip in the ratings, the show was quickly reduced back to thirty minutes. Given a chance, it is quite possible that viewers would have adjusted to the longer program, but that chance would have cost ABC too much money. The network was unwilling to take the chance, notwithstanding the potential dividends to society. If it is depressing that the networks maximize their profits even when that means minimizing their contribution to democracy, it is deplorable that they won't take chances on behalf of democracy.

Bill Moyers tells a sad and revealing story of what happened when the president of the CBS Broadcast Group asked how he could entice Moyers to remain at CBS:[7]

> [I said] "Give me a 52-week commitment, your worst time slot—a slot you haven't won for years. Give me a call on some of CBS News's best producers and reporters, and a little patience. In return, this is what you'll get: ratings as good or better than you've had in that slot, and—because of the lower costs—profits better than you can get in the same slot, the prestige of a first-class broadcast. . . . At the end of one year, you decide the success or failure. If it fails, send me $1 in the mail. . . ." He looked at me and said, "Bill, I'm going to stick with *West 57th.*"

The CBS aversion to creativity was, in this case, more lamentable than usual because Moyers was not some guy off the street with an off-beat grandiose vision, but an award-winning television essayist.

Even if the networks are correct in assuming that insufficient numbers of viewers will tolerate an hour of serious political dialogue, they needn't settle for political roundtables as the major genre of opinion commentary. The choice is not simply between *Firing Line* and *The McLaughlin Group.* Creativity is in order. Public television used to run a show called *The Advocates,* which offered debate on a public issue in the form of a trial, with the leading advocates cross-examining witnesses to help make their points. It was neither the best nor most widely watched show, but was at least an imaginative effort to stimulate viewer interest in major issues. More such efforts are needed.

Fred Friendly has lamented that "because television can make so much money doing its worst, it cannot afford to do its best."[8] If the airwaves must remain hostage to corporate profits, the least the profit-oriented owners could do is search hard for ways to make money while doing good. At the same time, without public pressure there is no reason to expect good consciences to prevail.

As noted, there is a second solution to the lamentable state of political commentary on television: to rely heavily on public television. A well-funded and truly independent public television system would serve our democracy well even if its audience were limited. As Hodding Carter says,[9]

> There are sufficient outlets and sufficient time slots and sufficient mandate for in-depth shows. I feel about public television the way I feel about small magazines. You don't measure it in the number of people. You measure it in the effect it has on the people who might themselves be energized, and you have a responsibility to those people. . . . We ought to feel responsible to segmented audiences who are committed to public affairs.

Carter's vision of a public television system truly responsive to public affairs devotees hasn't happened, and discussions in PBS quarters today are more often about ratings than about quality. It is no secret why this has occurred: the absence of independent funding makes public television dependent on underwriters who crave large audiences and no controversy.

Ultimately, the solution is the same for both private and public television: pressure from the people. There is no shortage of legislative steps that can be taken. For better public affairs programming, many propose a return to a more activist FCC. For a broader spectrum of opinion, Ben Bagdikian proposes a panoply of legislative measures designed to democratize ownership of the media, including limits on the number of newspapers a corporation could acquire; stricter limits on the numbers of radio or television stations a corporation can own; severe limits on cross-ownership among the media; higher corporate taxes; and a progressive tax on advertising. (Bagdikian fears that the measures won't be implemented because the owners of the media will resist them and they control the debate on the subject. Indeed, since his book was first published in 1983, corporate ownership has become more concentrated and the measures he recommended have not been adopted.)

Even if adopted, these measures alone would hardly ensure a broad, robust political debate. The first and most important step toward improving the media's contribution to political discussion is not any piece of legislation. Rather, it is a widespread recognition that our debate is impoverished. When this becomes a matter of consensus, we can appeal to all parties to make the public interest paramount.

Most journalists, including many of the regular participants on television's talk shows, agree that political commentary on television leaves a lot to be desired. Yet even those who do not blame the masses have not taken the issue to the masses. The people must enter the fray, for they alone are likely to force changes in the way things are done. They must send a message to those in control of the media: we want a better and broader debate.

We The People must pressure the elites. A campaign of protest over Sidney Schanberg's firing, for example, might have kept the *New York Times* from dismissing the next columnist to get bold. If the networks received enough letters insisting that the ideological base of their political programs be broadened, they would take note. A campaign to create a well-funded, independent PBS could bear fruit. Despite the left's complaints that political thought is dominated by a small band of wealthy, powerful corporations, those corporations are ultimately—at least potentially—at the mercy of consumers.

Of course, the interaction between elites and masses is reciprocal: a few brave elites can arouse the masses. Anthony Lewis could have helped create outrage by criticizing the firing of Schanberg. Such a protest would have been even more effective if William Safire recognized that it is Schanberg today, but could be a daring conservative tomorrow, and joined the cause. Indeed the complaints of both liberal and conservative commentators seem likely to result in the return of the "fairness doctrine," which required television and radio stations to give time to groups to respond when an opposing viewpoint was aired, and thus played a role in exposing Americans to more views.

America's public debate would be improved if many people in various positions—network executives, stockholders, journalists, statesmen, advertisers—placed the public interest higher on their agenda, made sacrifices and took risks. The general public, though, may have to make these risks and sacrifices more worthwhile for the elites to take. Unfortunately, too much of the public is unaware of the extent of the problem. And the media are rarely in the forefront of educating the public about their own deficiencies.

Again, whether corporations, the government, the American people, or inertia is to blame, our political debate is impoverished, and nowhere more so than on television. The word must get out that our democracy is undernourished. If there is nothing we can do about it, then it is not our democracy after all.

NOTES

Interviews with the individuals named in the text were conducted by the author on the indicated dates. Television programs are identified by the short titles used in the text, e.g., *Brinkley* for *This Week with David Brinkley.*

INTRODUCTION

1. Barbara Matusow, "Washington's Journalism Establishment," *Washingtonian,* February 1989, p. 94.
2. John Gregory Dunne, *Harp* (New York: Simon and Schuster, 1989), p. 160.
3. *Washington Post,* 18 April 1987, p. 6.
4. Interview, 18 September 1989.

ONE. TWO TRADITIONS AND TWO KINDS OF *Firing Line*

1. Edward Bliss, Jr., *In Search of Light: The Broadcasts of Edward Murrow* (New York: Knopf, 1967), p. 247.
2. Bruce Williamson, "TV's New Fun Game: Savagery," *Life,* 7 April 1967, p. 25.
3. "As Unrehearsed as a Hiccough," *TV Guide,* 6 November 1965, p. 34.
4. John Judis, *William F. Buckley, Jr.: Patron Saint of the Conservatives* (New York: Simon and Schuster, 1988), p. 265.
5. William F. Buckley, Jr., *On the Firing Line* (New York: Random House, 1989), pp. 9–11.
6. Interview, 16 January 1990.

7. Shana Alexander, "Even Better than Batman," *Life,* 5 August 19...

8. *Firing Line,* transcript, 13 November 1968.

9. *Life,* 7 April 1967, p. 25.

10. *Firing Line,* transcript, 8 April 1966.

11. Judis, *Buckley, Patron Saint,* p. 439.

12. John Leonard, *This Pen for Hire* (Garden City, NY: Doubleday, 1973), p. 297.

13. Buckley, *On the Firing Line,* p. 100.

14. Buckley, *On the Firing Line,* pp. 29–30.

15. Joseph Epstein, "The Politics of William F. Buckley," *Dissent,* Fall 1972, p. 615.

16. Interview, 16 January 1990.

17. Buckley, *On the Firing Line,* pp. 206–207.

18. Geoffrey Stokes, "Bulls'-Eyes and Misses," *Washington Post Book Week,* 30 April 1989, p. 8.

19. Buckley, *On the Firing Line,* pp. 64–65.

20. Buckley, *On the Firing Line,* p. 77.

21. William F. Buckley, Jr., "The Joys and Trials of Television Debate," *TV Guide,* 24 January 1970, p. 7.

22. Jay Rosen, "Chatter from the Right," *Progressive,* March 1988, p. 28.

23. Judis, *Buckley, Patron Saint,* p. 441.

24. Buckley, *On the Firing Line,* p. xiii.

25. William F. Buckley, Jr., "Notes and Asides," *National Review,* 30 September 1988, p. 21.

26. Buckley, *On the Firing Line,* p. xxxii.

Two. McLaughlin and Company

1. Interview, 12 October 1989.

2. Ben DeMott, "The Pursuit of . . . Charm," *Nation,* 27 March 1982, p. 353.

3. *King:* Larry L. King, "How Good Are TV's News Analysts?," *TV Guide,* 25 January 1986, p. 42.

   Fallows: James Fallows, "The New Celebrities of Washington," *New York Review of Books,* 12 June 1986, p. 42.

   Wainwright: Loudon Wainwright, "Masters of Babble," *Life,* December 1987, p. 26.

4. Larry L. King, "How Good?" *TV Guide,* 25 January 1986, p. 42.

5. *Washington Post,* 26 September 1986, p. B-2.

6. Michael Kinsley, "Jerkofsky and Co.," *New Republic,* 9 September 1981, p. 16.

7. David Remnick, "The McLaughlin Group," *Esquire,* May 1986, p. 80.

8. James Kilpatrick, *Washington Post,* 3 December 1987, p. E-9.
9. Axel Madsen, *60 Minutes* (New York: Dodd, Mead, 1984), p. 15.
10. Interview, 15 December 1989. See also "An Interview with James Jackson Kilpatrick," *Quill,* October 1975, p. 14.
11. Tom Shales, "McLaughlin, the Master Immoderator," *Washington Post,* 30 October 1985, p. B-11.
12. *McLaughlin Group,* transcript, 30 January 1987.
13. David Remnick, "The McLaughlin Group," *Esquire,* May 1986, p. 80.
14. *McLaughlin Group,* transcript, 6 May 1989.
15. *McLaughlin Group,* transcript, 20 September 1986.
16. Tom Shales, "McLaughlin . . . Immoderator," *Washington Post,* 30 October 1985, p. B-11.
17. Edwin Diamond, "Circus of the Stars," *New York,* 3 February 1986, p. 18.
18. *McLaughlin Group,* transcript, 12 December 1986.
19. *McLaughlin Group,* transcript, 14 November 1986.
20. *Powell:* Barbara Gamarekian, "Come the Weekend, It's Talk-Show City," *New York Times,* 1 March 1987, p. 52.
   Kinsley: Michael Kinsley, *Curse of the Giant Muffins* (New York: Summit, 1987), p. 93.
   Gergen, Russert, Reagan: David Remnick, "The McLaughlin Group," *Esquire,* May 1986, p. 80.
   Weisman: John Weisman, "Left! Right! The Gang of Five Throws Nothing but Haymakers," *TV Guide,* 20 July 1985, p. 11.
   Schram: Interview, 6 October 1989.
   Barnes: Remnick, "The McLaughlin Group," p. 80.
21. Sam Donaldson, *Hold On, Mr. President!* (New York: Random House, 1987), pp. 219–220.
22. Donaldson, *Hold On,* p. 219.
23. Donaldson, *Hold On,* p. 234.
24. Donaldson, *Hold On,* p. 234.
25. *Brinkley,* transcript, 26 May 1985.
26. *Brinkley,* transcript, 12 June 1987.
27. Interview, 21 September 1989.
28. Interview, 10 October 1989.
29. William S. Armistead, "Braden and Buchanan Attack in *Crossfire,*" *Conservative Digest,* January 1988, p. 18.
30. *Crossfire,* 15 June 1989.
31. Armistead, "Braden and Buchanan Attack," p. 25.
32. Armistead, "Braden and Buchanan Attack," p. 18.
33. Elisabeth Bumiller, "Pity the Victims Caught in the Crossfire," *TV Guide,* 16 June 1984, p. 35.

34. Michael Kinsley, *Curse of the Giant Muffins* (New York: Summit, 1987), p. 93.
35. Jack Germond and Jules Witcover, "In This Corner, Pat Buchanan," *Washingtonian,* June 1985, p. 98.

THREE. WHERE'S THE BEEF?

1. David Remnick, "The McLaughlin Group," *Esquire,* May 1986, p. 80.
2. *Broder:* Remnick, "The McLaughlin Group," p. 80.
    Fallows: James Fallows, "The New Celebrities of Washington," *New York Review of Books,* 12 June 1986, p. 41.
3. David Broder, *Behind the Front Page* (New York: Simon and Schuster, 1987), p. 364.
4. Interview, 18 September 1989.
5. William F. Buckley, Jr., *On the Firing Line* (New York: Random House, 1989), p. 171.
6. Fallows, "The New Celebrities," p. 45.
7. Interview, 16 January 1990.
8. Interview, 15 December 1989.
9. Interview, 19 September 1989.
10. Fallows, "The New Celebrities," p. 45.
11. Edward Diamond, "Circus of the Stars," *New York,* 3 February 1986, p. 20.
12. *Brinkley,* transcript, 19 December 1982.
13. *Brinkley,* transcript, 8 January 1988.
14. Jay Rosen, "Chatter on the Right," *Progressive,* March 1988, p. 26.
15. Anne Lewis, "The Pale-Male-Talking-Head Syndrome," *Ms,* December 1988, p. 6.
16. Interview, 24 October 1989.
17. Interviews: McGrory, 14 October 1989; Randolph, 28 September 1989; Roberts, 24 October 1989.
18. Interview, 28 September 1989.
19. Interview, 2 October 1989.
20. Interview, 18 September 1989.
21. Jacob Weisberg, "Buckrakers," *New Republic,* 27 January 1986, p. 18.
22. David Remnick, "The McLaughlin Group," *Esquire,* May 1986, p. 88.
23. Remnick, "The McLaughlin Group," p. 82.
24. Michael Kinsley, *Curse of the Giant Muffins* (New York: Summit, 1987), p. 93.
25. Interview, 3 November 1989.
26. Interview, 11 September 1989.
27. William S. Armistead, "Braden and Buchanan Attack in *Crossfire,*" *Con-*

servative Digest, January 1988, p. 24.

28. Barbara Matusow, "Washington's Journalism Establishment," *Washingtonian,* February 1989, p. 98.

29. Interview, 3 November 1989.

30. Interview, 21 September 1989.

31. Interview, 11 September 1989.

32. Interview, 17 October 1989.

33. *Brinkley,* transcript, 15 May 1988.

34. Loudon Wainwright, "Masters of Babble," *Life,* December 1987, p. 26.

35. Interview, 26 January 1990.

36. *Larry King Live,* 11 May 1989.

37. Christopher Hitchens, "Blabscam," *Harper's,* March 1987, p. 75, presents an interesting firsthand account of the nonspontaneity of the shows.

38. William A. Rusher, *How to Win Arguments* (Garden City, NY: Doubleday, 1981), p. 187.

39. David Remnick, "The McLaughlin Group," *Esquire,* May 1986, p. 82.

40. Remnick, "The McLaughlin Group," p. 80.

41. Remnick, "The McLaughlin Group," p. 88.

42. Letter to the editor, *New York Review of Books,* 23 September 1986, p. 74.

43. Barbara Gamarekian, "Come the Weekend, It's Talk-Show City," *New York Times,* 1 March 1987, p. 52.

44. Interview, 19 September 1989.

45. Interview, 6 October 1989.

46. Remnick, "The McLaughlin Group," p. 88.

47. Remnick, "The McLaughlin Group," p. 80.

48. Joseph Epstein, "The Politics of William F. Buckley," *Dissent,* Fall 1972, p. 615, attributing the phrase to Irving Howe.

49. Epstein, "Politics of Buckley," p. 616.

50. *Inside Washington,* transcript, 13 October 1989.

51. *McLaughlin Group,* transcript, 2 January 1987.

52. *McLaughlin Group,* transcript, 16 January 1987.

53. Neil Postman, *Amusing Ourselves to Death* (New York: Viking, 1985), p. 4.

54. Jonathan Alter, "The Performing Pundits," *Newsweek,* 16 June 1986, p. 62.

55. Interview, 19 September 1989.

56. Edwin Diamond, "Circus of the Stars," *New York,* 3 February 1986, p. 20.

57. Interview, 3 November 1989.

58. Jerry Mander, *Four Arguments for the Elimination of Television* (New York: Quill, 1978), pp. 323–327.

59. Interview, 18 September 1989.

60. Interview, 26 October 1989.
61. Interview, 16 January 1990.
62. Jonathan Alter, "Taking CBS to Task," *Newsweek,* 15 September 1986, p. 53.
63. Alter, "Taking CBS to Task," p. 53.

Four. The Perfect Participants

Pat Buchanan

1. Garry Wills, "Standing Pat," *New Republic,* 2 May 1988, p. 33.
2. Patrick J. Buchanan, *Right from the Beginning* (Boston: Little Brown, 1988), p. 3.
3. Buchanan, *Right . . .,* p. 384.
4. Buchanan, *Right . . .,* pp. 6–7.
5. Buchanan, *Right . . .,* p. 13.
6. Buchanan, *Right . . .,* p. 13.
7. Buchanan, *Right . . .,* p. 70.
8. Wills, "Standing Pat," p. 33.
9. Buchanan, *Right . . .,* p. 65.
10. Buchanan, *Right . . .,* p. 67.
11. David Brock, "Street-Corner Conservative," *Commentary,* June 1988, p. 4.
12. Buchanan, *Right . . .,* pp. 95, 99.
13. Buchanan, *Right . . .,* p. 210.
14. Buchanan, *Right . . .,* p. 218.
15. Buchanan, *Right . . .,* p. 261.
16. Buchanan, *Right . . .,* pp. 245–246.
17. Buchanan, *Right . . .,* p. 262.
18. Buchanan, *Right . . .,* p. 272.
19. Buchanan, *Right . . .,* p. 287.
20. John Judis, "White House Vigilante," *New Republic,* 26 January 1987, p. 20.
21. William Safire, *Before the Fall* (Garden City, NY: Doubleday, 1975), p. 100.
22. Safire, *Before the Fall,* p. 148.
23. Patrick J. Buchanan, *The New Majority* (Philadelphia: Girard, 1973), p. 67.
24. Buchanan, *New Majority,* p. 79.
25. Carl Bernstein and Bob Woodward, *The Final Days* (New York: Simon and Schuster, 1967), p. 288.
26. Patrick J. Buchanan, *Conservative Votes, Liberal Victories* (New York: Quadrangle/New York Times Book Co., 1975), p. 6.

27. Buchanan, *Conservative Votes,* p. 8.

28. Larry Speakes, *Speaking Out* (New York: Scribners, 1988), pp. 86–87.

29. Michael Deaver, *Behind the Scenes* (New York: Morrow, 1987), p. 182.

30. Pat Buchanan, "A Conservative Makes a Final Plea," *Newsweek,* 30 March 1987, p. 26.

31. *Washington Post,* 1 November 1987, p. C-2.

32. *Washington Post,* 19 July 1987, pp. C-1, C-2.

33. *Washington Post,* 5 March 1986, p. A-19.

34. William A. Rusher, *How to Win Arguments* (Garden City, NY: Doubleday, 1981), p. 192.

35. Buchanan, *Right from the Beginning,* p. 203.

36. James S. Kunen, "Patrick Buchanan," *People,* 29 August 1988, p. 72.

37. Lally Weymouth, "The Great Right Hope," *New York,* 10 June 1985, p. 53.

38. Buchanan, *Right . . .,* p. 98.

39. Buchanan, *Right . . .,* p. 374.

40. Buchanan, *Right . . .,* p. 345.

41. Buchanan, *Right . . .,* p. 357.

42. Buchanan, *Right . . .,* p. 363.

43. Buchanan, *Conservative Votes,* p. 8.

44. James Fallows, "Patrick Buchanan: He Can Be a Likable Character But His Politics Are Poisonous," *Washington Monthly,* April 1988, p. 42.

45. Fallows, "Buchanan . . . Poisonous," p. 54.

46. David Brock, "Street-Corner Conservative," *Commentary,* June 1988, p. 64.

47. John Judis, *William F. Buckley, Jr.: Patron Saint of the Conservatives* (New York: Simon and Schuster, 1988), p. 440.

Sam Donaldson

1. *Brinkley,* transcript, 4 January 1987.

2. William A. Rusher, *The Coming Battle for the Media* (New York: Morrow, 1988), p. 111.

3. Sam Donaldson, *Hold On, Mr. President!* (New York: Random House, 1987), p. 24.

4. "Donaldson: You've Got My Secret. Russell: Brevity," *TV Guide,* 4 January 1986, p. 29.

5. Stephanie Mansfield, "Big Mouth of the Small Screen," *Washington Post,* 24 July, p. C-12.

6. Donaldson, *Hold On,* p. 7.

7. Donaldson, *Hold On,* p. 17.

8. Donaldson, *Hold On,* p. 4.

9. *Brinkley,* transcript, 29 August 1982.

10. *Brinkley,* transcript, 28 February 1982.

11. *Brinkley,* transcript, 3 January 1988.

12. *Brinkley,* transcript, 19 March 1989.

13. *Brinkley,* transcript, 26 February 1984.

14. Jody Powell, *The Other Side of the Story* (New York: Morrow, 1984), p. 307.

15. *Brinkley,* transcript, 2 June 1985.

16. Donaldson, *Hold On,* p. 85.

17. Interview, *Playboy,* March 1983, p. 57.

18. Garry Wills, "Standing Pat," *New Republic,* 2 May 1988, p. 33.

19. Donaldson, *Hold On,* p. 155.

20. Donaldson, *Hold On,* p. 209.

21. Interview, 26 January 1990.

22. Donaldson, *Hold On,* p. 234.

23. Interview, 26 January 1990.

24. Interview, 17 October 1989.

25. *Brinkley,* transcript, 3 February 1985.

26. Interview, 10 October 1989.

27. *Brinkley,* transcript, 21 August 1988.

28. *Brinkley,* transcript, 9 June 1985.

29. *Brinkley,* transcript, 1 February 1987.

30. *Brinkley,* transcript, 22 February 1987.

31. *Brinkley,* transcript, 6 December 1987.

32. *Brinkley,* transcript, 22 June 1986.

33. *Brinkley,* transcript, 30 April 1989.

Five. Celebrity Journalists

1. Jacob Weisberg, "Buckrakers," *New Republic,* 27 January 1986, p. 16.

2. Weisberg, "Buckrakers," p. 17.

3. James Fallows, "The New Celebrities of Washington," *New York Review of Books,* 12 June 1986, p. 44.

4. Weisberg, "Buckrakers," p. 17.

5. Fallows, "The New Celebrities," p. 44.

6. Fallows, "The New Celebrities," p. 44.

7. Fallows, "The New Celebrities," p. 44.

8. Interview, 19 September 1989.

William F. Buckley, Jr.

1. Patrick J. Buchanan, *Right from the Beginning* (Boston: Little, Brown, 1988), p. 221.

2. Nicholas Lemann, "William Buckley: He Could Have Been a Great Thinker, but He's Too Busy Rushing to the Airport," *Washington Monthly,* April 1988, p. 46.

3. John Judis, *William F. Buckley, Jr.: Patron Saint of the Conservatives* (New York: Simon and Schuster, 1988), p. 241.

4. Judis, *Buckley, Patron Saint,* p. 248.

5. *New York Daily News,* 11 October 1965.

6. *New York Journal American,* 21 November 1965.

7. Norman Mailer, *Village Voice,* 28 October 1965, quoted in Larry L. King, "God, Man and William F. Buckley," *Harper's,* March 1967, p. 54.

8. *Life,* 29 October 1965, p. 84.

9. "The Gingering Man," *Time,* 17 June 1966, p. 59.

10. King, "God, Man, Buckley," p. 53.

11. Carlin Romano, "Marshall McLuhan: Hot, Cool and Tepid," *Washington Post Book Week,* 30 April 1989, p. 4.

12. Charles Lam Markmann, *The Buckleys* (New York: Morrow, 1973), p. 315.

13. Eliot Abrams, "Public Discourse," *Commentary,* April 1974, p. 78.

14. David Oshinsky, "Bill Buckley without a Cause," *New Leader,* 31 October 1988, p. 14.

15. Morton Kondracke, "Liberty, Equality and a Flat 25% Tax," *New York Times Book Review,* 5 January 1986, p. 14.

16. Interview, 16 January 1990.

17. Larry Dubois, "Slightly Less than the Speed of Sound," *Harper's,* March 1971, p. 134.

18. William F. Buckley, Jr., *Cruising Speed* (New York: Putnam, 1971), p. 250.

19. *Washington Monthly,* April 1988, p. 42.

20. Marquis Childs and James Reston, eds., *Walter Lippmann and His Times* (New York: Harcourt, Brace, 1959), p. 227.

21. Childs and Reston, *Walter Lippmann,* pp. 230–231.

22. Kondracke, "Liberty, Equality, 25%," p. 14.

23. Judis, *Buckley, Patron Saint,* p. 326.

24. Judis, *Buckley, Patron Saint,* pp. 442, 450–451.

25. Alan Brinkley, "The Conservative at Sea," *New Republic,* 30 May 1988, p. 31.

26. William F. Buckley, Jr., *The Unmaking of a Mayor* (New York: Viking, 1966), p. 324.

27. Wilfrid Sheed, "William Buckley's Several Selves," *Commonweal,* 4 November 1988, p. 587.

28. Robert Lekachman, "William F. Buckley, Jr., Alchemist," *Commonweal,* 1 March 1974, p. 533.

29. Lekachman, "Buckley, Alchemist," p. 534.
30. Letter to the editor, *Commonweal,* 19 April 1974, pp. 173–174.
31. Charles Lam Markmann, "Old Vinegar in an Old Jug," *Nation,* 13 April 1974, p. 474.
32. Garry Wills, *Confessions of a Conservative* (Garden City, NY: Doubleday, 1979), p. 37.
33. James Nuechterlein, "William F. Buckley, Jr. and American Conservatism," *Commentary,* June 1988, p. 34.
34. Judis, *Buckley, Patron Saint,* p. 467.
35. Jacob Weisberg, "Buckrakers," *New Republic,* 27 January 1986, p. 18.
36. Christopher Simonds, "Hagiographer with a Hamstring," *National Review,* 10 June 1988, p. 49.

George Will

1. William A. Henry III, "George Will Among the Polysyllables," *Esquire,* January 1987, p. 71. The Lippmann biography is: Ronald Steel, *Walter Lippmann and the American Century* (Boston: Little, Brown, 1980).
2. Sidney Blumenthal, "The Lightweight Philosopher," *Washington Monthly,* October 1987, p. 53.
3. George Will, "On Turning 40," *Newsweek,* 27 April 1981, p. 104.
4. *Washington Post,* 3 April 1977, p. C-7.
5. "An Interview with James Jackson Kilpatrick," *Quill,* October 1975, p. 13.
6. William F. Buckley, Jr., *Overdrive* (Garden City, NY: Doubleday, 1983), p. 76.
7. *Washington Post,* 15 December 1977, p. A-23.
8. *Washington Post,* 1 February 1981, p. C-7.
9. *Virginia Quarterly Review,* Autumn 1978, pp. 130–131.
10. Michael Sandel, "Up from Individualism," *New York Times,* 7 July 1983, p. 6.
11. William Kristol, "Conservative Statecraft," *Public Interest,* Fall 1983, p. 120.
12. Charles W. Griswold, Jr., "Soul Food," *American Scholar,* Summer 1984, p. 401.
13. James Fallows, "The Foundation of Liberalism," *Atlantic Monthly,* May 1983, p. 99.
14. M. J. Sobran, Jr., "The One True Conservative," *National Review,* 10 June 1983, pp. 696–697.
15. Ronald Steel, *Los Angeles Times Book Review,* 30 November 1986, p. 6.
16. Henry Fairlie, "Tory Days," *New Republic,* 10 November 1986, p. 32.
17. Robert Lekachman, "At the Presidential Starting Gate," *New Leader,* 14 December 1987, p. 22.

18. Sidney Blumenthal, "The Lightweight Philosopher," *Washington Monthly,* October 1987, p. 53.
19. *Washington Post,* 21 November 1980, p. F-3.
20. *Washington Post,* 14 January 1981, p. A-21.
21. *Washington Post,* 28 January 1981, p. A-21.
22. George Will, "Grading the President," *Newsweek,* 9 November 1981, p. 108.
23. Mike Royko, *Like I Was Sayin'—* (New York: Dutton, 1984), p. 213.
24. Michael Kramer, "Triumph of the Will," *New York,* 29 December 1980–5 January 1981.
25. Joseph Sobran, "George Will and American Conservatism," *American Spectator,* October 1983, p. 10.
26. *Washington Post,* 10 July 1983, p. B-7.
27. *Washington Post,* 27 September 1987, p. D-6.
28. *Washington Post,* 22 April 1984, p. D-7.
29. *Washington Post,* 15 February 1988, p. A-27.
30. James Fallows, "The New Celebrities of Washington," *New York Review of Books,* 12 June 1986, p. 47.
31. Fallows, "The New Celebrities," p. 44.
32. Hugh Sidey, "The Mick Jaggers of Journalism," *Time,* 5 October 1987, p. 28.
33. George Will, *The Pursuit of Happiness and Other Sobering Thoughts* (New York: Harper and Row, 1978), p. xv.
34. David Halberstam, *The Powers that Be* (New York: Knopf, 1979), p. 370.
35. *Schlesinger:* Marquis Childs and James Reston, eds., *Walter Lippmann and His Times* (New York: Harcourt, Brace, 1959), p. 191.
    Aron: Childs and Reston, *Walter Lippmann,* pp. 114–115.
    Simon: Paul Simon, *The Glass House: Politics and Morality in the Nation's Capital* (New York: Crossroads, 1984), p. 125.
36. Sidney Blumenthal, "The Lightweight Philosopher," *Washington Monthly,* October 1987, p. 53.
37. Nelson W. Polsby, "A Special Kind of Conservative," *Fortune,* 25 July 1983, p. 103.
38. Ronald Steel, *Los Angeles Times Book Review,* 30 November 1986, p. 6.
39. William A. Henry III, "George Will Among the Polysyllables," *Esquire,* January 1987, p. 92; Jane Mayer, "Tory Columnist," *Wall Street Journal,* 7 May 1986, p. 1.
40. *Washington Post,* 5 November 1981, p. A-29.
41. Owen Fiss, "Groups and the Equal Protection Clause," *Journal of Philosophy and Public Affairs,* **5,** p. 197 (1986).
42. Michael Kinsley, "Equal Lack of Opportunity," *Harper's,* June 1983, p. 107.

43. Interview, 28 September 1989.

44. Jude Wanniski, *The Mediaguide of 1987* (New York: Harpers, 1987), p. 278.

45. Marc R. Levy, "The Best In the Business," *Washington Journalism Review,* February 1985, p. 34.

46. Ronald Steel, *Los Angeles Times Book Review,* 30 November 1986, p. 6.

47. *Conversations with Walter Lippmann,* CBS Reports (Boston: Little, Brown, 1965), pp. 178, 187.

48. *Brinkley,* transcript, 8 May 1988.

49. *Brinkley,* transcript, 2 June 1985.

50. *Brinkley,* transcript, 12 June 1987.

51. Ben DeMott, "The Pursuit of . . . Charm," *Nation,* 27 March 1982, p. 379.

52. Joseph Sobran, "George Will and American Conservatism," *American Spectator,* October 1983, p. 10.

53. George Will, "The Last Word," *Newsweek,* 4 January 1982, p. 68.

54. *Washington Post,* 7 April 1983, p. A-23.

55. "Ring Lardner, Call Your Office," *Newsweek,* 14 April 1986, p. 84.

56. "It's April, So 'Work Ball'," *Newsweek,* 11 April 1988, p. 92.

57. *Washington Post,* 11 April 1985, p. A-21.

58. "U. S. Grant vs. Stonewall Jackson," *Newsweek,* 7 May 1984, p. 108.

59. *Washington Post,* 11 April 1985, p. A-21.

60. *Newsweek,* 15 April 1985, p. 102.

61. *Washington Post,* 29 March 1984, p. A-21.

62. *Washington Post,* 14 July 1988, p. A-18.

63. *Washington Post,* 13 October 1983, p. A-23.

64. *Washington Post,* 7 April 1983, p. A-23.

65. *Washington Post,* 18 June 1981, p. A-19.

66. Ronald Steel, *Los Angeles Times Book Review,* 30 November 1986, p. 6.

67. *Brinkley,* transcript, 1 December 1985.

68. *Brinkley,* transcript, 28 June 1987.

69. *Brinkley,* transcript, 21 September 1985.

70. *Brinkley,* transcript, 21 September 1985.

Six. Caricatures

James Kilpatrick

1. James J. Kilpatrick, *The Sovereign States* (Chicago: Regnery Co., 1957) p. 279.

2. Kilpatrick, *Sovereign States,* p. 281.

3. J. Harvie Wilkinson III, *Harry Byrd and the Changing Face of Virginia Politics* (Charlottesville: University Press of Virginia, 1968), p. 127.

4. Brent Bozell, "To Mend the Tragic Flaw," *National Review,* 12 March

1963, p. 199.

5. *Inside Washington Twentieth Anniversary Special,* transcript, 7 December 1989.

6. "A Conversation with James Jackson Kilpatrick," *Quill,* October 1975, p. 15.

7. James Kilpatrick, "George McGovern, Prairie Progressive," *National Review,* 18 February 1972, p. 147.

8. *Washington Post,* 21 September 1982, p. A-19.

9. *Washington Post,* 18 February 1988, p. A-23.

10. *Washington Post,* 24 June 1982, p. A-23.

11. Edith Efron, "Why Two Able Men Turn Themselves into Caricatures," *TV Guide,* 27 July 1974, pp. A-5, A-6.

12. Efron, "Two Able Men," p. A-5.

13. Interview, 9 November 1989.

14. Interview, 15 December, 1989.

15. Efron, "Two Able Men," p. A-6.

16. Interview, 15 December 1989.

17. Interview, 15 December 1989.

18. *Washington Post,* 30 October 1985, p. B-11.

19. *Inside Washington,* transcript, 30 April 1988.

20. *Inside Washington,* transcript, 30 September 1989.

21. Michael Kinsley, "Jerkofsky and Company," *New Republic,* 9 September 1981, p. 16.

22. Arthur N. Haupt, "Agronsky and Company," *Washington Post TV,* 26 April 1981, p. A-3.

23. *Inside Washington,* transcript, 11 April 1989.

24. *Inside Washington,* transcript, 6 May 1989.

25. *Inside Washington,* 10 April 1988.

26. Interview, 15 December 1989.

27. James Kilpatrick, "Hail and Farewell," *Nation's Business,* March 1986, p. 4.

28. Edith Efron, "Two Able Men," pp. A-5, A-6.

29. Interview, 15 December 1989.

30. Interview, 15 December 1989.

31. Interview, 21 September 1989.

32. Jacob Weisberg, "Buckrakers," *New Republic,* 27 January 1986, p. 18.

33. Interview, 15 December 1989.

34. Interview, 14 October 1989.

Robert Novak

1. William A. Rusher, "Reporting the President," *National Review,* 19 November 1971, p. 1307.

2. Rowland Evans and Robert D. Novak, *Lyndon B. Johnson: The Exercise*

of Power (New York: New American Library, 1966), p. 574.

3. David Remnick, "The McLaughlin Group," Esquire, May 1986, p. 82.
4. C-Span, 25 October 1989.
5. Interview, 17 October 1989.
6. Loudon Wainwright, "Masters of Babble," Life, December 1986, p. 26.
7. Interview, 3 November 1989.
8. Interview, 26 October 1989.
9. Interview, 28 November 1989.
10. Vic Gold, "Saturday Night Fervor," Washingtonian, June 1984, p. 72.
11. McLaughlin Group, transcript, 29 May 1987.
12. McLaughlin Group, transcript, 5 June 1987.
13. Interview, 8 September 1989.
14. McLaughlin Group, transcript, 12 December 1986.
15. McLaughlin Group, transcript, 22 August 1986.
16. McLaughlin Group, transcript, 15 June 1987.
17. McLaughlin Group, transcript, 16 January 1987.
18. McLaughlin Group, transcript, 23 August 1986.
19. McLaughlin Group, transcript, 17 October 1986.
20. McLaughlin Group, transcript, 30 January 1988.
21. McLaughlin Group, transcript, 11 October 1986.
22. William S. Armistead, "Why Liberals Call Robert Novak the Prince of Darkness," Conservative Digest, May–June 1988, p. 14.
23. Eric Alterman, "Mr. Nice Guy," Washingtonian, November 1989, p. 140.
24. Interview, 2 October 1989.
25. Armistead, "Why Liberals Call," p. 14.
26. Interview, 19 September 1989.
27. Interview, 14 October 1989.
28. Interview, 17 October 1989.

III. BETWEEN THE FORTY YARDLINES

1. Marc R. Levy, "The Best in the Business," Washington Journalism Review, February 1986, p. 24.
2. Interview, 8 September 1989.
3. Interview, 18 September 1989.
4. Washington Times, 26 July 1989, p. D-3.
5. Washington Post, 9 July 1989, p. F-2.
6. Interview, 18 September 1989.
7. Interview, 6 November 1989.
8. Interview, 16 January 1990.
9. Interview, 9 December 1989.
10. Interview, 18 September 1989.

11. Interview, 8 September 1989.

12. Interview, 18 September, 1989.

13. William A. Rusher, *The Coming Battle for the Media* (New York: Morrow, 1988), p. 110.

14. Interview, 10 October 1989.

15. Interview, 10 October 1989.

16. Patrick J. Buchanan, *Conservative Votes, Liberal Victories* (New York: Quadrangle/New York Times Book Co., 1975), p. 73.

17. Nancy Collins, "The Smartest Man on TV," *New York*, 13 August 1984, p. 22.

18. Interview, 17 October 1989.

19. Robert Karl Manoff, "Quick-Fix News," *Progressive*, July 1987, p. 15.

20. Alexander Cockburn, "The Tedium Twins," *Harper's*, August 1982, pp. 26–27.

21. Interview, 8 September 1989.

22. Jerry Mander, *Four Arguments for the Elimination of Television* (New York: Quill, 1978), p. 264.

23. Mander, *Four Arguments*, p. 264.

24. Noam Chomsky, *Manufacturing Consent* (New York: Pantheon, 1988), p. 298.

25. Ben Bagdikian, *The Media Monopoly* (Boston: Beacon Press, 1987), p. 4.

26. Fred W. Friendly, *Due to Circumstances Beyond Our Control* (New York: Random House, 1967), pp. 96–97.

27. Edwin Diamond, "The 'Times' That Try Men's Souls," *New York*, 9 September 1985, p. 32.

28. Alexander Cockburn, "Beat the Devil," *Nation*, 21 September 1985, p. 231.

29. Bagdikian, *Media Monopoly*, pp. 38–39.

30. Bagdikian, *Media Monopoly*, p. 47.

31. Eric Barnouw, *The Sponsor* (New York: Oxford, 1978), p. 57.

32. *Broadcasting*, 5 November 1979, p. 52.

33. Ben Bagdikian, "The Media Grab," *Channels*, May–June 1985, p. 18.

34. S. L. Harrison, "Prime Time Pablum," *Washington Monthly*, January 1986, p. 38.

35. Harrison, "Pablum," p. 38.

36. Marvin Kitman, "MacNeil/Lehrer: Twice as Long, Half as Good," *New Leader*, 17 October 1983, p. 21.

37. Pat Aufderheide, "What Makes Public TV Public?" *Progressive*, January 1988, p. 38.

38. Bagdikian, *Media Monopoly*, p. 229.

39. Ben Bagdikian, "The Lords of the Global Village," *Nation*, 12 June 1989, p. 807.

40. Bill Moyers, A World of Ideas (New York: Doubleday, 1989), p. 65.

41. Interview, 19 September 1989.

42. Christopher Hitchens, "Blabscam," *Harper's,* March 1987, p. 76.

43. The sources who claim that Buchanan essentially vetoed Green and that Douthit preferred Green spoke on the condition that they remain unnamed.

44. Interview, 18 September 1989.

45. Interview, 19 September 1989.

46. Bagdikian "Lords of Global Village," p. 812.

47. Gore Vidal, "Cue the Green God, Ted," *Nation,* 7–14 August 1989, pp. 171–172.

48. Chomsky, *Manufacturing Consent,* p. 305.

49. Interview, 11 September 1989.

50. Buchanan, *Conservative Votes,* p. 73.

51. Barry G. Cole, ed., *Television* (New York: Free Press, 1970), p. 317.

CONCLUSION

1. Interview, 10 October 1989.

2. Fred W. Friendly, *Due to Circumstances Beyond Our Control* (New York: Random House, 1967), p. 95.

3. Ann M. Sperber, *Murrow: His Life and Times* (New York: Freundlich Books, 1986), p. xvii.

4. Interview, 10 October 1989.

5. Interview, 12 October 1989.

6. Interview, 8 September 1989.

7. Jonathan Alter, "Taking CBS News to Task," *Newsweek,* 15 September 1986, p. 53.

8. Friendly, *Due to Circumstances,* p. xii.

9. Interview, 18 September 1989.

SELECTED BIBLIOGRAPHY

This bibliography lists books cited or quoted in the text. All newspaper and magazine articles cited or quoted are referenced in the preceding notes.

Bagdikian, Ben. *The Media Monopoly.* Boston: Beacon Press, 1987.

Barnouw, Eric. *The Sponsor.* New York: Oxford University Press, 1978.

Bernstein, Carl, and Bob Woodward. *The Final Days.* New York: Simon and Schuster, 1976.

Bliss, Edward, Jr., ed. *In Search of Light: The Broadcasts of Edward Murrow.* New York: Alfred A. Knopf, 1967.

Broder, David. *Behind the Front Page.* New York: Simon and Schuster, 1987.

Buchanan, Patrick J. *Conservative Votes, Liberal Victories.* New York: Quadrangle/New York Times Book Co., 1975.

Buchanan, Patrick J. *The New Majority.* Philadelphia: Girard Co., 1973.

Buchanan, Patrick J. *Right from the Beginning.* Boston: Little, Brown, and Co., 1988.

Buckley, William F., Jr. *Cruising Speed.* New York: Putnam, 1971.

Buckley, William F., Jr. *Four Reforms: A Guide for the Seventies.* New York: Putnam, 1973.

Buckley, William F., Jr. *God and Man at Yale: The Superstitions of Academic Freedom.* Chicago: H. Regnery Co., 1951.

Buckley, William F., Jr. *On the Firing Line.* New York: Random House, 1989.

Buckley, William F., Jr. *Overdrive.* Garden City, New York: Doubleday, 1983.

Buckley, William F., Jr. *The Unmaking of a Mayor.* New York: Viking Press, 1966.

Buckley, William F., Jr. *Up from Liberalism.* New Rochelle, New York: Arlington House, 1968.

Buckley, William F., Jr., and L. Brent Bozell. *McCarthy and His Enemies: The Record and Its Meaning.* New Rochelle, New York: Arlington House, 1954, 1970.

Childs, Marquis, and James Reston, eds. *Walter Lippmann and His Times.* New York: Harcourt, Brace, 1959.

Cole, Barry G., ed. *Television.* New York: Free Press, 1970.

Conversations with Walter Lippmann. CBS Reports. Boston: Little, Brown, 1965.

Deaver, Michael. *Behind the Scenes.* New York: William Morrow, 1987.

Donaldson, Sam. *Hold On, Mr. President!* New York: Random House, 1987.

Dunne, John Gregory, *Harp.* New York: Simon and Schuster, 1989.

Evans, Rowland, and Robert D. Novak. *Lyndon B. Johnson: The Exercise of Power.* New York: New American Library, 1966.

Evans, Rowland, Jr., and Robert D. Novak. *Nixon in the White House: The Frustration of Power.* New York: Random House, 1971.

Evans, Rowland, Jr., and Robert D. Novak. *The Reagan Revolution: A Blueprint for the Next Four Years.* New York: E. P. Dutton, 1981.

Friendly, Fred W. *Due to Circumstances Beyond Our Control.* New York: Random House, 1967.

Grauer, Neil A. *Wits and Sages.* Baltimore: Johns Hopkins University Press, 1984.

Halberstam, David. *The Powers that Be.* New York: Alfred A. Knopf, 1979.

Herman, Edward S., and Noam Chomsky. *Manufacturing Consent: The Political Economy of the Mass Media.* New York: Pantheon Books, 1988.

Hertsgaard, Mark. *On Bended Knee: The Press and the Reagan Presidency.* New York: Farrar Straus Giroux, 1988.

Judis, John. *William F. Buckley, Jr.: Patron Saint of the Conservatives.* New York: Simon and Schuster, 1988.

Kilpatrick, James J. *The Foxes' Union; and Other Stretchers, Tall Tales, and Discursive Reminiscences of Happy Years in Scrabble, Virginia.* McLean, Virginia, EPM Publications, 1977.

Kilpatrick, James J. *The Southern Case for School Segregation.* New York: Crowell-Collier Press, 1962.

Kilpatrick, James J. *The Sovereign States.* Chicago: H. Regnery Co., 1957.

Kinsley, Michael. *Curse of the Giant Muffins, and Other Washington Maladies.* New York: Summit Books, 1987.

Leonard, John. *This Pen for Hire.* Garden City, New York: Doubleday, 1973.

Madsen, Axel. *60 Minutes.* New York: Dodd, Mead, 1984.

Mander, Jerry. *Four Arguments for the Elimination of Television.* New York: Quadrangle/New York Times Book Co., 1978.

Matusow, Barbara. *The Evening Stars: The Making of the Network News Anchor.* Boston: Houghton Mifflin Co., 1983.

Moyers, Bill. *A World of Ideas.* New York: Doubleday, 1989.

Novak, Robert D. *The Agony of the GOP 1964.* New York: Macmillan, 1965.

Parenti, Michael. *Inventing Reality.* New York: St. Martin's Press, 1986.

Postman, Neil. *Amusing Ourselves to Death: Public Discourse in the Age of Show Business.* New York: Viking Press, 1985.

Powell, Jody. *The Other Side of the Story.* New York: William Morrow, 1984.

Royko, Mike. *Like I Was Sayin'—.* New York: E. P. Dutton, 1984.

Rusher, William A. *How to Win Arguments.* Garden City, New York: Doubleday, 1981.

Rusher, William A. *The Coming Battle for the Media.* New York: William Morrow, 1988.

Safire, William. *Before the Fall.* Garden City, New York: Doubleday, 1975.

Simon, Paul. *The Glass House: Politics and Morality in the Nation's Capital.* New York: Crossroads Pub. Co., 1984.

Speakes, Larry. *Speaking Out.* New York: Charles Scribners Sons, 1988.

Sperber, Ann M. *Murrow: His Life and Times.* New York: Freundlich Books, 1986.

Wanniski, Jude. *The Mediaguide of 1987.* New York: Harpers, 1987.

Wilkinson, J. Harvie, III. *Harry Byrd and the Changing Face of Virginia Politics.* Charlottesville: University Press of Virginia, 1968.

Will, George F. *The Morning After.* New York: Free Press, 1986.

Will, George F. *The New Season: A Spectator's Guide to the 1988 Election.* New York: Simon and Schuster, 1988.

Will, George F. *The Pursuit of Happiness and Other Sobering Thoughts.* New York: Harper and Row, 1978.

Will, George F. *The Pursuit of Virtue and Other Tory Notions.* New York: Simon and Schuster, 1982.

Will, George F. *Statecraft as Soulcraft.* New York: Simon and Schuster, 1983.

Wills, Garry. *Confessions of a Conservative.* Garden City, New York: Doubleday, 1979.

INDEX